Praise for *Your Way There*

Therapist Gretta Keene's magical guidebook, *Your Way There*, tackles how we get stuck and shows you, step by step, how to unlock better ways to be happy. You will find yourself getting caught up in the stories in each chapter, eager to learn new skills for breaking through old patterns. Lively watercolor illustrations throughout the book by her partner-in-therapy, Bill Murray, make *Your Way There* a joy to read. Who knew self-discovery could be so rewarding?
       —JoAnne McFarland, artistic director of the Artpoetica Project Space

Thought-provoking and transformational. If you read this book, get ready for your perspective, and your life, to change!
                                                —Douglas Roest-Gyimah, LCSW,
                                                founder and CEO, Upstate Counseling

Did you ever get the feeling that everyone else was issued a map that shows them how to navigate intimate relationships but, somehow, you never got one? If the answer is yes, buy this book. Gretta Keene writes, "Humans are quite capable of remaining blissfully unaware of the complexity of their own inner reality," and then proceeds to provide a guide to unpacking those complexities in accessible, clear, humanistic, and compassionate terms. Coupled with William Murray's beautiful and evocative illustrations, this book is a sort of owner's manual for becoming an emotionally mature, psychologically skillful, more connected, and more contented human being.
                                 —Peg Tyre, Pulitzer Prize–winning journalist
                                 and *New York Times* bestselling author

To say my work with Gretta has changed my life is an understatement. I'm so glad there is a book that holds all her teachings and expertise that I can flip through again and again and gift to everyone I know. I am most excited about the "Toolbox" at the end where I'll be able to refresh myself on Gretta's unique concepts that have helped me become a more mindful human. And, as an extra added bonus, this book has glorious colorful illustrations that both teach and delight. This is a book to cherish!
                                 —Julia Rothman, *New York Times* Scratch columnist,
                                 best-selling author and illustrator

Your Way There is different from other psychology self-help books. With cutting-edge information from a lifetime of professional experience, Keene offers easy-to-understand, step-by-step processes for developing emotional maturity and finding satisfaction in relationships with self and others. William Murray's delightful illustrations add lightness while clarifying challenging concepts. Keene and Murray bring wisdom—and compassion!—to their teaching.

—**Lavinia Plonka, author of** *What Are You Afraid Of?*
A Body-Mind Guide to Courageous Living

If I've learned one thing from Gretta, it's that there are few things braver than facing our anxieties and our unhappiness head-on. By facing the thorniest aspects of life, we have the chance to really, truly love—or at least tolerate—every moment as it happens. This book is an intimate look into Gretta's mind, where personal anecdotes and life experiences are shared as the sort of *aha!* moments that come from a great therapy session. That Gretta's vast knowledge and uniquely comforting perspective—along with William's beautiful illustrations—are now collected in one place for all of us to learn from and absorb, is truly a life-improving gift.

—**Elazar Sontag,** *Bon Appétit* **editor and cookbook author**

Your Way There is wise and compassionate. Reading this book is like spending a sunny afternoon on a porch with a patient friend who also happens to know a lot about therapy. It offers readers a way out of the old stories that can turn into traps and a way into the new stories that we need in order to live. Highly recommended.

—**Peter Blauner,** *New York Times* **bestselling author**

I adapted Gretta's Full Spectrum feeling chart to use with an adult support group. They were pleased to discover words to describe the different feelings they didn't realize were part of their experience. It was an excellent way to introduce the psychoeducational part of the grief program and to validate each participant while also promoting good sharing, support, and bonding.

—**Joan Sudmann Shapiro, LCSW, grief group facilitator**

Gretta Keene has written a guide to a spiritual journey that leads to wholeness and to happiness. The book is full of wisdom that recognizes our fears and foibles and gently leads us to see them as the tools of transformation. Her stories are told with great compassion for the human condition and great hope for the power to change. They contain jewels of guidance to move us out of our unhappy stuck places toward a more satisfying and fulfilling life. This book leaves one feeling upbeat and hopeful about our ability to deal with life's struggles.

—**Joan Hoeberichts, LCSW, Zen Buddhist Roshi**

YOUR WAY THERE

YOUR WAY THERE

To Being Fully Alive

CONCEPTS and TOOLS
for MINDFUL TRANSFORMATION

Written by
Gretta Keene

Illustrated by
William Murray

To protect the confidentiality of my clients, I have created characters that are fictionalized composites based on the emotional content of real situations where the details of the precipitating events have also been combined and altered. Any similarities between the identifying details of the fictional characters and clients I have seen are coincidental. The concepts and tools presented in the book, especially those discussing trauma, are not meant to be in place of work with a psychotherapist.

ISBN 13: 978-1-63489-505-7
LCCN: 2021920284

Printed in the United States of America
First Printing: 2022

26 25 24 23 22   5 4 3 2 1

Illustrations by William Murray
Design assistant: Hong Wu
Cover and interior design by Francesca Richer

Wise Ink Creative Publishing
807 Broadway St NE
Suite 46
Minneapolis, MN, 55413

A Dedication to Our Readers

How great a mud pie, this our newborn book!
Imperfect, yes, like us, yet may it be
Of benefit to you who choose to look,
Engage, and hope, heeding an inner plea.

To enter into transformation calls
For courage as we meet the dragons of
Our minds, scale fortified defensive walls
To face our fears. And courage calls for love.

And love? Connection brings it to our heart
Through words, new thoughts, through kind and gentle looks,
Through recognizing others play a part
In how we grow, through songs and even books.

So may you find your way and learn to thrive,
Hopeful, awake, alive while you're alive.

Contents

1

2

3

4

5

6

10

11

12

13

14

15

16

So join the campfire and bring your stories held with heart and mind...

Here's a treat, Ukie!

17

...a human amongst humans.

I realize now...

18

CHAPTER 1

A Double Rainbow

That morning, land was far away and the water deep. Wind was whipping up peaks as ominous dark swallowed pale sky. Thunder rumbled. Guiding my slim, spring-green kayak into the four-foot waves of Lake Champlain, I was reminded of diving into hurricane surf when I was a young teen. Scary? Yes, but doable. I was brave. Bill, my husband and partner in our psychotherapy practice, was up ahead in his red kayak. His curly, white mane streamed out from under his floppy hat. We had spent the night camping on an island accessible only by boat. Other campers had warned us of the approaching storm and told tales of the treacherous lake. But we had stayed, and now we had to get back. We had no choice. We couldn't be late for my elder daughter's very important party. Better to face an actual storm rather than an emotional one.

The week before, I had dubbed my gleaming, newly purchased kayak "Greenie." Humans turn objects into symbols by naming them and connecting them to an idea or an object that has symbolic weight. "Greenie" was a subtle reference to Bluebird, my childhood bike, vehicle to freedom and adventure, conduit to my Whole Self.

I conceive of my Whole Self as that sense of being in which I experience my complex and contradictory thoughts and feelings as unified and connected to a life force and awareness that is greater than the sum of those parts. I visualize the disparate aspects of my personality, each with its distinct perceptions, interpretations, and reactions, as parts of a circular spectrum of colors contained in the light of my spirit. The various hues and shades of color are imagined as perpetually expanding and contracting slices of what I identify as my Full Spectrum pie.

In Whole Self moments, I experience myself as in the center of my Full Spectrum, where my light is undivided and connected to the universal light. I become aware and in touch with the circularity of life, where energy flows in and out, and I am both giving and getting. The contradictions inherent in my Full Spectrum of thoughts and feelings are acknowledged but irrelevant in those Whole Self experiences. Pain and joy, birth and death, self and other, fear and faith—all become one, joined, not separate.

Kayaking was a recent passion, a symbolic "Yes!" to being strong and capable, choosing to seize life rather than retreat into the limitations of sickness and old age. Bill and I are not ancient humans, but since the number of years we can possibly live is fewer than the years that are behind us, we are not exactly "middle-aged" humans either. We are experienced humans. That day, neither one of us was an experienced kayaker. But one of us had more fear.

As a therapist, I often use the metaphor of "heading into the waves" as a way to encourage my clients to go toward what is painful. This helps them consider other interpretations and responses rather than react with one of the Big Four deeply embedded defenses: Fight, Flee, Freeze, or Fawn. I have dived into my own high waves of hurt and trauma and understand the healing that can happen when those emotional waves are faced.

Unfortunately, at that moment, confronting high waves was the opposite of what I needed to do. The strong winds were headed in the same direction as the small beach where we needed to land.

Sounds good, but not for a newbie kayaker. The wind-whipped, four-foot, white-peaked waves were heading to where I had to go, which meant maneuvering the fifty-pound, seventeen-foot piece of Kevlar so that the waves would first hit the side of Greenie and then come from behind, surprising me with every lift. Every fiber in my being told me, "Not safe!"

"You have to turn!" Bill yelled.

"I can't!" I wailed, obstinately heading farther away from Bill and the beach.

There was a Full Spectrum of contrasting thoughts, feelings, and possible actions twirling around inside of me. In the grip of fear, I chose Flee, avoiding what I didn't want to face, and Freeze, beginning to numb and shut down. All the paddling techniques I had learned in lessons were there, but by focusing on my fear, they seemed inaccessible, vanished from my brain. I was in what Bill and I refer to as an "activated state."

My mind became flooded with images of all the terrible things that would happen if I turned my boat. I imagined waves whacking the back of my kayak, dumping me into the churning, deep, cold water. The headlines would read, "Grandma Capsizes in Kayak and Drowns!" The subhead would reveal, "Husband watches, unable to save her." I envisioned Bill calling the kids, family, and friends to tell them the tragic news. How awful to cause such a mess! My daughters would never forgive me for abandoning them due to my own inept stupidity.

"It was her own fault!" others would cluck. "Gretta was never athletic. Just like her arthritic mother. She should have stuck with crocheting." Images of my failure in childhood sports played like a cheesy TV-movie montage, with shame-filled memories of the gawky girl who couldn't catch or hit the ball, the one no one wanted on their team. How could I be so stupid as to think I could kayak in a big lake? My body further stiffened in response to my internalized damning and judgmental inner parent.

Fear had pushed the alarm and activated my entrenched beliefs about my athletic inadequacy. I was in Trauma Land, the mental place where old, traumatic experiences become superimposed on the present moment. My defenses, those loyal, hypervigilant Bodyguards, recruited and trained during past times of hurt and threat, seemed to shout in my brain. "Stay with what you know!" those familiar inner voices yelled. "Keep the waves in front! Then you'll be in control, safe." A sneakier Bodyguard, the Fawning defense long ago named Poor Pitiful Pearl, whispered, "Be helpless. Then you'll get saved. Someone else will take care of you."

Bill, suddenly much farther away, called again: "Gretta! There is nowhere to land in that direction! You have to turn!"

Greenie and I lifted and slapped against the water, lifted and slapped, lifted and slapped. A gust of wind had yanked my hat off my head. The hat strings tugged at my throat. My face and hair were wet from the spray. I resisted the urge to cry. Where was the fast-forward button that would instantly change the scene to safe and cozy, Bill and me cuddled in front of a toasty fire?

The only way to that longed-for future moment was via actions taken in the present moment. The only one who could get me there was me.

I struggled to get back to the center of my Full Spectrum of thoughts and feelings, where I had access to possible interpretations of the moment that could lead me to more constructive actions. Old Bodyguards ruled by judgment and fear didn't need to run the show. I could choose to listen to a kinder, wiser internalized perspective with a more effective response.

"Breathe!" said that inner, calming voice.

I'd been holding my breath, grabbing quick, shallow gulps of air. I took three slow, deep abdominal breaths, and with a long exhale I imagined myself releasing the fear. My wiser self encouraged me to center, come back into my body, into the present, out of dire past and future stories. "YES— you are scared—AND you're going to be okay. You can do this."

I would trust Greenie and myself, stroke by stroke, to make it home. Concentrating on the physical sensations of the paddle in my hands, thighs pressed against the sides of my kayak and feet pushing on the pegs, I was in the now. I stopped watching the scary movies in my head and got attuned to the lifting swells. My muscle memory returned, and my stroke miraculously improved. Using my emotional and physical core, I shifted our direction, turning alongside the waves. Water sloshed over the spray skirt, but we stayed upright. The urge to tense was strong, but focusing on my breath helped me relax into a different kind of control. My eyes no longer needed to identify each rising, threatening wave. Paddling with renewed determination, I pointed Greenie in the direction of the distant landing. The waves rose from behind.

THAT EVENING, ON THE PORCH overlooking the lake, we saw a hue-drenched double rainbow. Bill took my hand as we stared at the magical arc of colors. "That was the most fun I ever had kayaking," he said, turning toward me, excitement glinting in gray-green eyes. I hesitated, looking up at his dear, enthusiastic, expectant face.

It matters how we tell the story. I wondered, could I have compassion for myself and how I reacted, not add more evidence to the belief that I was "helpless and incompetent"? What could I learn by being curious about my inner experience?

In my mind, the tale ends with an image of the double rainbow, the ancient symbol of renewed hope after a storm. I kissed Bill, and we gazed out toward the horizon.

Our adventure on that stormy lake reminded me that I have a choice in how I meet life's events—especially the ones that threaten to swamp my metaphorical boat. Viktor E. Frankl, a psychotherapist who survived Nazi concentration camps during World War II but lost his family, later wrote in *Man's Search for Meaning*, "Everything can be taken from a man but one thing: the last of the human freedoms—to choose one's attitude in any given set of circumstances, to choose one's own way."

Everything can be taken from a man but one thing: the last of the human freedoms – to choose one's attitude in any given set of circumstances, to choose one's own way.

Looking back on my kayaking adventure, I recognize that attachments to old, shame-ridden identities, self-imposed or laid on my self-image by the judgment of others, were interfering with what was in this case a life-saving moment. Whether life's challenges are physical or emotional, we can free ourselves from being ruled by toxic, unhelpful self-beliefs. Instead, when we access our Full Spectrum of thoughts and feelings, we can identify, strengthen, and act on what is capable, courageous, and compassionate within us.

We humans are complicated critters. As psychotherapists, Bill and I provide tools and a safe place for our clients to explore, understand, and transform their Full Spectrum of contradicting (useful and not so useful) beliefs, Bodyguards, and comments from the internalized voices from our past. People come to us because they are confused, disappointed, and un-comfortable—maybe to the point of life-altering emotional pain. Habitual remedies such as numbing, avoidance, and distraction become solutions that destroy the ability to feel joy, love, and satisfaction—to be wholly alive. We help each person find their way to the life they really want, not necessarily the life they think they should want or the one that others want them to have.

It's a brave thing to do, to work at identifying the reasons for our un-happiness and begin the process of change. We are afraid of the unknown, even if the known is not what we want. This is a guide based on concepts and tools that Bill and I, as well as hundreds of our clients, have used to radically change our lives.

There is a way there, to that fully lived life.

CHAPTER 2

A Full Spectrum Perspective

Suddenly, the ground drops away and you are in a mind movie, on your inner horror film network. You've been mentally transported to some scary Trauma Land, battling for your life, Fighting, Fleeing, Freezing, or Fawning to protect yourself from your particular brand of monster or dangerous situation. Searching for a way out, you crawl through a thicket of thorns and find yourself in a swamp of despair, breathing in the fog of hopelessness. Wandering around, you enter a cave and are in a hall of glass and mirrors that leads to a room filled with hundreds of televisions showing scenes from your past. There is a flashing red exit sign, and you slam open the metal door and find yourself outside, blinking in the sunlight, standing where you were before and not sure how you got there. There is no hole in the ground, birds are singing, and you hope a sudden trip to Trauma Land will never happen again. But it will.

I'll often ask a client (and myself): "Where are you today? What's the landscape? What's your inner weather?" We have a sign on our door with the motto "Like weather, life happens. You can't choose the weather, but you can choose your response." As with my kayaking experience, how we choose to interpret a situation radically impacts our response. But can we really choose how we respond? Yes and no. Upsetting things happen, and we get upset. We report to ourselves and possibly others that we are some version

> *Like weather, life happens.*
> *You can't change the weather,*
> *but you can change your response.*

of angry, sad, happy, worried, or "fine!" Someone tells us or asks us what we are "really feeling," and we get defensive and confused. Or feel ashamed that our feelings are wrong and that for whatever reason we shouldn't feel that way.

Emotionally exhausting trips through the horror fun house of our mind are especially distressing because we don't know where we are, how we got there, if we will be there forever, or what could happen next. We feel lost and don't know how to get back home. It happens to all of us. We enter an inner landscape that feels uncomfortable, painful, or frightening. What if there was someone with satellite information who could identify where you are and suggest several routes back home? What if that someone was you?

"I KNOW I SHOULDN'T FEEL this way," said Wren, my twelve-year-old client. "But I still love my mom and want to see her even though she is the bad one who left. My dad is so mad and wants us to be mad at her too and tells us all the bad things she did, and I am. Really mad. And sad. But I remember fun times too, and then I think that if she was actually bad like my dad says and we just didn't know it, then maybe I shouldn't believe my memories. Maybe it was all a lie."

We were in my office sitting at the table, and Wren was working on a page of a mandala coloring book as we talked.

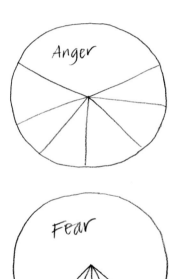

"What if you didn't have to choose and could just be curious about all your thoughts and feelings, even opposite ones or those you think you aren't supposed to feel?" I opened to a blank page of my sketchbook and drew a circle and divided it into different size pie pieces.

"What happens when your mom isn't there and you want her, right then? Imagine this like a color wheel of your thoughts and feelings. We could imagine this pie piece of anger as red and make it really big so other thoughts and feelings in different, maybe cooler, colors, become much smaller, to the point where you are no longer aware they exist. If someone else, or the voice in your head, keeps telling you over and over why you should be mad and hate your mom, then that anger pie piece will get even bigger and firmer, with thick walls around the edges. You can get locked in that feeling, fed by those thoughts. The anger feels right—what you should feel and will always feel."

I drew another circle with pie pieces and labeled the biggest piece "fear."

"What if after or instead of feeling angry, you got scared? Maybe you had the dark thought you might not see your mother ever again and maybe your dad might leave or die and you kids would be abandoned and sent to live with strangers or your aunt who you said was smelly and didn't like cats? You imagine all kinds of awful stuff and get so scared it feels like the monster under your bed has grabbed your foot. The thoughts get creepier and feel truer than true. Then your mom calls and tells you about plans for the weekend and suddenly you are in another pie piece. The black piece becomes much smaller. You feel like you will be okay. Life will be okay. Even fun."

The third circle I divided into equal sized pieces. "Let's name all the thoughts and feelings you have had in the last few weeks." Wren described the time in the school bathroom when she couldn't stop crying and then told me about seeing her mom's new place and how quiet and comfy it was

YOUR WAY THERE

and the feeling of relief knowing there wouldn't be fighting with her father there. We labeled those pieces "sad" and "comfortable/safe."

"I feel awkward sometimes with Dad," she said. "I don't know what to say or do. He lets us get by with stuff and buys us things, then all of a sudden he's pissed off over something that was fine before." I labeled that pie piece "confused and awkward."

"Don't forget the angry and scared pie pieces," Wren reminded me. "Because I'm always mad she left. And scared about what happens next. But there is a part of me that maybe understands. She got sort of crazy and really sad after her mom died. I never met her dad."

"Yep," I said. "Adults are just as complicated as kids. We all have what I call a Full Spectrum of thoughts and feelings, a changing wheel of pie pieces that each lead to different reactions. So. Imagine you are in a certain emotional pie piece, but another part of you, one I think of as the watching, wise Whole Self, is in the center of the circle and has a window into all your thoughts and feelings, the big ones and the slivers. If you tune into her, you might get some useful instructions, like, 'It makes sense that you get sad, confused, and angry. But those aren't all your feelings, all the time.' When you recognize your painful parts and give them understanding, then they don't need to fight so much for your attention and can make room for other, more comfortable thoughts and feel- ings. Focusing on those happier, wiser pie pieces helps them get bigger, and then they will be more likely to direct what you do instead of you acting out of your painful thoughts."

I told Wren, like I tell all my clients and remind myself, that learning a new way of navigating life takes practice before it becomes just what you do. We all want that super pill, secret tool, magic wand, or time machine that will transport us instantly to who and where we want to be. Oh well. I learned from a kayaking instructor that any kind of change, psychological, behavioral, or emotional, goes through four stages—and you can't skip from one to four!

Unconscious Incompetence is the first stage, where we are doing what we have always done, seeing things like we've always seen them, and are unaware that the way we know is outdated, useless, or, in some cases, a detrimental navigation system. A. A. Milne's Pooh Bear experiences that twinge on the edge of consciousness, as he is "coming downstairs now, bump, bump, bump on the back of his head, behind Christopher Robin. It is, as far as he knows, the only way of coming downstairs, but sometimes he feels there really is another way . . . if only he could stop bumping for a moment and think of it."

A Full Spectrum Perspective

Sometimes he feels there really is another way... if only he could stop bumping for a moment and think of it.

We all go bumping along, reacting to each next thing as our dreams slip and slide and morph into lives that aren't quite what we envisioned. We keep on this way until something or someone propels us into thinking about where we are, how we got here, and what we want instead.

Stage Two, Conscious Incompetence, is not at all comfortable! We see what we are doing and why it is not working so well, but we are still doing it all the same. Ugh. The discomfort leads some people to work even harder at being unconscious. (And there are so many methods to choose from! What are yours?) The problem is, once we know there's a more effective way, those twinges suggesting it might be time for change can become painful spasms and much harder to ignore.

So, we become super conscious and work with energy and focus to do things differently. This is Conscious Competence—Stage Three. Also hard. We need lots of positive reinforcement from ourselves and others to keep it going.

Eventually new habits of thinking and acting begin to become normal, natural, and what we do without thinking. Yay! Stage Four, Unconscious Competence, has arrived! We just don't know we are there until we slip back into Stage One or Two and think, "It's been a while since I've done this!"

Stage One: Unconscious Incompetence
Stage Two: Conscious Incompetence
Stage Three: Conscious Competence
Stage Four: Unconscious Competence

We go back and forth through all the stages, in all areas of our life, as we keep moving toward being more conscious and more competent. Increased awareness of the Full Spectrum of thoughts and feelings offers us choices and gives us the ability to direct our experience and actions toward the life we want.

YES, IT IS HELPFUL WHEN two people in a relationship have a Full Spectrum perspective and approach to communication. But most work done to change an operating system is done on our own, increasing and strengthening our lines of communication between the self in the experience and the wise, watchful Whole Self who is manning central control.

Here's another example: I get a notice from my bank that I'm overdrawn. I forgot to transfer funds to cover the monthly bills on autopay. A pie piece of shame blasts in my head, over and over—the mind-loop audio file, downloaded many years ago, of who and what I really am: "I am so unorganized and irresponsible! [Bad!] If I were who I should be, I would never make such a stupid mistake!"

At that moment, the critical judgment feels totally true, the only possible interpretation of my actions. Alternate interpretations, more useful pie pieces in my Full Spectrum, are obscured from view. I react to the shameful meaning of the action. My face gets hot, my chest gets tight, and my shoulders tense. I call the company, pay the bill with my credit card (making long, unnecessary apologies) and transfer the funds for next month. I feel foggy, agitated, and distracted by the damning soundtrack playing in my head. I eat a handful of peanuts (activating more critical thoughts) to distract me and soothe my discomfort. Then I remember to tune in to good old wise and watchful Whole Self in central control.

She understands why I'm upset and agrees that I might need to adjust my system for keeping track of funds. She also reminds me of all I have responsibly taken care of during an exceptionally busy month and the fact that it has been years since I last bounced a check. Nope, I'm not perfect and never will be. But I do okay. I extend my compassionate thoughts to Bill and decide not to give him a hard time about the fact that he forgot to take out the recycling.

Sitting quietly, I join my wise, watchful Whole Self and survey all my coexisting and contrasting realities. There are landscapes of memories and stories about other people being irresponsible. That place is dark and threatening. There are practical thoughts, viewed from a renewed commitment to being responsible, about what to make for dinner and whether I should buy those new shoes I liked. A bit more sun there. Following my breath back to center, I am comforted by the presence of my nurturing, compassionate Whole Self. She encourages me to look out through other portals and remember joyful times where my actions have been of benefit. I am complex and multifaceted. And so is life.

> *I welcome in whatever comes,*
> *for I know that all will change.*
> *Whatever life may send me,*
> *however life may bend me,*
> *I trust the light I hold within*
> *to guide and to befriend me.*

IMAGINE THIRTY WOMEN WITH LONG, dark hair dressed in colorful saris, smiling, clapping, and singing, "The night is cold, I'm feeling scared, but I know that this will change." Bill and I and the other singers improvise the verses of Bill's song, changing the weather and time of day and to reflect a correlating mood. "The sun is bright, I'm feeling joy, but I know that this will change," and "The clouds are gray, I'm feeling sad, but I know that this will change," until the verse "I welcome in whatever comes, for I know that all will change. Whatever life may send me, however life may bend me, I trust the light I hold within to guide and to befriend me."

Five weeks after the devastating tsunami that hit the day after Christmas, our friend and colleague Joan Hoeberichts, a Zen Buddhist Roshi as well as a psychotherapist, flew to Sri Lanka to do relief work. Joan forged connections with Sarvodaya, a powerful collective of mostly volunteers that depend on shared Buddhist values and Gandhi's principles for creating sustainable methods of self-help and empowerment. Joan organized a group of eight mindfulness-based therapists from the United States to help train thirty counselors to work in villages throughout Sri Lanka. Bill and I were part of her Psycho-Spiritual Healing Project.

Every few months for four years, two therapists from our group would travel to Sri Lanka to spend a week leading intense workshops, integrating the Sri Lankan counselors' cultural systems of faith with more Western approaches to healing through psychotherapy. We remained curious about their experience and customs, as they were curious to learn about ours.

As the Sri Lankan counselors learned new psychological methods for healing to use with the villagers, they processed with us many of the traumas they had also endured. Close family and friends had been lost to the tsunami as well as in the conflict between the Tamil and the Sinhalese. We met their vulnerability with teaching, using stories from all aspects of our lives. We were Buddhist, Hindu, Christian, and Muslim, from all parts of Sri Lanka and from many different backgrounds in the United States. We were not there to impose the "right" reality. We were there to share our Full Spectrum of thoughts and feelings, interpretations, and responses impacted by our experience as psychotherapists with a Western point of view.

Before the tsunami, there was almost no practice of psychological treatment in Sri Lanka. These thirty counselors became responsible for implementing techniques for working with trauma and grief in villages all across the country. Thousands of Sri Lankans flocked to their groups where the counselors shared approaches for healing they had experienced in our workshops. These brave young women traveled alone, via public transportation, often walking many miles to reach remote areas to conduct their groups and hear the stories of grief and loss.

As the counselors expanded their Full Spectrum to understand the tools we taught, we struggled to enlarge our Full Spectrum of awareness to understand their realities. This kind of growth happens when the question shifts from, "But what are you *really* thinking and feeling?" to a compassionate, nonjudgmental, openly curious, "What are *all* the thoughts and feelings you are aware of at this time?"

Within each of the counselors' "realities" were many thoughts and feelings all happening at the same time, some surprising and some contradictory. The counselor who had seen her husband and grown son swept away by the tsunami still held the sorrow but was also able to open her heart wide enough to laugh and sing and show great concern for others. "Yes, I am grieving to my core, and yes, I am able to smell the flowers, and yes, I can have the thought about a friend in pain and send her compassion, and yes, I can pay attention to a grandchild and find pleasure in reading her a book." She did not allow her tragic experience to become her sole identity and was able to experience life through other filters of perception.

THERE IS A BUDDHIST CONCEPT about being able to open your heart wider and wider, as if your consciousness and spirit were as wide as the vast blue sky and you were viewing the moment from that openhearted metaperspective. Another metaphor describes a tablespoon of salt in a glass of water versus a tablespoon of salt in a large blue lake. The salt is still there in the lake, but it will not taste the same as the salt in the small glass. There are many benefits to enlarging our focus.

Many psychological maladies involve fixating on one thought and one feeling. Someone having a panic attack or in the grip of a phobia, paranoia, or obsession has a very narrow focus. They see only the object or physical symptom they believe is generating the feeling. Someone quick to rage focuses on whatever, or whomever, that person thinks caused the anger. Addicts believe there is only one solution to discomfort—the object of the addiction.

We often huddle thoughts and feelings under the heading, "I am depressed." We concentrate on the physical experience of lethargy and ennui with the repeating refrain of "What's the point?" It is important to separate clinical depression from the more culturally prevalent description of a state of mind. Clinical depression is actually often not recognized, hidden behind other explanations for mood and behavior. When the Full Spectrum of thoughts and feelings is ignored, grief, frustration, and past traumas that tattooed toxic beliefs on the soul about self-worth or the chance for happiness and love are not recognized and therefore not addressed. We stick with one interpretation. All other possibilities are no longer considered.

Becoming aware of the Full Spectrum of existence allows life to be experienced as an ever-unfolding tapestry or bolt of cloth made of hundreds of colorful threads that weave in and out, changing in tone and hue throughout the tapestry, contrasting and complementing with the neighboring threads, and creating patterns and designs.

Embracing the complexity of life means becoming comfortable with the idea that there will always be aspects of our self and the situation that remain unknown. Some thin, clear nylon threads may add invisible strength and never be identified. Some aspects of life are buried during times of crisis or adverse conditions.

During the trip to Sri Lanka, I remembered and reconnected to forgotten threads that once nourished my soul. Aware of how easily life can be suddenly extinguished, I vowed to be as fully awake and alive as possible during my time as a human on Earth. The threads of my existence, changed by my experience in Sri Lanka, continue to run through my life.

The tools, concepts, and stories in this book all hinge on the idea that there is not just one way to experience a situation or tell the story of a life. Our lives have radically changed, and our clients' lives have changed through this practice. There is always more to learn and improve on. We are always a work in progress, moving through the stages of change—unconsciously incompetent, then uncomfortably consciously incompetent, struggling to be consciously competent, and finally, incredibly, feeling the relief and vitality of a life attuned to a Full Spectrum perspective. Step by step, day by day, you will find your way there.

CHAPTER 3

Nurturing Parent or Judging Parent?

can't believe I was such a scaredy-cat!" my thirty-something client, Julie, snapped. "I should have been able to ski that slope with Pete, even if it was a Black Diamond. But I got off the lift, looked down the mountain, and freaked. Everyone, including Pete, was sympathetic when I had to go down in a special vehicle. I could have taken lessons, gone on easier slopes, but I felt so humiliated. So instead I shriveled up like a stupid, wimpy girl during the day, huddled in front of the fire, scrolling on the internet, drinking way too much hot cocoa and at night slurping way too many martinis. Pete kept encouraging me to try again, but I was stuck, useless. Didn't even read my book. When I think about it, I just want to vomit with shame!"

I nodded. "That must have been painful and confusing. You're used to playing sports and spend a lot of time and energy being physically fit. I know that's often what you and Pete do together. The vacation weekend wasn't what you imagined. Must have been disappointing."

"Disappointing? I was a mess! When Pete began making moves in bed, I shut it down. I didn't want to have anything to do with my body. All weekend I was a cranky bitch. He probably hates me. I hate me!" She took a tissue to wipe the tears, then reached for her coffee.

Julie and I had worked together for almost a year, and I knew she had always been high achieving academically and athletically, fashionable, successful, and well liked. Her parents and older brothers were prominent professionals. Failure was for other people, other families. In a previous session, Julie revealed that her father had recently been diagnosed with Parkinson's disease. He'd had symptoms for a while but refused to see doctors. Her family was also embroiled in her older brother's divorce proceedings, blaming the soon-to-be ex-wife and refusing to acknowledge the role of Julie's brother's addictions.

Every week seemed to present a new challenge. She felt fear, sadness, and hope as she supported her cousin who was undergoing treatment for breast cancer. We diagramed Julie's equally complicated Full Spectrum of thoughts and feelings when we processed the news that her newly married best friend was now pregnant. Julie had concluded, "Life keeps changing and moving way too fast."

Julie's hand shook slightly, and a few drops of coffee spilled on her yellow silk blouse. She scrubbed at the stain with another tissue, then wailed, "I can't fall apart! Not now!"

I paused. "Was there ever a time when you felt okay to fall apart?"

She shook her head. "You know the answer. Not really."

"You hold yourself to a high standard."

"I expect more from myself than I do from others. I grew up privileged. I have no excuse."

"And that belief supports your description of yourself as a scaredy-cat or cranky bitch? Seems those descriptive names might have originated from comments made by someone else."

"My oldest brother called me a scaredy-cat when I wouldn't go along with his crazy schemes. And I guess my college boyfriend called me a cranky bitch if I got pissed off when he was acting like a jerk or if I was upset and emotional. In his mind, it was all hormonal. Maybe it is. I'm being ridiculous."

"Maybe there were real reasons for your reactions then and now."

"I refuse to feel sorry for myself and be a victim."

"Yet you are caring and supportive when others are suffering. Why do you deserve shaming and judgment and others deserve kindness and compassion?"

"I expect more of myself. I don't let myself off the hook."

"Sounds like you are a fish ready to be reeled in, not allowed to swim free. What are you hooked to? Who controls the line?"

Julie was quiet, then said, "The voice inside me that says if I'm not perfect, I'm a failure. I get tugs on that line all the time."

"You were hooked on that belief a long time ago. The bait that lured you was the praise given when you were judged as wonderful, 'perfect.' We all hunger for more of that delicious reward.

"Let's try a thought experiment. Imagine you're a little girl and you climb the ladder to the biggest slide in the playground. You've never done it before, and when you look down, it looks too long, too high, too scary, and you start to cry. What happens next?"

you're perfect!

"Depends on who is with me. If it's my brothers, they laugh and call me scaredy-cat. If it's my father, he gets super stern and tells me to be a big girl, pull myself together, and get on with it; don't be a quitter. My mother explains all the reasons why I'll be fine, and if I make her proud, she'll buy me an ice cream."

"Any other options?"

Julie thought for a while. "My Nana. I forget about her because she died when I was eight, but she was different. She might have climbed up the ladder and gone down the slide with me or helped me off the ladder and said it was okay, I'd do it another day. Maybe she'd show me how to slow the ride down using my feet and promise to catch me and hug me when I got to the bottom. Things seemed easier, less pressured with her.

"I remember my parents complaining because when I stayed with Nana we didn't 'do' anything. But that wasn't true. We'd feed ducks and make necklaces out of clover. Stuff like that. Nothing won prizes or got hung on the wall."

I drew a large circle on my pad. "This time it is the Full Spectrum of you as that little girl. Describe the pie slices."

"Well, when that little girl—me—is at the top of the ladder, the biggest pie slice is fear. She imagines going really fast and falling off or crashing onto the ground. Another pie slice is shame, imagining her mother and father disappointed in her and her brothers laughing. Label that one 'scaredy-cat.' There is a small pie piece imagining her success, proud that she is a 'big girl,' but it isn't very big. There is another small piece that I'd call 'baby' where I am sitting in Nana's lap, safe, cozy, and taken care of, not having to do brave things."

I smiled. "Now imagine yourself at the top of the mountain, spooked by the steepness and height of the slope. How would you describe your Full Spectrum?"

"Fear and shame. Lots of judgment. Not much else. Later, I needed to spread the judgment around and I found ways to criticize the place, the other people, and Pete."

"What if you add some Nana to the scene?"

Julie laughed. "I picture her knitting by the fire, asking people about where they're from and offering them mints."

"And what would she say to you?"

Julie was silent a moment, then looked like she might cry. "She would have given me a hug—and a mint. Said something like, 'There, there. That must have been scary, and you are scared about a lot these days—your dad, your brother, your friend, and whether or not you and Pete will get married and have kids. So many things you can't control. But it's okay. You're okay. Don't worry so much. You don't have to be perfect. No one is.'

"I wish my Nana was the voice in my head. Wish I sounded more like that. I judge people who talk like that—so sweet and gentle. I think they are soft, sappy. They'll never succeed. Maybe even simple. Tough and judgmental is for winners. Superior. I think my mother was embarrassed by Nana, where she came from, and my father treated her with disdain."

Then Julie's tears came freely, and we paused as she sat with her love and loss.

"SO AS A YOUNG CHILD, you experienced both nurturing and judgment. I want to introduce you to another way to conceptualize these internal systems, one we've adapted from theories described by Eric Berne, a psy-

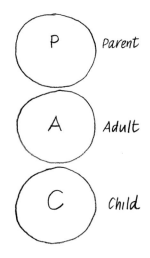

P — Parent

A — Adult

C — Child

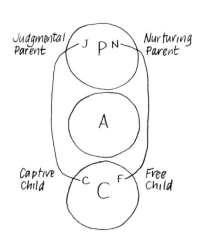

Judgmental Parent — J P N — Nurturing Parent

A

Captive Child — C C F — Free Child

I bet it's the best in the class!

Experiencing a pride memory

chiatrist. He identified three self-states we all go in and out of every day, through every stage of life. They are Parent, Adult, and Child." On my pad, I drew three circles, one on top of the other. I labeled the top one *P* and the bottom one *C*, with *A* in the middle.

"The P is for Parent," I told Julie. "The Parent is the part of us that is the caretaker, overseer, the one in charge, doctor, guide, judge, and teacher. We internalize the Parent self-state at an early age, according to what we see modeled by our own parents.

"A young child might offer his or her stuffed bear to another child who is crying or help care for a pet. We could identify those actions as evidence of ways the child has assumed the role of a nurturing parent. A child might also exhibit other kinds of behavior learned from parents when they discuss who should be allowed in the clubhouse and make judgments about which kids are cool, cute, or smart and which kids are not. We absorb what we experience. From birth we are solidifying systems of nurturing and judgment that, unexamined, will continue into the years when we are actual parents."

Julie looked wistful and shook her head. "So much time I spent mimicking my older brothers, wanting approval from my parents. And, I'm ashamed to admit, I used to follow the mean girl who ruled our group, dressing like her, talking like her, wanting her acceptance. I kept it hidden that I still loved my dolls and my crayons, and enjoyed it when our neighbors had me babysit."

I nodded and added a *J* on the left and an *N* on the right side of the circle labeled *P*.

"According to this model, the Parent aspect has two forms: the critical, Judgmental Parent, *J*; and the compassionate, Nurturing Parent, *N*. Corresponding to each of those internalized parents are the Captive Child and the Free Child."

I placed a small *C* on the left of the *C* for Child and an *F* to the right of the circle. I then drew a line between the *J* for Judgmental Parent and the *C* for Captive Child and another line connecting the *N* for Nurturing Parent to the *F* for Free Child.

"Our Parent aspect usually echoes our actual parents as well as other authority figures from our childhood. The Judgmental Parent doles out both praise and blame, creating and then reinforcing their child's Pride and Shame identities. They may mean well when they say, 'What a beautiful picture. I bet it's the best in the class! You are such a good little artist!' But the Captive Child identity is born, trained to seek the sweet judgment of praise. The Captive Child relinquishes the ability to assess and navigate his or her own experience and, instead, depends on others to issue the verdict on the value of their own efforts and how to proceed in life. It's like having a sugar addiction. We become programmed to seek the reward rather than take in the nourishing satisfaction available through attention to the process. We become hooked to the Judgmental Parent within us and those around us who take on that role.

"A different version of the Captive Child emerges from a steady dose of disappointment and disapproval from parents and other voices of authority. At the sight of the child's picture, these Judgmental Parents proclaim, 'What a mess! Cats don't have red dots, and they're not purple. You're never going to succeed if you don't learn to do things right and stop being such a clown.'

Experiencing a shame memory

"The criticized and humiliated child will, nonetheless, remain dependent on the Judgmental Parent, hoping to change the script and someday win the longed-for reward of praise. The child who rebels and reacts in defiance of both the real and internalized Judgmental Parent is still captive to the system, focused on the other's reaction rather than focused on his or her own experience.

"When, as adults, we are in the position of Captive Child, we need someone else to tell us who we are and evaluate how we've done. Our actions are in reaction to the anticipated judgment of a real or imagined someone else. The child or adult who declares, 'You're not the boss of me! I'm doing the opposite of what you want!' is still guided by the expected judgment of someone else, rather than an inner assessment."

Experiencing a defiance memory

"So, what about the Nurturing Parent connected to what you called the Free Child. How is that different?" Julie asked.

"The Free Child aspect is conceptualized as spontaneous, curious, sensual, and attuned to the visceral experience of life. In an actual child, the Free Child self would savor experiencing all aspects of an ice cream cone, laugh with glee rolling down a grassy hill, delight in spontaneous games of make believe, and, eventually discovering sexuality, use all that curiosity and playfulness and sensual attunement in the art of making love. The Nurturing Parent observes and reflects back the child's actions and emotions, expressing interest and curiosity about the child's experience.

"A nurturing, curious response to the child's artwork could be, 'Wow! You spent a long time drawing, and look at all that purple! Do you want to tell me about your picture?' The Nurturing Parent is helping the child to focus on his or her own experience rather than look to the judgment of others. The child might answer, 'It's a special cat that nobody has seen before, and the red dots are ladybugs. I was drawing another cat, but it didn't go right so I turned it into a rock and made bugs be her friends.' A Nurturing Parent might say, 'Yeah. It's disappointing when things don't turn out the way we plan.' The message is not, 'You shouldn't feel that way,' but rather a validation of what the child is actually feeling. After the child has felt understood, then a possible way to address the problem might be suggested.

Experiencing a satisfaction memory

"A Free Child develops confidence in his or her own abilities and perceptions as well as remaining interested in, and able to take into consideration, the perspective of others. They are not without rules and boundaries. They learn to share and put crayons away so they don't get stepped on or lost. They also know that purple cats are fine when drawing for fun and when shown to specific adults, but not all adults will have the same reaction."

"That's for sure!" agreed Julie. "The teachers who I'd call nurturing were the ones I really wanted to please. I feared the ones who were strict judges. And you know what category was prevalent in my house. But then what is the *A* for in this diagram if the Parent and Child roles are both in us as children and adults?" Julie asked.

I explained, "This model identifies the Adult as the problem solver, investigator, and negotiator. The Adult aspect in a child would be the part that works at learning how to stack blocks, say the alphabet, then drive a car, pay bills, discuss problems, and plan a vacation. Maybe a ski vacation?"

Julie laughed. "Ha! What a fiasco. My Judging Parent is furious I made such a mess of things. My Captive Child felt so ashamed, but I guess I was also saying 'You can't make me' by refusing to take lessons and eating and drinking my way through the weekend."

"You got it!" I said. "How else can we use this model to conceptualize what happened on the ski weekend?"

Julie took over. "Captive Child Julie, wearing the golden chain attaching her to Mr. and Mrs. Judgmental Parent, got scared and freaked. The Judgy *P*s were ashamed of their Captive Child who wasn't being who she should be, so they began transmitting nonstop angry messages. Captive Child Julie wanted comfort, and to quiet the blaring, blaming voices, she went for the hot chocolate, cozy fire, snacks, and sweets, with plenty of alcohol. Adult Julie was iced out of the interaction and had no opportunity to problem solve and calmly suggest a lesson or easier slope. Judgmental Parent and Captive Child were too busy fighting over who had control of the situation. At one point I went into the arcade and got obsessed playing this violent game that expressed exactly what I wanted to do. Makes sense why Adult didn't stand a chance. Pete was in the line of fire of the ongoing battle and got shot at by both angry Parent and angry Child. No Nana. No Nurturing Parent. No Free Child. How does that sound?"

I laughed. "That sounds about right. It's a lot to think about."

Julie sighed. "And talk to Pete about, Adult to Adult. He was so confused and hurt by my reaction. He didn't understand because I didn't understand. I was just reacting."

"Reacting to interpretations you were taught to have about yourself in similar situations. And now you've considered other interpretations and are considering a character more like your Nana to be your wise, watchful Whole Self in charge of central control."

"Yeah. I think I might tweak that a bit!"

"And you can. It's always just you. Doing life. Finding your way."

THE VOICE WE HEAR MOST often coming out of central control and making a running commentary on what we and others do can emerge from a Nurturing Parent and become a wise, compassionate Whole Self, able to discern the complexity and nuances of our Full Spectrum and anticipate repercussions based on awareness and consideration of others' Full Spectrums. Our Whole Self has the ability to comfort, encourage, and guide us along the path.

Or, our central control can be ruled by a rigid, narrow-sighted version of a Judgmental Parent, acknowledging only good or bad, right or wrong, success or failure, and other black or white, either/or interpretations, issuing defining verdicts about our identity and experience. Their praise often involves comparison to others, and verdicts of success contain the unspoken threat of future failure. The feeling that one is never good enough usually indicates a never-satisfied Judgmental Parent installed in central control.

Childhood is the time when so many of our systems are put in place, systems of communication that continue throughout all stages of life. We live in a world of judgments and verdicts. There is no escape. We aren't always going to say the perfect Nurturing Parent words, just like others aren't going to say them to us. Our internalized Judging Parent and Nurturing Parent are permanent entities.

The adjustment we can make is a matter of choice. Which one do we give the greater say in determining the meaning and guiding the process of our actions? Which one takes over in our central control, either tuning us in to our Full Spectrum or focusing our attention on reactive pie slices? The power struggle between those two forces, with their divergent agendas, can create quite an energetic inner conflict. First, we need to get conscious of which voice already rules. Power will not be easily relinquished. Compassionate understanding is key.

CHAPTER 4

How Interpretation Directs Our Path

Charlie, a relatively new client who'd started therapy for "self-improvement," thought he was being the best husband ever, and instead his actions led to the biggest fight ever in his three-year marriage.

What is the meaning of a vacuum cleaner? Not its use, its meaning. What does it mean when someone gives someone else a vacuum? Answer: there is no intrinsic meaning to a vacuum cleaner or the gift of a vacuum cleaner. The meaning changes according to the interpretation of the person getting or giving the vacuum. Vacuums operating with artificial intelligence might eventually have an opinion on the matter, but for now they are not included in the conversation.

We think that a certain action causes a predictable reaction. This holds true for physics but becomes much more complicated when humans are involved. How we interpret the action, what meaning we give to the action and objects involved, is key to what happens next.

Sandra, Charlie's wife and mother of their two-year-old daughter and three-month-old son, had been complaining since before they were married about the ancient vacuum she had inherited from a roommate. Charlie had never owned a vacuum cleaner. When he was single, a cleaning service came once a month and used their own vacuums. Before that, floors were never much of a concern.

Birthdays were important to Sandra, and this was a big one. She was turning forty. You might guess where this is going.

Charlie decided that a big birthday warranted a big, expensive present, something he felt confident that Sandra really wanted. So, he asked his mother—always proud of her meticulous housekeeping abilities—what vacuum he should buy for Sandra. His mother, as usual, had strong opinions. They never discussed the fact that the house his mother had maintained for many decades was furnished with wall-to-wall carpeting, while the co-op Charlie and Sandra had recently purchased had hardwood floors decorated with rugs Sandra had collected during her travels.

Charlie researched where to get the best deal on the recommended vacuum and bought every accessory possible, along with extra bags and a warranty. He got super-wide wrapping paper and used a whole roll of ribbon to make an elaborate bow. There the present sat, under a blanket in the back of the closet until the moment he triumphantly presented it to Sandra, just after she blew out a bonfire of candles in front of a gathering of friends, family, and many of Charlie's coworkers that Charlie had organized. Sandra smiled as she unwrapped the box, and he snapped pictures.

Moments after the vacuum was revealed, Charlie's mom was by Sandra's side explaining why this was best and how much cleaner Sandra's house would be now that she had a suitable machine. Sandra nodded, said, "Thanks. It's a great vacuum. Now who wants cake?"

The fight didn't happen until they were cleaning up and all the guests were gone. Charlie opened with, "Is there something going on, Sandra? I don't understand how you could be so rude. You barely looked at my present. It was humiliating. Everyone knew how much research I'd done. Are you getting your period?"

Sandra countered with, "No! It is not 'that time'—your convenient explanation for whenever I might get upset by your stupid behavior and remarks. What's wrong is that I'm married to someone who has absolutely no clue who I am and has no interest in finding out!" The activated interaction continued with raised voices, tears, the throwing of a pillow, and doors slamming; it ended with Charlie sleeping in the living room. Charlie did not follow Sandra's suggestion (or Freud's interpretation), which was to "Go sleep with your mother! She's the one you care about!"

The baby woke, adding his wails, and their daughter wandered in, rubbing her eyes and asking, "What's going on?" while Charlie made his bed on the couch. In our session the next day, Charlie was still so mad he could hardly sit still. I brought him a glass of water.

"It was the most expensive present I ever bought! And I wrapped it myself! I was so mortified! What are my coworkers going to think about me, seeing her react like that? My mother told me as she was leaving that she would have been very grateful if my father had ever bought her such a wonderful present. I know I'll hear more about Sandra's reaction from her."

I spent some time focusing on Charlie's hurt feelings and how he viewed the evening, inviting him to express all that the buying and giving of the vacuum had meant to him.

"The vacuum was an expression of my appreciation, an act of love and devotion. Sandra is a wonderful wife and mother, an amazing person! Beautiful, smart, funny! She'd been asking to get a new one, but I kept saying we should wait until she went back to work and we had more money. That's why I thought she'd be so pleased, react so differently."

"You imagined Sandra's reaction to your actions according to how you interpreted the buying and giving of the vacuum. I suspect her interpretation was quite different. We react according to our interpretation of an action, then our reaction becomes an action that is interpreted by the other person, and that interpretation leads to their next reaction. The vacuum meant one thing to you and something else to Sandra. Your mother had yet another interpretation, I'm sure. How did you interpret her reaction to your present?"

"It wasn't just a random interpretation! It was rude! She was so ungrateful. She could have at least pretended to be excited."

"What did she say about her reaction?"

Charlie folded his arms across his chest. "She said when she saw the vacuum she had to work hard to not burst into tears. That it was just another example of my wanting her to be my mother. That all anyone wanted her for was to cook, clean, and be a milk machine. When I said she was being ridiculous and she had no reason to feel that way, she threw a pillow at me and began yelling that I didn't understand—would never understand—and that if I hadn't been raised to think I was God's gift to the world, I might be able to see someone else's point of view."

"In other words, the meaning for her of that moment was extremely different from the meaning that moment held for you and what you wanted that moment to mean to her. Rather than being curious about her experience and why she reacted that way, you argued that your interpretations of the gift and the moment were the only true, right interpretations."

Charlie looked uncomfortable. I softened my voice. "I know you meant well and were trying to please. You were disappointed."

"And she said she knew that. That's why she tried to control her reaction. But turning forty and stepping back from her career to be with the kids was hard, and then she went on and on about all the changes. I tried to comfort her by telling her I liked her bigger and wrinkly, and she didn't have to be Sexy Sandra for me to love her, and she flew into a rage. That's when I went and slept on the couch."

I was quiet a moment. "And how might she have interpreted your words?"

Charlie unfolded his arms, reached for his water, took a sip, and sighed. "I know. It was a stupid thing to say. And too close to another sore topic. We've only had sex once since the baby was born, and it wasn't that great. Her boobs hurt. Actually, a lot of places hurt, and I was awkward. She ended up crying, and we decided to eat ice cream and watch a show."

Charlie was getting the point, so I pressed forward. "The meaning of things can change when roles change. Including parts of our body. Breasts mean one thing when we're fifteen and wanting to be seen as attractive, and another when they are a utilitarian tool to feed our baby. Think of all the meanings connected to sex. That's why communication is so important. Actions that were interpreted as exciting, daring, and adventuresome become dangerous, irresponsible, and even emotionally wounding in another context.

"In our Full Spectrum, the old meanings attached to staying out drinking until 3:00 a.m. or surfing in the high waves of an oncoming hurricane might coexist with newer, contrasting, and opposing interpretations of those actions. Contradicting interpretations within our Full Spectrum interact with contradicting interpretations within another individual's Full Spectrum—a definite challenge to communication and fertile ground for misunderstanding."

"I'm always feeling misunderstood. I know she is too."

"Tell me about other arguments, those about the truth of what something meant."

Charlie dove into multiple accounts of conflicts that had left him baffled. "I don't understand myself sometimes. I find myself arguing positions I don't really believe. And I get stubborn, denying that some of my old patterns might still be there. With the vacuum, I wanted to please Sandra. But I also wanted to please my mother. That's hard to admit."

"Hard and confusing. We change, but old stuff remains, and we feel like a bundle of contradictions. Then we interact with others who are just as complicated and inconsistent. Not easy! Hopefully, as we get older, we are more able to understand and accept that nobody has interpretations exactly the same as ours. For the sake of community and to avoid conflict, we emphasize commonality and agree to meanings, but when we get into it, get the details, there are surprising differences, even with people we see as like us."

Charlie finished his water. "I married Sandra because I didn't want to be like my parents. Didn't want to be so locked in to my mother's judgment. It was presumptuous of me to buy the vacuum without Sandra's input. I get controlling about money, and that was in there too, in our fight. She was always fiercely independent, and I love that about her. I want to be needed, to be the generous provider, but I can understand that would have a different meaning for her. I'm going to suggest we return the vacuum and maybe go somewhere fun, just the two of us. But we'll talk about it. See what she wants."

I smiled. "Sounds like a plan."

CHANGE IS A DIFFICULT PROCESS. It doesn't happen instantly, even with new awareness. Remember the four stages of change? Charlie moved from

Stage One, defensive and bewildered, unconsciously incompetent, unaware of how the difference in their interpretations was creating conflict, to Stage Two, consciously incompetent, still making some of the same activating comments and behavior choices, but more able to understand Sandra's reactions and to adjust his actions.

Sandra was able to recognize his efforts and explain her reactions, rather than merely take the experience as more evidence that he didn't care enough about her to understand her point of view. Both were encouraged when humor, compassion, and curiosity about the other's interpretations replaced hurt, blame, and estrangement. Eventually, Stages Three and Four become more the norm, with both parents modeling what they told their children, using their words and making the effort to communicate and understand their own and the other's Full Spectrum of interpretations. Changing habitual patterns of perception and reaction is hard work.

WE HUMANS ARE MEANING MAKERS. Conversations involving only ourselves are no exception. A destructive argument and a solo panic attack both follow a similar domino-effect trajectory. Bill had a client, Shawna, who had been in a bad car accident. She was fine when driving on city streets, but every time she drove on the expressway, she had flashbacks of the accident. Her palms would sweat, her heart would race, her chest would tighten, her breath would become short and gasping, and she'd feel a little light-headed. This physical reaction would lead to the fear that she was about to pass out—never a good idea when driving. The interpretation that she was going to faint would lead her to exit the expressway.

In the office, Bill had her induce the same physical sensations she would have when panicked. She ran in place, breathed into a paper bag, and remembered scenes from the accident. She experienced the scary thoughts and physical sensations but added other less scary thoughts and feelings. Without denying the sensations and thoughts or making them "wrong," she was able to expand her awareness to consider that, yes, she might be afraid and "excited" driving on the expressway—and—she might not faint.

Interpretations that impact identity increase fear. Her thought, "Panic reactions prove I am weak and ridiculous," had become an entrenched and toxic belief. She feared both the situation and her judgment of herself in

Interpretations that impact identity increase fear.

the situation. Fear of judgment was added to the fear of an accident. Bill encouraged her to consider adding to her Full Spectrum an interpretation that included compassion and validation, such as, "It's understandable that I get spooked by the situation and my heart begins racing." The other, more threatening interpretations were still there, but Shawna learned to focus on more helpful pie slices.

Shawna recounted how her mother had been terrified of driving and never got her license. She died of breast cancer during the time Shawna was taking driving lessons in high school. "She always encouraged me to do what was scary and learn to drive. I was upset I couldn't show her my license before she passed. She would have been real proud. My dad is more of a pessimist. I think he liked that Mom was dependent on him. He doesn't understand why I don't just give up and take public transportation or a car service. I think there's a part of me that agrees with him, thinks I should be dependent—and safe. Rely on others. But Mom wanted me to dare more, not be held back like she was in so many ways."

Bill asked, "Can you imagine your mom cheering you on?"

Shawna nodded, tears coming. "'You go, girl!' That's what she'd say."

"And maybe give you a hug when you succeeded?"

Shawna nodded.

"Maybe you can imagine her when you start to feel anxious."

The Nurturing Parent in the form of Shawna's mother was a way for Shawna to give herself the encouragement and compassion she needed when caught in the grip of fear. Self-compassion loosens the grip of anxiety-provoking, paralyzing judgment. The Nurturing Parent within us can diminish the influence of the Judgmental Parent. When we are activated, our focus zooms in on one interpretation. That interpretation feels "truer than true" and is also usually attached to the belief that this is the way it has "always" been, and things will "never" be any different. There are no other possible interpretations, no other possible reactions.

Bill gave Shawna tools to help her recognize and evaluate her interpretations. Rating her reactions on a scale of 0 to 10, Shawna was able to determine her level of distress and observe the levels fluctuating over the course of the drive. A large, fast vehicle passing on her left was a 9, but most of the drive fluctuated between a 4 and a 6. She decided it was okay if she'd had enough and wanted to get off the expressway and take local streets. Shawna still felt panicky, but she widened her focus to include a Full Spectrum with many possible points of view, including, "I'm worried I'm going to faint and cause an accident and die; I'm having the thought that I'm weak and ridiculous; I know how to drive, and I'm a safe driver; my reaction is understandable; my level of panic is slightly lower; other people have panic attacks; the more times I successfully change the course of the panic attack, the more confidence I have; and it's okay if I sometimes have heightened reactions." Shawna allowed herself to have *all* her thoughts and feelings—not just the "right ones." She focused on the interpretation, "I know how to get where I want to go." And she did.

SOMETIMES, WHEN ALL INTERPRETATIONS ABOUT our life and who we are seem bleak and miserable, we need to actively find meaning that can give us some hope. My mother certainly felt friendless and hopeless the New Year's morning when she found the Potato Rock.

It was the year my parents separated. I was home from college. My mother was living in the house with my younger brothers, and my father had moved to an apartment. We had muddled through the rituals of tree trimming, gift giving, and an elaborate holiday dinner, although it had all seemed rather hollow and pointless. My brothers and I tried to lift spirits by holding an indoor, homestyle Olympics and playing every game in the house. Before midnight my mother wistfully commented that in all the years she had lived on the East Coast, she had never seen dawn break over the ocean. We seized on that as the ultimate goal. We would carouse until dawn, then go to the beach.

The beach was about an hour away, and we set off in the dark. A long stretch of sand separated the parking lot from the sea. A thick fog made it impossible to see beyond an arm's length. My mother's severe rheumatoid arthritis made ordinary walking difficult.

"You all go on," she told us. "I'll stay back here in the car."

I could hear the despair and discouragement in her voice. Years later she confessed that she had been suicidal, with a plan. Hope was gone. She had reasons. She had suffered with arthritis since she was a young child. Her parents were killed in a car crash on Christmas Eve when she was thirteen, and she was left an orphan, not taken in by family. Life had been hard. Her marriage had been hard. She worked at seeing the positive, like in her favorite childhood books *Pollyanna* and *Heidi*, and making "lemonade out of lemons," but she'd lost access to any of those indomitable, defiantly positive pie pieces in her Full Spectrum.

My mom was being swallowed by the dark, and I was desperate. We kids convinced her to let us hold her tightly on each arm and walk at her pace across the wide beach. The walk to the shoreline seemed interminable. The fog remained, and only the increasing

loudness of crashing waves assured us we were getting close. A few feet from the water, the low cloud began to dissipate, and the colors of the world reemerged. My brothers ran to the water. My mother looked down at the sand near her feet.

"Oh look!" she exclaimed. "Someone left a potato!"

My mother was half Irish, which meant that potatoes were her sacred food. Mashed potatoes, boiled potatoes, baked potatoes, scalloped potatoes, fried potatoes, and all other kinds of comfort-food potatoes were what my mother cooked when she was depressed, which was most of the time. My mother reached down to pick up the discarded potato. Just then, the sun popped up over the ocean's horizon and shed golden rays on the rock, shaped just like a potato, that my mother held in her hand.

"I know what this means," she said, tears trickling down. "God is giving me the promise of a potato. Life for me may not be fancy, but it can be like a potato and that's good enough! There can be moments like this. I'll be okay. We'll all be okay."

My mother held on to the Potato Rock during the drive home and kept it on the nightstand by her bed. Sometimes she would carry it in her purse. Whenever she needed to feel the promise of the moment on the beach, she would hold it in her hands and feel comforted. Her enthusiastic curiosity about life returned and sustained her. She bought a VW microbus and took a road trip across the country the year after my youngest brother graduated from high school. She took college writing classes and learned computer programming. When my girls were born, she moved close and while babysitting would recount the stories I heard as a child.

She was never well. When there was a crisis, like a trip to a hospital, the Potato Rock was packed first. She told the story of the Potato Rock to all who would listen. Nurses and doctors would sometimes inquire about the pale brown rock on her hospital tray.

"It's my secret medicine. You think you are curing me, but actually it's this rock."

I think she was only half kidding. She began to lend the rock to her friends, my friends—anyone who was going through hard times—with the firm agreement that when the crisis passed, she wanted the Potato Rock back. Yes, her life was hard, filled with pain, and she savored the daily discoveries, touched joy, felt hope. When she died, I inherited the Potato Rock.

I also inherited my mother's inquisitive nature with an ability to navigate a life full of contradicting interpretations resulting in many ways to tell a story. The Potato Rock was just a rock. There was no intrinsic meaning, only the meaning she chose to give it. My mother's interpretation of the finding of that rock on that particular New Year's morning was what gave her the strength to continue her life journey. She chose to recognize and remember an essential slice of her Full Spectrum, the pie slice of hope.

We have choice in how we interpret situations and how we react. Understanding how we and others are interpreting a situation is essential for successful communication and crucial to changing reactions. Is it just a rock, or is it a Potato Rock? Does having an accident mean we aren't meant to drive? Does the gift of a vacuum mean love and appreciation or a slap in the face? Our interpretation makes all the difference.

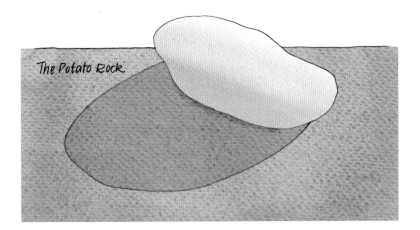

The Potato Rock

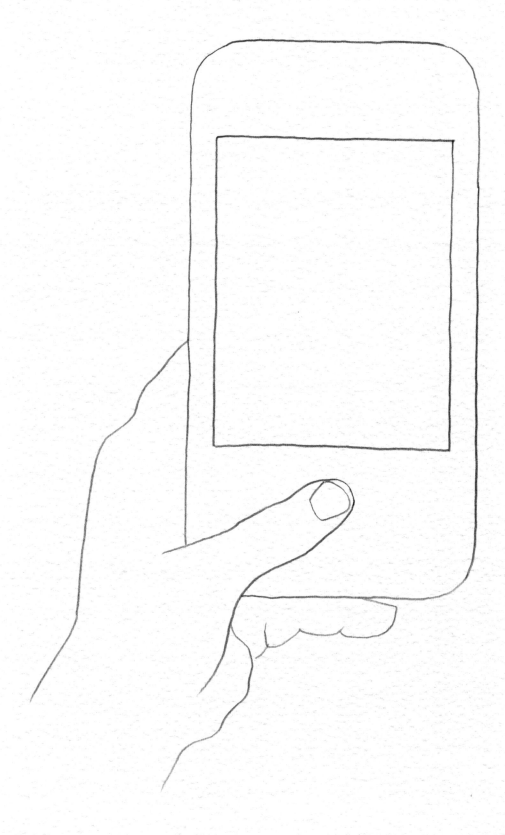

CHAPTER 5

Inner Camera or Outer Camera?

P atrick was anxious. Anxiety can be like an internal smoke alarm that is continually blaring warnings: "Danger! Not safe! Something's wrong! You're not okay!" Intrusive thoughts provide an endless supply of evidence supporting the interpretation that a threat is imminent. The body responds by activating that person's particular brand of defense.

Patrick arrived in my office after both his doctor and his physical therapist recommended that he see someone. "I guess they think my mind was broken in the accident along with my body. I do feel crazy sometimes. My wife, Kathleen, made me promise not to tell anyone I was seeing a shrink, but she told her sister and now her whole family knows."

"And asking for help is shameful?"

"Well, yeah! But that's my life now," he said, the knees of his long legs bobbing up and down as if he were running while sitting on my couch. I found out that redheaded Patrick had been the star basketball player at St. John's College when he married his high school sweetheart, Kathleen. He was signed by a semiprofessional team and had two great years. Everyone was sure he was going pro. Then, when he and his snowboard crashed into a tree and he was seriously injured, his potential career was over before it started. Their son, Todd, was two months old, and Kathleen was pregnant with their second son, Terry.

"It was bad. I almost died. They said I might never walk. Kathleen was furious, refused to come to the hospital that first week. She thought I was stupid to take the risk, and her family thinks I was *really* stupid. Even with insurance, the bills were enormous, and we had a lot of debt because Kathleen had been spending as if I was already making the big bucks. Her father bailed us out, and he never lets me forget it. I spend a lot of time with the boys, love it, but that's not going to count when they get older. Nobody wants a failure for a father."

"You seem pretty certain that you are and will always be a failure," I said in response to his rapid-fire monologue.

"The verdict is in, and I doubt I'll ever be able to change it. Nothing I ever do can earn the same big bucks as being a basketball star."

"And that's the only measure of success?"

"In their eyes, yes."

"Are they the only eyes that count? What about other people in your life?"

"My mom, my sister. When I was a freshman in college, Mom moved to Portland to help my big sister with her son, who has cerebral palsy. After my smash-up, they kept saying how I'd be on my feet and succeeding in no time, but now we stick to safe topics. Too painful. Mom tells me I'm on her prayer list, but I know my sister's son gets more of her prayers. She's basically told me that she regards him as an innocent victim of circumstance, but my situation is my own damned fault. That's one place where Mom and Kathleen see eye to eye. And Kathleen doesn't let me forget it. Everyone agrees, I'm a loser."

"Seems Kathleen and her family play a big role in how you see yourself."

"My father was long gone when we got together, and Kathleen's family became my family. My other world was basketball. Lost that. When I was able to walk again, my father-in-law got me a job with his friend who sold cars and promised I would be flush in no time. But I sucked. The boss kept telling everyone I used to be this great player. Me. The gimp. It was humiliating. I started to find reasons not to go in. Finally, I was fired. That clinched it. The only thing I could do was work for my father-in-law handing out keys to customers in his rent-a-car business. At work I have to call him Mr. O'Malley, and he makes jokes to the other workers about me 'dropping the ball' or 'being lame.' Can't argue. It's true."

Patrick was a Captive Child chained to a Judgmental Parent, represented by an entire tribe of judgmental O'Malleys. He was not allowed a dominant role in any category. The more I suggested alternative possibilities to a life of shame and failure, the more Patrick brought in opposing evidence provided by his adopted family. Joining in judgment while perfecting the art of ridicule and slipping in jabs of sarcasm was the family sport—toxic rituals that served as both glue and control. Judging others as inferior gave the clan assurance that they were superior, beating the competition. It left them feeling certain that the imagined audience of "people who matter" would continue to clap, agree that the O'Malleys were doing everything "right," and rate them The Best! Judging Patrick as an inferior failure provided them with evidence of their contrasting success and superi-

> Joining in judgment while perfecting the art of ridicule and slipping in jabs of sarcasm was the family sport—toxic rituals that served as both glue and control.

ority. His unacknowledged function in the familial system was to reinforce the power and control of the other family members.

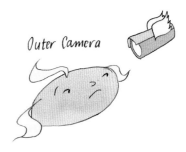

Outer Camera

I often use the metaphor of viewing our life through an Outer Camera, as if we are seeing ourselves through the eyes of a Judgmental Parent who is intent on declaring a verdict of good or bad, right or wrong. An Outer Camera emphasizes a quick and easy, superficial judgment on how we imagine our appearance and actions would be rated by others. Our Inner Camera, on the other hand, is focused on our Full Spectrum, inner experience. It is a metaphor for a sense of agency, confidence, and reliance on our own perceptions and capabilities—qualities that are best put in place in the early years with a Nurturing Parent or a Nurturing Parent figure supporting our emerging Free Child. They encourage a compassionate curiosity.

Are we satisfied, disappointed, challenged, frustrated? How are we energetically connecting with others? When we rely on our Inner Camera, we take into consideration other people's perceptions and interpretations but are not governed by their judgment. We control our Inner Camera. When we find ourselves performing for an Outer Camera, we may be in the imagined audience as well as on stage, but forces outside us control the lens.

Patrick's mom, raising two kids on her own, overworked and distracted, would overcompensate for her insecurities by heaping on praise. Her two kids took the praise in as nourishment, just as candy or a glucose drip can be a substitute for a well-balanced meal. They were trained to look outside of themselves, toward the metaphorical Outer Camera, to assess how they were doing, rather than check in with their own experience. Patrick's mother was familiar with the currency of judgment, and her praise quickly turned to blame when Patrick couldn't just bounce back. In sessions, we worked on the notion that Patrick needed to develop the ability to see himself through his Inner Camera.

In our first months of sessions, Patrick could only repeat, like a memorized mantra, a litany of examples proving he was a failure. And permanent failure meant permanent anxiety. He had a hard time accessing his own thoughts and feelings, and when he did, he didn't trust that they were real. He could only see himself through the O'Malleys' judging eyes. They controlled his Outer Camera. Their interpretation of reality had to be true.

Patrick was near tears as he told me, "Kathleen is so mad. I am not what she signed up for. She hates her life. She hates me. When Terry dropped and broke his plate, she asked him if he wanted to be a loser like his father. She thinks Todd was fighting because he's embarrassed that we don't have a big house like his friends. She's right. I can't give them the life they should have. Feels like the other me, the successful me, was some strange dream."

I reminded him of times he had told me about, where he offered his boys an alternative, more compassionate, complex, Full Spectrum way of

Inner Camera

interpreting the things that happened to them and to others. Patrick sheepishly smiled. "I know that you think I'm a hard nut to crack and get frustrated because every week I bring in more evidence of failure, but I am listening to you. And being there for my boys is the one thing I do that feels important. I walk them to school, talk to the teachers, set up their playdates, and take them to doctors. Kathleen hates doing that stuff."

I agreed. "So important. Makes a difference!"

A few sessions later, Patrick, with a big grin, announced a plan. He would go back to school to become a teacher and coach. But by the next session, Kathleen had already popped that balloon with her reaction. "All your decisions are ridiculous! You make me sick! You don't care about us! You only care about playing hero to a bunch of adoring kids! You think it's okay we'll always be poor! I've married a loser!"

The O'Malley family worked hard to present an image of success to an imagined Outer Camera, by which everyone who mattered would see them and judge them winners. Teachers were considered low-paid do-gooders or losers who taught because they couldn't succeed in the real world. Patrick's presence spoiled the desired family portrait of perfection.

Patrick and Kathleen lived in an apartment in a building his father-in-law bought for an investment. Kathleen spent most of her time in her parents' house. Discouraged from any social interactions not part of the O'Malley circle of acceptable people, Patrick had no friends he could talk to who could give him another perspective. As Patrick began to question Life According to the O'Malleys, he realized how much he systematically edited out thoughts diverging from what his wife and in-laws believed, avoiding the reaction that his ideas were wrong or stupid.

"It's like I'm in a cult or trance. I am dependent on the O'Malleys for everything, and I never was good with conflict except on the basketball court. Even then, I wasn't a fighter. I was a team player. The O'Malleys are my team. And I am the guy who keeps losing the game!"

Awareness for Patrick was slow and arduous. There were no easy answers. His sadness increased as the numbness subsided and he began to recognize the extent of his wife's verbal abuse and how much he had been hypnotized by the O'Malleys' harsh, judgmental view of every situation. Kathleen refused to come to couples therapy, claiming that Patrick was the problem. The heavy drinking that was part of the O'Malley family culture made serious discussions even more difficult. Eventually he found support in an Al-Anon group that he secretly attended.

"She'd kill me if she ever found out!"

He surfed the O'Malleys' waves of ridicule and gave up his dream of becoming a teacher. Instead, he began training as a radiologist, a profession that promised to make more money and sounded more important than teaching, but had flexible hours that allowed him to be home in the afternoons when the boys got out of school. Kathleen was not completely happy, but tensions eased.

Patrick practiced seeing through his own Inner Camera, encouraged by an internal Nurturing Parent to have confidence in his own perceptions. The habit of seeking approval from a judging Outer Camera slowly shifted. His developing Nurturing Parent found a voice as he worked with his sons and with the children he coached at the community center. Patrick realized that he could never "make Kathleen happy" and that her habit of ridicule was starting to have an effect on the boys.

"I get my little guys to tell me what's going on with them. I want them to know that I'm interested in how they see things, so that they feel confident and don't get hypnotized. I offer that alternative interpretation you're always talking about—a judgment-free zone. Kathleen works hard performing for her Outer Camera, rating her worth by the number of 'likes' she gets on social media. I don't know that she'll ever change. She's chained to powerful Judging Parents, real ones and the ones inside her. But me judging her only keeps us both in that prison."

Patrick became more aware of his complicated Full Spectrum of thoughts and feelings. There would always be the harsh, judgmental thoughts and a longing for the sweet reward of praise, but there were also Inner Camera perceptions—feelings of frustration and disappointment, but also of satisfaction, acceptance, and encouragement. He reflexively still looked first to his Outer Camera for approval but was more likely to use the perceptions of his Inner Camera to guide his actions. He began to ask, "What is my experience and

> There would always be the harsh, judgmental thoughts and a longing for the sweet reward of praise, but there were also Inner Camera perceptions— feelings of frustration and disappointment, but also of satisfaction, acceptance and encouragement.

how do I interpret this moment?" instead of the habitual, "What will others think of me? How will they judge my actions?" He was not as quick to look to others to determine or define his decisions.

"I'm Catholic. Not going to get divorced. At least not until the boys are out of the house. I'm learning to let the judgments whiz by. If I dodge, don't catch it or pick it up, then it's just someone else's ball. Not my responsibility. I've got my own game."

Attentiveness to how others interpret and experience our actions is an important, useful skill. But increasing awareness of the perceptions of others, and taking what we understand about them into consideration, is different than relying solely on the judgment of others.

The Outer Camera, as I envision it, is cultivated by the Judgmental Parent intent on dividing the world into two distinct choices, good or bad, right or wrong, us or them. The Outer Camera is designed to detect and reinforce judgment. When we are performing for the Outer Camera, we are asking the presiding judges, "How do I rate? Do I deserve pride or shame? Success or failure? Am I an accepted member of the tribe?" Sometimes the only judge sitting on the bench is me judging me.

We can abdicate our self-determination to codes created by ancestral figures, outmoded rules of behavior that were necessary for survival in the past but are no longer relevant. In those cases, the person or people we are performing for, the ones we imagine scrutinizing us through an Outer Camera, are powerful ghosts who haunt our imagination. They are long gone or were never really there.

SARAH CAME TO THERAPY BECAUSE she worried that she was a "bad mother." According to her version of parenting, mothers should not feel annoyed by their children. And she did. Often. She was caught between powerful judges with conflicting criteria for success or failure. If she spent time playing with her daughter but toys were everywhere, was she a good mother or a bad housekeeper? If her daughter cried, was she a bad mother? Or, if she gave in so her daughter didn't cry, was she a bad mother?

She had known how to be a good daughter, good student, and good employee. There were rules to follow, and she was very good at following the rules. But lately it felt like every decision led her down a twisting maze of rights and wrongs. The Judgmental Parent in her head was always annoyed at her, and she passed that annoyance on to her daughter, who, it seemed, was making her feel that way.

I suggested we focus on one reoccurring source of tension. Sarah said her daughter's requests for snacks evoked almost instant anger. We began filling in the parts of her Full Spectrum, on the lookout for judgments and anxiety-provoking beliefs. Sarah's daughter, Ani, was rail thin, like her mother and father. Sarah was not currently worried about her daughter's weight, but she admitted to harshly judging other people she viewed as overweight.

"I thought that if I'm always giving my daughter snacks, she might form a snack habit, develop a weight problem, and get rejected for being fat. So I made the rule that we only eat at mealtimes. But I felt so mean, so unloving, so I changed the rule. As long as it was healthy, I would give her a snack when she asked. But then she was asking all the time! I didn't want to be seen as raising a spoiled, manipulating, entitled child. It would be my fault if she has no self-control. That's why I get angry when she asks for a snack. I don't know what to say, to do! I don't want to be too lenient or too strict! I don't want to be like my mother," said Sarah, near tears. "I hated how my mother controlled everything I did!"

"When you say that your mother was controlling, do you have an image of her when you were a child?" I asked.

"Brushing my hair. She'd pull it very tight into perfect pigtails. She dressed me in old-fashioned, perfectly pressed dresses and would get so angry if my hair got untidy or my clothes got dirty. Less than an A in school meant I failed. The house had to be immaculate, always. Everything, including me, had to be perfect."

"What do you know about why that felt so important to her?"

"My mother did have to be perfect. Or at least try to be. My grandmother was from Tokyo and my grandfather was a soldier from Kansas stationed in Japan in World War II. He met and married my grandmother and brought her back to the States. My mother was half Japanese and half Midwest American. She and my Japanese grandmother never felt fully accepted. My mother once told me that eyes were always on her, waiting for her to do something wrong. There were always whispers and snickers and sometimes mean things written or said.

"My father met my mother in college and saw her as smart, capable, and beautiful. He never understood why she was anxious, angry. They'd have fights over her judgments and fears. He'd tell her she was paranoid and too sensitive. 'Take a chill pill,' he'd say and walk away. Finally, he left. Just me and Mom. And her anger. He remarried, had another family. She didn't make it easy for him to see me, so eventually he stopped trying."

"It's understandable why you would believe that if you aren't perfect, you'll get left, or at least harshly judged, shamed. And, like your mother, you want to keep your daughter and yourself safe by being perfect. But there are no clear rules about how to be a perfect mom."

The Outer Camera judges watching Sarah's every move felt very real. We spoke about ways in which they were real for her mother and grandmother, and how their fears had been transmitted and tattooed into Sarah's core. The threat of ridicule and rejection reinforced habits of behavior. The experienced threat of starvation and death were also added to that inherited emotional response. Her grandmother lived in Japan in the 1930s and '40s when there was food scarcity and rationing. Specific attitudes about food, the ability to control greed and hunger—attitudes necessary for survival during war—had been passed down from mother to daughter. A strict, Judgmental Parent was needed to keep the family safe.

When Sarah reflected on these things, she felt compassion for her mother, her grandmother, and herself. "I can do things differently with my daughter," she told me. "I can be a good-enough mother, a Nurturing Parent respectful of my daughter's inner experience while also teaching her useful rules. I won't let old fears dictate my actions." Sarah felt relief and hope. The potential behavior was to discuss healthy snack options with her daughter and to create a "snack box" with healthy snacks she and her daughter could make together. Sarah envisioned her own internal Nurturing Parent encouraging her to check in with her Inner Camera. As she became more aware of all the contradicting thoughts and feelings swirling around—some useful, some not, some from new sources, some from old, ingrained experiences—she was able to choose which ones she wanted to direct her response. The threatening "other" she imagined observing and judging her via her Outer Camera no longer felt as powerful.

THERE ARE TIMES WHEN IT feels like our survival depends on our ability to successfully perform for those Outer Camera judges. That may be true when an individual or group of people are threatened by those with the power to control. We can't stop the judging eyes of others, but we can choose how that judgment impacts our life.

Think of how an audience experiences an artist. Sometimes we have the sense that the performer or writer is declaring, "Look at me! Aren't I great at showing emotions?" It's likely they are energetically coming from their own Outer Camera, focused on how they and the imagined others are judging the character they are creating. Another actor or author has the

We can't stop the judging eyes of others, but we can choose how that judgment impacts our life.

ability to embody a character, empathetically writing or performing from the character's imagined Inner Camera. Energetically, the audience knows the difference, although they might not be able to identify why one performance feels off, false, and another rings true.

We can't avoid being influenced by our Outer Camera, but we can avoid an addiction to obsessively checking. An alternative is to pay attention to our Inner Camera. With our Nurturing Parent as watcher and guide, we can give ourselves comfort and compassion while having the courage to be curious, contemplating our interpretations and reactions. Are we going to let the imagined audience of other people and their judgments write the story of our life? Or do we get to write our own story, its meaning formed by information gathered from our Inner Camera? Can we be wholly alive, both a Nurturing Parent and a Free Child? We have a choice.

Paying attention to the Inner Camera
in my heart

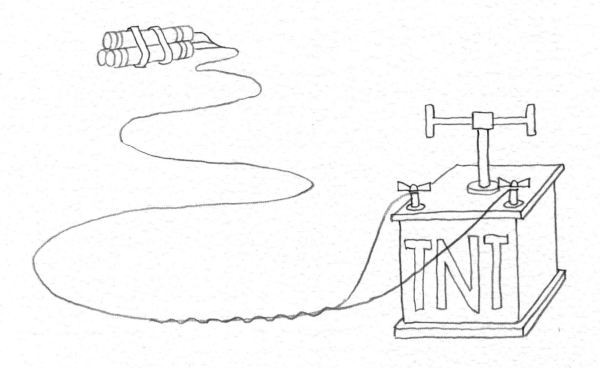

CHAPTER 6

Activation! Do We Fight, Flee, Freeze, or Fawn?

The action happens, the conflict starts, we interpret that we are in some way at risk, and we react. Since the beginning of life on Earth, the impulse to stay alive has produced an elaborate array of survival mechanisms. As demonstrated in my kayaking adventure, four standard categories of response to a threat are Fight, Flee, Freeze, or Fawn.

A lion will roar and attack with claws and teeth, a rhino will charge and impale with its horn, rabbits and mice will run and hide, a lizard will go motionless and attempt to blend into the environment, a hen will pretend to have a broken wing, and a dog will crawl on its belly—tail between its legs—and lick the hand of the man with a stick.

Humans have similar defenses. One human might experience another as suffocating, slippery, sneaky, poisonous, roaring, barking, or biting—in other words, dangerous. In response, they might get prickly and make biting or stinging remarks back, while a different human might clam up and go into their shell. Some humans will divert attention, muddy the waters, or Freeze like a deer in the headlights. Others emphasize their subservience and act like a helpless victim to avoid attack, or camouflage, hide, and bury their feelings. We're just another kind of critter hoping to survive.

A sense of threat activates an automatic response in the amygdala, which is often referred to as our primitive or lizard brain. We often say we are "triggered" when we shift into that emotional danger zone and the panic, anger, and desire to escape the moment become unbearable. The image conjured is of a finger on the trigger of a gun ready to shoot the threat. But not all humans react to perceived peril with the urge to Fight. Rather than using the term *triggered* to refer to the defensive response, we use the term *activated* to include the other defensive reactions that are often less obvious than an attack response. Not everyone carries an emotional assault rifle. Gunless folks respond to danger, but not by pulling a trigger.

Our own style of activation, reduced to its essential meaning, is the method we use to stay alive. This is why conflicts, which we later regard as "about nothing," can feel like life-or-death battles in the moment.

Physical sensations are a good clue that we are activated. There can be a tightening of shoulder muscles, squeezing of the chest, or a clenching of the jaw or fists. Others feel a shift in the stomach—nausea or churn-

> *Our own style of activation, reduced to its essential meaning, is the method we use to stay alive.*

ing. Heads hurt or eyes squint. Some people get jittery, jiggling legs or fingers. Some get hot and red in the face—or cold, like a block of ice. All are activated.

The activated person believes something dangerous or uncomfortable either has happened or is about to happen and they need to engage their habitual defense. Even one-celled organisms are programmed to do whatever they can to avoid the threat and stay healthy and alive. Understanding what actions are interpreted as a threat—and why—is essential to altering our activated interactions to more constructive, comfortable, and compassionate systems of behavior.

BILL AND I HAVE EXPLORED the trajectory of activation on many occasions. One such time is particularly memorable. We had been camping and kayaking our way from North Carolina to Nova Scotia when a storm had us packing up our tent and heading to a dry bed and shower in Montreal. The drive had been horrendous with blinding rain, slick roads, and confusing directions. Finally, we reached a small hotel in the center of the city, took showers, and were ready to eat. Bill looked at the brochures in the guidebook provided by the hotel and suggested Indian food.

"Indian food?" I said, incredulous. "No way! We are in Montreal! We have to go to a French restaurant!" Bill interpreted my tone to mean, "You're crazy to have that idea." I wasn't considering his suggestion. He felt judged and dismissed.

With a glare, he snapped, "Fine! Then you choose." He went into what he conceives of as his Periwinkle self, a mollusk reacting to aggressive stimuli. I interpreted that self-state of Bill's as Mr. Silent and Grim, a powerful and punitive figure of authority, proclaiming me "guilty" and sending me off to solitary confinement.

I reacted with an annoyed, impatient, "It's not fair for you to be mad just because I didn't like your suggestion. I'm allowed to have an opinion!"

In that moment, I perceived myself as rational and assertive—the Suffragette, oppressed by male authority and standing up for her reasonable rights. I didn't hear the sarcasm in my voice, nor was I aware that I was getting louder. Bill perceived me as the Army General, moving in with troops. He imagined himself as the Pacifist, doing civil disobedience with silent, passive resistance. I perceived him as sulking. He perceived me as attacking.

This was a familiar set of interpretations, and we were stuck with them inside a tiny hotel room, with torrential rain outside and nowhere to flee.

Back and forth we went on that rain-soaked evening in Montreal, defending our reactions and accusing the other of not responding in the way they should have responded. We were each doing what we knew, those methods of activation we had absorbed from our family culture, the perceptions and behaviors that were both instinctual and habitual. Like an intense game of ping-pong, each reaction was hit back with another correspondingly forceful reaction, retaliation upon retaliation until I put down my paddle and called a halt to the game.

What changed? I'd widened my focus, checked in with my Full Spectrum, remembered the relentless downpour and Bill's difficult drive. This gave me access to pie slices that included empathy for his experience and my desire to feel close. I then made behavioral choices supporting my more compassionate thoughts. My wise Whole Self got control.

"I know you just finished an awful drive. I really don't want to fight. I may have reacted with more force to your suggestion than I realized." Bill responded to my white flag and offered that he would be willing to have French food instead of Indian. Still grumpy, hungry, and tired, we made our way through the rain to the nearest French restaurant.

We were both quiet, focusing on food and sipping our wine. What hidden pie slices might be at play? Something important needed to be understood. Of course! The last and only time I had been in Montreal was when I was about eight years old and with my family. Our family never ate out. Restaurants were considered an unnecessary luxury. But on this weekend trip to Montreal, we were all going to eat at a fancy, real French restaurant. However, my brothers, ages two and three, had other ideas. So Gretta, the in-charge-and-responsible older sister, was sent to amuse them outside the restaurant while my parents enjoyed their white tablecloths and coq au vin.

I told Bill the story and explained why my need to eat in a French restaurant in Montreal held a hidden imperative. I didn't want to be denied the chance again. This time I wanted my feelings to count. Bill acknowledged that the drive had left him on edge and vulnerable. Plus, when he was little, he felt like his older sister and brother had often laughed and told him his ideas were stupid. My response to his Indian restaurant suggestion was proof that I didn't respect him.

Understanding hidden, relevant scenes from our past helped us to find compassion for each other and ourselves and enjoy our real French meal. Our intimacy was restored, as was our ability to be alive and enjoy the moment by being curious about all that was going on within the swirl of our reactions. The present moment had been directed in more than one way by our past.

> We want to leave the uncomfortable past in the past. Easier to believe is that we are who we are, we do what we do, end of story.

HUMANS ARE QUITE CAPABLE OF remaining blissfully unaware of the complexity of their own inner reality. We want to leave the uncomfortable past in the past. It is easier to believe that we are who we are and we do what we do, end of story. Self-reflection isn't always comfortable or natural, but when we become habitually curious about what we do and why, we gain more control of both our experience and our reactions.

Albert Einstein said, "The important thing is to never stop questioning. Curiosity has its own reason for existing." Awareness encourages greater acknowledgment that we, not the activating action, are responsible for our behaviors. To pause and survey our thoughts, feelings, and potential behaviors allows us to choose from a wider repertoire of responses. The more often we mindfully and calmly do this in-depth survey in calmer waters, the less time is needed to consider possibilities and accurately identify the Something Important that needs to be understood during an unfolding, activated situation. Practice brings knowledge and skill. Knowledge and skill connect us with the power of choice.

Three common defensive strategies interfere with an awareness of the wider scope of our Full Spectrum when we are activated: compartmentalization, tunnel vision, and dissociation.

The tendency to compartmentalize—keeping the pie slices of our Full Spectrum separate—can be a useful coping mechanism when life feels like "too much" but will eventually lead to difficulties navigating relationships and life. We compartmentalize when we are activated, and as a result, our inter-

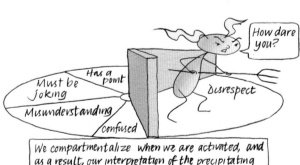

We compartmentalize when we are activated, and as a result, our interpretation of the precipitating action seems "truer than true."

pretation of the precipitating action feels truer than true. We believe with certainty that the menace is real and will never change without our action. To contemplate another interpretation or point of view is experienced as vulnerable and dangerous. The resistance to consideration of an alternate reality gets greater as the demands to recognize the thoughts and feelings of the "threatening other" increase. Our defensive behavior, ruled by the amygdala, takes over, and we lose the ability for rational thoughts and appropriate action. People will say "I wasn't in my right mind" or "I don't know what came over me" as they look back on their defensive reactions.

Most of us can identify with statements like, "I'm of two minds. I want to go and I don't want to go. I love him and I hate him," without worrying that we have multiple personalities, or what is now diagnosed as dissociative identity disorder. Activation can bring out personality traits so different and confusing that others may say, "When you get mad, I hardly recognize you!" A confident, accomplished woman may find herself becoming a giggly little girl around certain male authority figures or, when frustrated, suddenly sounding just like her critical mother. A man may be gentle and loving when getting along with his wife and children but be cutthroat and cold as the boss facing a business problem.

A single-minded focus is more efficient than a scatterbrained or paralyzed response to tasks and crisis, but tunnel vision limits our access to subtle, often important, information. Carriage horses were fitted with blinders to limit focus and make them put their trust fully in the signals from their drivers. They had a task to perform and a master giving directions. When survival is involved, our brain usually switches to a very narrow focus and quick reaction. Someone "quick tempered" goes immediately from zero to sixty without a pause or widened awareness. This is useful for a shoot-out at the O.K. Corral but is not the best way to win friends and endear family. We need to step back and be our own rational, broad-seeing, wiser master situated in the center of our Full Spectrum, with access to all our possible interpretations and reactions.

Dissociation, numbing, and denial can be effective survival strategies but have serious drawbacks as permanent solutions to conflict. If we have strong opinions about how we should think and feel, or have a belief that we should behave a certain way to support a specific identity, then we tend to avoid awareness of aspects that are contrary to that belief. Pie slices that are too shameful or that connect to uncomfortable events can get pushed down and hidden. To conform to images of who we think we should be and how we want to be seen by others, we create secret compartments to hide those disgraceful thoughts and feelings. When we avoid our own awareness of contradictory and uncomfortable thoughts and feelings, though, the banished ideas and emotions resort to oozing out as nagging sensations of

unease through the crack beneath the door or bursting through the locks and shouting, "Surprise!" when we least expect or want a reunion.

If, however, we can become curious about all the possible pie slices in our Full Spectrum of thoughts and feelings, then we are less likely to react impulsively to what we initially perceive as the true meaning of the situation. An attitude of compassionate curiosity gives us the courage to open those locked doors and see what—or who—is there, wanting attention. We may discover that an invigorating sense of freedom accompanies our welcome of all we find. Mewlana Jalaluddin Rumi, a poet from the thirteenth century, says it so eloquently in "The Guest House."

> *This being human is a guest house.*
> *Every morning a new arrival.*
>
> *A joy, a depression, a meanness,*
> *Some momentary awareness comes*
> *As an unexpected visitor.*
>
> *Welcome and entertain them all!*
> *Even if they're a crowd of sorrows,*
> *who violently sweep your house*
> *empty of its furniture,*
> *still treat each guest honorably.*
> *He may be clearing you out for new delight.*
>
> *The dark thought, the shame, the malice,*
> *meet them at the door laughing,*
> *and invite them in.*
>
> *Be grateful for whoever comes,*
> *Because each has been sent*
> *as a guide from beyond.*

When we view the experience of activation as bad or wrong, as a mistake or evidence that a relationship is a failure, then we are losing an opportunity to understand more about ourselves and the other person and make useful changes in our interpretation and resulting behavior. When activation is regarded as a signal that there is Something Important that needs attention, then we are more apt to feel invited rather than forced to explore the meaning and associations we have to the precipitating event.

We can choose to be bravely vulnerable and open ourselves to our own Full Spectrum of thoughts, feelings, and associated experiences *and* be curious about the other person's equally complex Full Spectrum. We can find a new way to navigate through the challenges life and others present.

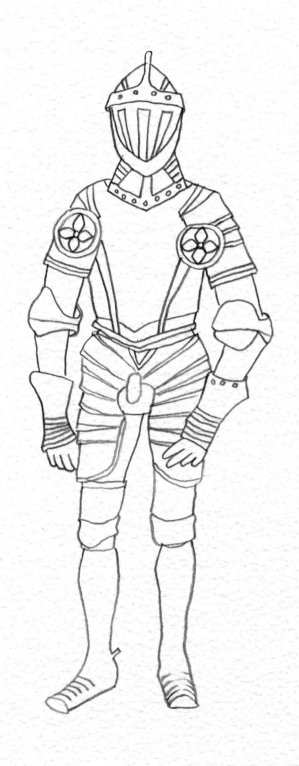

CHAPTER 7

Bodyguards to the Rescue!

Life feels precarious. Life *is* precarious. When threatening forces are detected, defenses are activated. Our human styles of defensive activation may fit under the general categories of Fight, Flee, Freeze, or Fawn, but it is useful to identify and examine more closely our own unique personas of defense—our Bodyguards.

Bodyguards need compassion and understanding. They are aspects of our personality brought into existence through early conditioning and traumatic experiences. Who are our Bodyguards? And why do they keep arriving on the scene, pushing their way into situations with their (often misguided) attempts to keep us safe? When we can answer these questions, we become able to enter into dialogue with our stalwart defenders and negotiate plans for their retirement.

The Traffic Cop

Remember Sarah's powerful urge to refuse her daughter's requests for snacks? Sarah acknowledged that a part of her strongly believed that she was keeping her daughter safe by saying "No!" We can think of that part as one of Sarah's Bodyguards. In working with our Bodyguards, it helps to get a little distance from them. We can do that by giving them a name and imagining their persona. In this instance, Sarah might imagine a stern traffic cop, standing in front of a refrigerator and holding a stop sign. When she notices the associated defensive thoughts and behaviors becoming activated, she can say to herself, "Here comes my Traffic Cop!"

A hypochondriac might imagine his or her Bodyguard as a serious-minded doctor, the Doc, with light and stethoscope, always ready to examine. A client recognized how her husband kept his anxiety at bay and avoided uncomfortable emotions by being constantly active—Doing! Doing! Doing! This resulted in a successful business that kept his family financially safe but also prevented any real awareness and intimacy with his wife and children. She named his Bodyguard Dan the Doer, picturing him with his headset on, phone in one hand, and coffee in the other. She also identified her own tendency to fantasize about others as a defense, frequently going down the rabbit hole of gossipy shows and social media, as well as drifting into long, elaborate fantasies of herself in some other life. The one she was in felt unhappy and painful, but the idea of change felt terrifying. So, she'd call in her Bodyguard Fantasy Fran, the romance novelist, and, focusing elsewhere, feel soothed and comforted.

The Doc

Dan the Doer

Fantasy Fran

Jumpy Jack

Peggy Perfect

Poor Pitiful Pearl

Patrick pictured his anxious Bodyguard as Jumpy Jack, a basketball player in a perpetually tied game, grabbing the ball, desperate to score the winning point, and terrified he will fail. In one tearful session, Julie identified her mean-girl, quick-to-judge Bodyguard, who always wore the coolest outfits and was up on all the hottest restaurants, books, and topics, as Peggy Perfect. To be seen as doing things "right" was to be safe. Judgment was the armor.

Nature and nurture are intricately intertwined, working together to create both our inner experience and how others experience us. Add some chronic abuse or early trauma and you've got some finely tuned Bodyguards who can grab the wheel, call the shots, or run the show.

Some people's Bodyguards are curse-flinging witches, gun-slinging sheriffs, or backyard bullies. The subtler Bodyguards are like Charlie's Good Boy persona, seeking approval by picking the dandelions and getting As. I've had clients identify their Bodyguards as Mother Teresa, Busy Bea, and even Michelle Obama. All are aspects of personality who believe they, and often they alone, are keeping us protected. When I got scared kayaking on Lake Champlain, my motley squad of Bodyguards came rushing in. The Bodyguard attached to the most shame is the one I long ago dubbed Poor Pitiful Pearl from a popular 1950s doll.

The ability to evoke pity was her secret weapon. Facing someone in power, or a situation where I felt at risk, Poor Pitiful Pearl would take over, go belly up, and plead, "Help me! Don't hurt me, don't judge me! I'm crippled, damaged, and weak!" Her sob stories were based on real traumatic events. Some I had actually experienced, but many were internalized stories of pain, deprivation, abandonment, and abuse from my parents' and grandparents' past. I was fed the anecdotes of my parents' suffering as if they were beloved fairy tales or memorized nursery rhymes.

I was a clumsy, bucktoothed bookworm, five years older than my skeletal, sickly brother who was labeled "brain damaged" and six years older than my chubby, musical clown of a brother with the vivid freckles and brilliant red hair. We were all odd ducks, outsiders who never quite fit into the cultures where we landed. Defenses that are not recognized and transformed get stronger, bolder, and passed on.

Poor Pitiful Pearl was birthed as a protector, a first responder helping me to steer through the judgments that came from every direction. She provided an excuse for inadequacies and failure and deflected outright bullying attacks. Hidden beneath the disguise of rags and tales of woe, like Gollum, she begged for pity, claiming, "I'm not a threat!" Poor Pitiful Pearl would keep me safe. Or so I thought. Now, I cringe when she arrives, feed her a cookie, and send her away. "I've got this!" I tell her.

SOMETIMES THERE ARE DANGERS OUR Bodyguards are not equipped to address. Celeste was the top sales rep for a pharmaceutical company until her splitting headaches could no longer be controlled by an ever-increasing supply of painkillers. The brain tumor was operable and benign. She was vague when she told others about the growth, making it sound more like a boil on her neck. Her parents lived in a small town in Wisconsin. They sent a card and flowers. Her company gave her a few weeks' leave. Celeste's friends bought food delivery from a well-known restaurant and a spa package. Her last boyfriend was already engaged to someone else.

"It was me and my cat," Celeste recalled in a session. "I thought I would manage on my own. That was my way. But after the operation, my attention span was that of a gnat. I couldn't even successfully distract myself by reading or watching shows. I was dizzy and exhausted and so disoriented. I didn't recognize me. Then the seizure happened. That was when I first started coming to see you." She gave a little laugh. "Wow. Nearly a year. I've changed. Madame X only makes rare appearances."

Madame X was what Celeste named her mind-reading hypnotist Bodyguard. Early on in our sessions, Celeste identified how she used to navigate life and how, after the brain tumor, those honed skills were no longer working. "I used to think I could anticipate what the other person was thinking and feeling by accurately reading their signals," she told me. "Once I had an image of how they worked and what they wanted, I could manipulate the situation, get them to like me and do what I wanted. If the relationship or situation didn't work the way I imagined it, then I only had myself to blame. I was responsible, in control. People who didn't cooperate, I tended to judge 'losers' and not worth my effort. The friends I kept were the ones who would join me in judgment. I believed if someone truly loved me, they would think and feel like me. Any annoying differences, Madame X, my mind-reading hypnotist Bodyguard, would easily change."

Madame X

Celeste was the only child in a house that she described as "neat as a pin and quiet as a tomb." Her family went to the Lutheran church every Sunday and vacationed at a small cabin on a lake in northern Wisconsin. "My father was always annoyed at someone or something," she recounted. "My mother either agreed or ignored him. She focused on her projects. They never kissed or laughed. I couldn't wait to get out of there."

Trained to tolerate strict rules and harsh judgments, Celeste combined her ample intelligence with an ability to observe and assess human behaviors and created a self-assured, self-sufficient persona. Seizures and debilitating migraines altered everything. Celeste had judged her life through an Outer Camera. Then what was, was no longer. She came to acknowledge that, even before her world fell apart, her inner experience felt quite different from the successful image she presented to others and that she herself wished she could believe. Her faithful Bodyguard, Madame X, was good at creating the illusion of happiness, but those projected fantasies were only as real as the shows Celeste watched while hugging her cat.

During high school, Celeste worked at her father's drugstore, which led to connections to pharmaceutical companies, where she began working as a sales rep to pay for college. She chose Columbia University because it was as far as possible from her family. She was soon earning six figures, and her goal to become a research chemist morphed into how to own a condo with a river view. She never graduated. Tall, blonde, and successful, Celeste seemed like the perfect catch, but relationships never worked out.

Over the course of many sessions, Celeste realized how much she went through life reacting to "imaginary people [she] constructed in [her] head." Like a fairground fortune teller, she gathered information about the person in focus, then made mental models of how they worked based on assumptions of how she would think and feel.

"I couldn't imagine there would be another way to experience the situation. That seemed impossible—or at least implausible. It really didn't occur to me to ask what they were experiencing. I thought I knew. I was like my father, judging everything they did as wrong or not good enough. But I was also my mother, never saying my feelings, smiling, not making a scene, but complaining to friends and finding ways to sabotage the relationship. No one was ever good enough. Too boring. Too poor. Too something." Now there was someone new, Gus. And Celeste had changed. Madame X was no longer running the show. "I don't want to lose Gus! He's different. I'm different. And I don't want to blow it!"

Celeste's vulnerability after the brain surgery had made her more able to replace knowing with curiosity. She worked on relaxing into what had always been uncomfortable—uncertainty, confusion, chaos. And when she couldn't get comfortable, she learned she could tolerate discomfort rather than flee it. Becoming aware of her Full Spectrum of sometimes contradicting thoughts, feelings, and potential behaviors felt at first like "a big mess!"

"It's so strange," Celeste told me. "With Gus I can relax into the idea that I have no idea what he is thinking and feeling. And I'm not focused on figuring him out because he actually tells me. Instead I work at identifying what I'm thinking and feeling because he wants to know! It sounds so simple, but it is not at all what I was doing before. If only I could stop my judgments. I'm always adjusting him, correcting him. I get apoplectic if he cuts the onions the wrong way!"

Celeste realized how much the voice she was using on him was the voice she used on herself. "Instead of Madame X reading his mind, I'm reading my mind, and what's there is another Bodyguard, the Sergeant, barking orders. I'm treating Gus like I treat me."

The Sergeant

When Celeste judged previous boyfriends, she distanced herself emotionally with what she identified as "smiling contempt." Now she was open to being "the real me," and that was terrifying. Judgments, so a part of her family environment, were flooding her thoughts. "The radio station in my head is like a continuous stream of public service announcements telling me what is right and wrong. Not much music! Who'd want that?"

CELESTE AND I HAD DONE a lot of work helping her to recognize when she was operating out of her internalized system of Judgmental Parent–Captive Child. The strict household rules of her childhood provided steady training in this orientation toward life and produced her stalwart Bodyguard, the Sergeant. Once this pattern became clear to both of us, I invited her to imagine a Nurturing Parent speaking to her Free Child as an alternative pie slice in her Full Spectrum. At first, she was resistant. "Being what you call 'compassionate' feels like letting myself off the hook, not holding myself, or the other person I judge to be wrong, accountable—deserving punishment for bad behavior."

"Spare the rod and spoil the child" was the rule of life she unconsciously followed. Judgment not only dominated her relationships with others but controlled how she spoke to herself as well. The Sergeant never let up and had her convinced that the threat of the whip was responsible for all her success, her attractiveness, and her intelligence. To replace the whip of judgment with the carrot of compassion was, to use a phrase her parents often repeated, to "go to hell in a handbasket."

Healing emotionally as well as physically meant that she had to learn more about her fears and how to nurture herself with patience, care, and compassion. This process led her to develop a Nurturing Parent she imagined as a different kind of protector. She envisioned this aspect of her personality as a Wise Spirit, a rather wild-looking, white-haired, witchy woman with kind eyes—a figure unlike her own mother in as many ways as possible. Her judging, barking Sergeant no longer ruled, and her relationship with Gus continued to flourish. She often wondered what her life would have been if she had never had a brain tumor.

Radical change often comes unbidden. How we respond makes all the difference. Are we desperate to get back to what was, or are we open to new possibilities?

OUR BODYGUARDS TEND TO RULE different pie slices of our Full Spectrum, influencing how we interpret and react to situations. Sometimes they get into conflict about who is in charge. It is useful to know the Bodyguards on your squad and make sure you are the captain. Over the years, I have come to identify many of my Bodyguards and understand the

It is useful to know the Bodyguards on your squad and make sure you are the captain.

fears that brought them into existence and what fears cause me to summon them.

Bodyguards were formed to protect us, so we can have a life. They can create a life we don't want to live. We have a choice. We are the boss. Thank them for their years of service and offer early retirement with a generous package and a ticket to Florida. They may leave, but they'll probably keep in touch when activation occurs. You can acknowledge their input in a friendly way while making it clear that you're in charge and you've got this.

RETIREMENT HOME
FOR BODYGUARDS

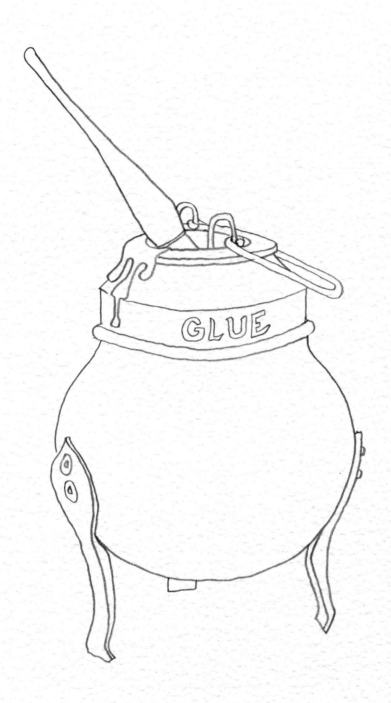

CHAPTER 8

Sticky Beliefs

Our Bodyguards are summoned and fueled by what we call our Sticky Beliefs. They are beliefs about our selves, life, and others that feel truer than true, stuck to us with super glue. Sticky Beliefs determine how we interpret and react to a given situation, and we defend them with all the self-righteousness of a true believer. The hidden or not so hidden thought, "God and/or everyone [sensible, smart, and good] would agree with me," eliminates consideration of another point of view. An all-knowing, internalized Judgmental Parent issues the verdict in absolutes: good or bad, smart or stupid, love or hate, and on down the list of possible true or false, black or white Sticky Beliefs.

In our sessions with couples, Bill and I are both in the room, as a couple, using what we have learned from conflicts we have personally "researched," and bringing our different experiences and personalities to the work. A married couple, Artie and Amy, came to us for help with "communication."

"We are either having a big fight, getting over a big fight, or picking at each other with little jabs, looking to start a big fight," Artie reported. One evening, as they were leaving the apartment on the way to a concert, Artie made a comment about having to wear a tie, and Amy, certain of her mind-reading abilities, insisted that Artie admit to what he "really felt" and said something like, "You say you want to go to the symphony, but I know you really would rather stay home! You really don't like anything about me or what I love, which means you don't really love me! We have nothing in common and never will! We should call it quits and get a divorce!"

In that moment, Amy's interpretation of the situation felt truer than true. An alarm had been set off, and her Bodyguards had barricaded her into one pie slice that she believed encompassed the entirety of her Full Spectrum. Forget having a wise, calm, compassionate Whole Self in the center of her circle, encouraging her to be curious about what else might be at play for both her and Artie. She knew what she knew, she was right, and she needed Artie to admit it.

If partners in a relationship subscribe to the One-True-Thought-and-Feeling belief system, then there has to be one and only one true and right answer, resulting in one possible interpretation and one possible reaction.

TRUTH

Every argument becomes a power struggle with our Bodyguards battling over whose Sticky Belief version of the truth will be declared the winner. Having the attitude that, in any given situation, there are always a few more pie slices to discover in our Full Spectrum increases our awareness, helps maintain a nonjudgmental attitude, and gives us greater control and more choice in how to interpret and react.

We are not looking for the answer or uncovering the Truth about what he, she, or we *really* feel; we are embracing the process of compassionate curiosity. A better image would be strolling on the beach hunting for pieces of beach glass. Little ones, big ones, old ones, new ones—each becomes part of that day's collection, an awareness of the beach, the movement of tides, and the history of objects that have found their way to the ocean. Some imagined calming wave action might also help to dial down the intensity of the activation. Unfortunately, when we are activated, our inner weather feels more like a seashore hit by a hurricane!

Artie at first denied that he had any reluctance to go to the symphony, but Amy insisted she knew "the truth." Artie finally blurted out, "You're right! I hate the symphony, and if that means that I don't love you, then maybe we should get a divorce!"

If we are forced to answer either true or false, this or that, then we end up choosing and defending a "that" that does not include unconscious but controlling beliefs and important, contradictory thoughts and feelings. Bill and I both empathized with Artie and Amy about how fights like that can happen when a seemingly small and insignificant comment or action sets off a firestorm of reaction. We now know that Something Important is at play and needs to be uncovered and understood. We look for Sticky Beliefs connected to the various components in both parties' Full Spectrum. I drew two large circles to map out what was going on for Artie and Amy around the action "going to the symphony."

What did the action mean about them as a couple and each of them individually? What did classical music and going to the symphony represent and symbolize? What were associations from the past? Identifying Sticky Beliefs helps us get to the heart of the matter more quickly when tensions are escalating. When we can recognize old Sticky Beliefs from our past hanging about in the shadows of our current Full Spectrum and sounding the alarm, we can deactivate the system and call off the Bodyguards. Our experience has taught us

When we recognize old Sticky Beliefs from our past hanging about in the shadows of our current Full Spectrum and sounding the alarm, we can deactivate the system and call off the Bodyguards.

how Sticky Beliefs we don't consciously or even rationally believe are often a driving force in a disagreement.

"Can each of you tell us more about your experience of going to the symphony?" Bill asked. "Let's see if we can get a better understanding of what's going on."

Artie began, "My family and the people I grew up with made fun of what we thought of as snobs who listened to boring classical music and fat, screeching opera singers." Amy rolled her eyes and shook her head. Artie reached out and touched her arm. "But I liked you, so I decided to be a good sport and agreed to go. It wasn't that bad. In fact, it was okay. The music sounded like film soundtracks, so I'd come up with scenes. I'd have these secret mind movies with some pretty wild and crazy stories while you were just calmly sitting there," he told Amy. "That was—is—fun! I enjoy it!"

I made a pie slice in Artie's Full Spectrum where I wrote, "Class identity—my people don't like classical music— don't want to go." I made another labeled, "Good Sport identity—reluctant but agree to go" and another, "mind movies—enjoy—want to go."

Amy crossed her arms and frowned. "That's not what you communicate. You always look bored, close your eyes and go to sleep. I nudge you when you begin to snore! You never will talk about what we just heard. How is that enjoying the music?"

Artie turned away and looked out the window. "Yep. Of course, you know more about what I think and feel than I do. And if I'm not just like you, then I'm wrong. Why would I ever tell you about my mind movies? I knew you'd just laugh and make fun of me." His voice got sarcastic as he turned to her and mimicked, "Artie is such a peasant! He can't listen to serious music without imagining cartoons!" He glared. "You think you are so superior."

We were all silent a moment. I asked, "And when you have that thought, 'Amy thinks she's superior,' what comes up in you? What do you feel?"

Artie snorted, but his eyes looked like he might cry. "I get pissed. Don't say anything because I don't want to explode, but inside, I'm seething. Want to hit something." After a pause, he continued. "Feelings? Really? Stupid. Exposed. Ashamed. Going to the symphony is like being with all your relatives at Thanksgiving. They're all professionals with PhDs, name-dropping important books they've read and important people they know and sneering at folks like me who grew up eating white bread with mayonnaise from big jars and processed cheese!"

In a previous session, Bill and I had drawn diagrams and explained the concept of Parent-Adult-Child, and Amy and Artie had identified ways in which the dynamic of Judgmental Parent–Captive Child played out in their relationship. Amy spoke quietly. "So, are you feeling like a Captive Child at the symphony, dragged there by your Judgmental Parent?"

"Sort of, but not completely," said Artie. "When we were dating, it wasn't as serious. I remember us laughing more after a concert. Then we got married and had Andy and Esme, and suddenly we had to act like your idea of adulting and buy a Volvo because it was safe, save for retirement, and get season tickets to the symphony. Everything had a lecture. Parenting. Food. What I should know about the composers and music. Always a test."

Amy gave him a half smile. "And you felt I was always giving you an F."

He nodded. "You don't believe me, but I'm actually interested in learning more about classical music. I want our kids to be exposed to all kinds of things my family never did. I don't want them to feel insecure because they don't know about something. I want them to attend good schools, travel, go to museums, and hear all kinds of music. They learn different things from my family, who have their own judgmental attitudes about what's worthwhile and who's an idiot. You've heard my grandfather go on about highfalutin snobs who may have lots of degrees but can't cook an egg, hammer a nail, or wipe their own ass. He's convinced that they invented 'high-class culture crap' and endure going to it just to make others feel inferior."

"Yes," said Amy. "I've had the pleasure of hearing his philosophy of life, many times."

Artie chuckled. "His bark is worse than his bite. He'd slip me a few hundred-dollar bills when I was in college and ask about my grades. Tell me to put it to good use. He'd tell me, 'You're smart, but don't get too big for your britches.' He didn't want me to judge him as stupid. I hope our kids can decide what they like, not what either of our families says they should like." He smiled at her. "I'm game. I'd even go to an opera. A short one."

Bill and I both know how much family culture and what is identified as belonging to our class or our partner's class have an impact on our Sticky Beliefs. Bill calls it "the stew we were simmered in." We often create genograms, drawing diagrams of each person's family tree going back several generations, collecting descriptions of each person and the relevant experiences, personalities, and beliefs. What is normal for us is accepted as true until we encounter other ways of perceiving and behaving. We don't know what we don't know. I filled in some more pie slices with what I heard about Artie's thoughts and feelings and what I'd identified as Sticky Beliefs. Certainly a full, Full Spectrum!

I asked Amy, "Are you ready to tell us about your movie connected to going to the symphony?"

"I'm sorry I took up so much of the time," said Artie.

"Don't be," said Amy. "I've been listening and thinking, and my Full Spectrum is spinning so fast it's just a blur. All the talk of family, that's what this is about. Of course. I do lecture you. I am testing you. Judging you. Just like my father did with me. But I was a good student, and he'd give me an A. That's how we were close, how we connected. I was like him, not my mother.

The irony here is that she was the one from Pilgrim stock who rebelled against her family by blasting Jimi Hendrix and then anything that came along that was loud, electric, and railed against the establishment. My father grew up on a small dairy farm started by his great-grandfather, and he learned to love classical music all on his own. Actually, it was the music teacher in his elementary school who got him playing the violin for the school orchestra she single-handedly created in rural Vermont."

She smiled sadly at Artie. "I imagine I'm being the inspiring music teacher, and you just hear the judgment. But you aren't wrong. It's there. I get embarrassed when you look like you're asleep. And when you snore, I want to die. I imagine everyone judging the both of us.

"My father became a doctor and his sister a professor, but the farm was sold when my grandparents died before you met me. Thanksgiving's with my mother's family. Yes. They are self-righteous and judgmental, and they judge my mother. But she doesn't care because her second husband takes her on fancy vacations and buys her expensive jewelry and never makes her go to a museum or concert.

"The woman my father married grew up with season tickets and museum memberships to everything happening in New York, and now they do it all together. He doesn't need me as his partner. Not since the affair was discovered and the divorce happened when I was twelve. My mother and father disagreed about everything and had nothing in common. I think he married her because he considered her 'rich and classy,' and she thought he was 'salt of the earth.' They didn't take the time to see who the other actually was. I don't want to make that same mistake.

"If I had to come up with the Sticky Belief that activates me the most, it would be this: If we aren't on the same page, if we don't agree and don't share interests, then we don't really love each other, and one of us will leave to find someone who is a better fit." Amy began to cry and reached for a tissue. "But I do love you. When I get anxious, I get controlling and nag. I don't want to make mistakes. I want to do things right. I'm sure I have some Sticky Beliefs there, but that's not important now. I heard your Sticky Belief was that I think I'm better than you. Or maybe your Sticky Belief was that you think I *am* better than you. Or maybe both. But I want to get back to when we were able to laugh. Have more fun. I want to hear about your mind movies. I just wish you wouldn't snore."

Artie agreed that snoring was embarrassing and gave her permission to pinch him if he seemed like he was really asleep. They agreed to communicate more often and openly about what they were aware of in their Full Spectrum, even if it was uncomfortable.

Both had feared that the other would judge, ridicule, not believe, or react with anger or disappointment and possibly abandon them if they revealed all they were thinking and feeling. Each had retreated further and further into their own world, afraid to know the other's thoughts, afraid to know their own internal thoughts. The more they didn't communicate, the more they focused on imagining what the other was thinking and feeling and the less they paid attention to their own Full Spectrum. The fortress walls became thicker and judgments firmer. They became more afraid to know.

Previously they had instituted a "don't ask, don't tell" policy with each other and within themselves. Now they were learning to be curious and compassionate toward all their possible pie slices. The scariest thoughts and feelings were just one part of the Full Spectrum. Even the thought "maybe we aren't a good match and should divorce" could be considered with much less fear. Amy had a T-shirt made with Bugs Bunny conducting the symphony and gave it to Artie for his birthday. He decided to wear it with a tuxedo jacket to the season premier.

Amy experienced a full range of pie slices when she heard his plan. She communicated them all. He listened with compassion and curiosity, validating, saying he understood. He could more easily take in and consider the pie slices that were judgmental because she acknowledged they were "just thoughts" and not "true." He expressed to her his Full Spectrum. She worked to understand his perspective. They negotiated that he would wear a scarf, making the T-shirt less obvious. He wore the T-shirt, scarf, and tuxedo jacket. He did not doze. They both enjoyed the evening. And laughed. But did not giggle during the concert.

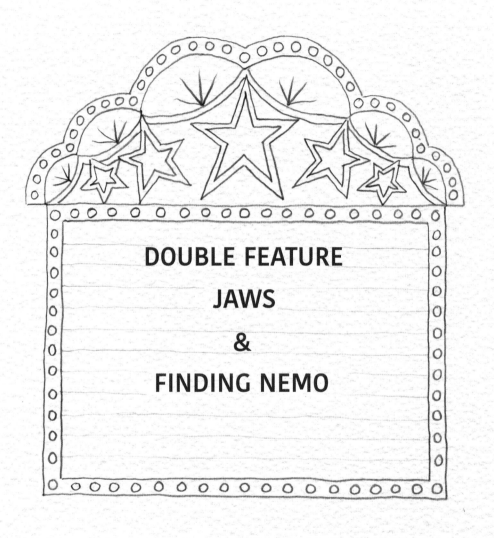

DOUBLE FEATURE

JAWS

&

FINDING NEMO

CHAPTER 9

How Do We Communicate When We Are in Different Movies?

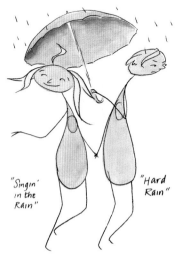

"Singin' in the Rain"

"Hard Rain"

Sticky Beliefs provide many of the themes for our inner movies. By paying attention to the movie-like quality of our inner experience, we can learn to change the script. Curiosity about the filmmaking going on in our heads is an essential part of mindfulness-based therapy. The movie we make and replay about our third-grade backyard carnival birthday party is different from the movies made by our mother, father, little sister, and each of the guests. But we tend to assume we were all in the same movie.

When we communicate what we know about our movie and do not demand that our movie is the only possible movie, we invite dialogue and connection. We tell clients (and remind ourselves) that it is useful to communicate the details of our current movie way more than we think should be necessary. Our movies seem so vivid and real, yet other people's movies can be so amazingly and confusingly different!

What to do? We become aware, as much as we can, of our Full Spectrum of thoughts and feelings in a given moment and the beliefs and experiences associated with each of them. With openhearted, nonjudgmental curiosity, we expand that awareness to what we know about the Full Spectrum of others impacted by our actions. We consider what we know and the interpretations that are available to us, then make choices on how to proceed according to our best guess of how our actions will impact what happens next. Based on previous experience, we can anticipate possible, perhaps probable, reactions, but we are not mind readers or fortune-tellers. We do the best we can, considering our inner movie and what others have communicated about their inner movies.

This creates a much different dynamic than when we believe we are responsible for somehow knowing what another person wants, providing or being what that other person thinks they want, and making sure life proceeds as planned. That is a recipe for guilt, resentment, shame, and blame. A recipe for fear and disdain is very much related: the belief that our reality—our movie—is the only reality, and that we can and must cajole, persuade, or just plain force others to accept it.

An attitude of compassion and kindness to ourselves and others allows us to acknowledge that our awareness of a situation and ability to control an outcome are always incomplete and imperfect. Rather than turn to the Outer Camera of judgment to guide our actions, we can commit to awareness, consider options, and own what we choose to do.

WHEN BILL AND I SEE couples and the two people sitting on the couch across from us get activated at the same time, the conflict can get intense and sometimes destructive. To work with this situation, we use a tool we call Speaker-Listener to slow down the conversation so that each person can truly focus on, and work to understand, what the other is attempting to communicate. By the couch, there is a table with a collection of palm-sized objects—stones, a ceramic heart, a glass star. We ask the person sitting next to the table to choose one of the objects. The person holding the object is the speaker. That person explains in small chunks, only a few sentences at a time, their experience when the sense of Something Important arose and they became activated. We encourage an attitude of compassionate curiosity.

The other individual, the listener, attempts both to understand what the speaker is explaining and to communicate that understanding back to the speaker. Following the basic formula, the speaker says, "When such and such [the action] happened, I had these interpretations and these reactions," and the listener paraphrases what they heard the speaker say, without commentary. Layer by layer, the speaker uncovers their Full Spectrum, made up of contradicting thoughts and feelings, Sticky Beliefs, old memories, traumas, and all the complicated repercussions of that moment when the Something Important made its appearance and the Bodyguards were alerted.

The object is passed back and forth as each person takes on the roles of speaker and listener. Sometimes we spend a whole session having just one action-interpretation-reaction sequence understood as much as possible. No one can ever completely understand someone else's reality. We get, at best, only a glimpse of their inner movie. But we can feel the energy of those thoughts and feelings, whether it is fear, judgment, pain, or love. Our pets don't use words. We have little idea what it's like to be in our pet's movie, but we can feel the connection.

The listener doesn't have to agree with the speaker's memory of what happened or their interpretation of what the action meant. They are both paying attention, expanding the focus to include more than one interpretation. One person's version is not truer than another, although that is often hard to accept. The lingering story each person tells is more important to understand than deciding whose version is right. Bill and I are not the official judges determining whose reality is the true reality. We do support and expand interpretations that are more effective in coping with a situation and creating optimal connection, communication, and collaboration. Clients learn to recognize and avoid interpretations aimed only at establishing who is to blame.

The process we call Speaker-Listener has many purposes. Slowing down the interaction allows time for greater awareness. The listener practices suspending or at least restraining their defensive responses in order to focus on understanding what the speaker is saying about what they experienced. Imagining what the speaker thought, felt, and believed in the situation is different than if the listener were to imagine what they would have done if they were in the position of the speaker. The distinction is important.

A human's first level of empathy is to imagine themselves in a situation and think, "Well, if that happened to me I would have acted *this* way, not *that* way!" The next level of empathy is the attempt to imagine themselves as the speaker, with the speaker's personality and their experiential history. This requires a relationship built on asking questions and paying attention to the answers as well as a commitment to allow both realities to be part of the expanding awareness.

The struggle to understand each other's movies through a Speaker-Listener dialogue yields two basic results. In the role of speaker, each person ultimately feels more seen, heard, and understood, and that alone shifts the couple's dynamic. In the role of listener, each person practices expanding their awareness to include both interpretations of the Something Important that needed to be understood. Both the listener and the speaker learn to consider more than one interpretation of an action, more than one possible reaction. Compassionate curiosity is a trusty guide. The volatile and vindictive retaliation of Bodyguards is not useful.

I was upset last night when you and my dad talked politics. The anger scared me. Mom and I tried to change the subject, but you two wouldn't listen.

I hear you didn't like me and your dad talking politics.

Sort of. More like the level of anger was frightening and I felt you both were ignoring how we felt—like our needs didn't matter.

So our discussion got scary for you and you felt invisible—that I didn't care about your reality. I was just paying attention to what I wanted.

Yes! I know the issue is important to you - to me too- but it didn't feel like a conversation. It felt like a fight. I want us to figure out a better way.

So you understand that I'm passionate about the subject, and you're with me. You just want us to find a way to talk that's not so heated.

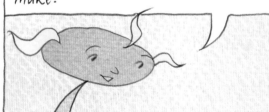

Yes! That's what I wanted you to understand, and I'm interested in hearing your ideas about changes we could make.

You're saying it feels like I understand you and you'd like to hear what I think we could do differently. Okay, pass the rock!

TERRY WAS A MUSIC TEACHER and jazz performer—and her partner, Sam (short for Samantha), was a journalist. They had been arguing more than usual, and the "Dirty Dishes Fight" was the last straw. Terry had been seeing me for over a year, and Sam agreed to have some couple's sessions to see if they could have compassionate dialogues and get to a better place. Sam would get activated when she interpreted Terry's actions to mean Terry "doesn't appreciate me and just attacks." Terry's Sticky Beliefs were that Sam was "cold, controlling, and abandoning."

Sam was the foodie. She followed chefs and restaurant news and knew which establishment would be the perfect match for the person she was interviewing. She also loved to cook and pored over recipes, often making themed dinners with multiple courses. Terry had always liked to cook before she met Sam, but she felt her lasagna and stir-fry could never compete and so left making meals a joy of the past. The kitchen became Sam's domain. Except for the dishes. Since Sam did all the cooking, it seemed only fair that Terry do all the cleaning up.

"Except everything for Terry is a huge production," said Sam. "She gets really angry about nonsense, and we have a fight—and sometimes the dishes don't get done."

Terry could feel herself getting activated. "Can you describe your feelings?" Bill asked her. "Where do you feel it in your body?"

Terry breathed for a moment. "Pit of my stomach and my shoulders."

Bill nodded. "Is there a thought with those sensations?"

"It's too much. I'm always left all alone with the mess."

Sam started to interrupt and comfort Terry, but I signaled for her to pause.

"Just softly, without trying too hard, see if any scenes from your past emerge with those thoughts and those feelings," said Bill.

Terry closed her eyes. After a moment, she spoke. "I'm in my room. It's a Saturday just after my mother died, so I'm eleven. My room is a mess. My father comes in, tells me I'm a slob and lazy and why don't I understand how hard it is for him to have to do everything."

"Picture yourself looking at the scene as if it were a movie. What do you know about the characters?"

"They're both sad about the mother's death. My father is scared so he's judging everything, including me, as wrong. I'm still a child, dependent on him for love and approval, safety. But I want to hold on to some sense of my mom by pushing back against my father's iron grip of judging control. Really, I didn't have a clue how to keep up with all that had to be done. My mom was a school teacher and busy and, though the house was messy then, there still was a sense of order. Now things are out of control. Laundry and dishes and floors, everything is dirty. Friends are coming for a visit and they both are ashamed. They will spend the whole day making it clean enough, but they both know the truth. They are slobs and don't know how to keep house."

Sam interjected. "But our apartment is never that messy! You freak out when I suggest you leave that night's dishes for the morning, and you start cleaning baseboards when I invite friends for dinner and are really angry. Like I'm making you do it!"

Bill brought her back to the form of Speaker-Listener. "You are going into your reality. Stay with what you understand Terry is saying."

Sam sheepishly smiled at Terry. "I'm sorry. I guess your pain felt like an accusation. I hear that after your mother died things got pretty overwhelming and chaotic and neither you nor your dad was able to stay on top of the cleaning. Your mom was doing cleaning that nobody noticed or learned how to do. When someone came over there was fear of judgment, so you'd clean like crazy, but that didn't change the belief that you were slobs."

"Yeah," said Terry. "That's about right. My anxiety is like having a chronic low-grade fever. I don't know the rules, so I can never do it right. Letting things get a bit messy feels wrong, but being obsessed about it also feels wrong. When you get annoyed and aloof and tell me to 'get a grip,' I feel judged and rejected."

Sam looked directly at Terry. "When I get activated and shut down or go away, you feel criticized and abandoned. Your anxiety is always dialed up and then unexpected things happen, and your anxiety gets big fast. Your Sticky Belief is that you don't know how to be this neat, organized person you think you should be."

"Yeah. Here," said Terry. "You take the stone."

Sam held the heart-shaped stone with both hands, staring at it. Looking up at Terry, she said, "When you go into a shame spiral, your fear feels to me like anger. I want to get away from anger. It feels dangerous, attacking. It's not rational, but I feel like you will hurt me."

Terry nodded sadly. "I know. My fear reads like anger, and that's scary for you."

Sam sighed. "My mother was an accountant who liked precision. At exactly six thirty she would serve a nutritious but unimaginative meal. We all helped with the dishes. There were dated labels on the food in the freezer. I don't want to live like that. I decide how much I'm going to do, and then I do that. If my goal is to get the food away and that's all I do, then I've succeeded. If I decide to do the dishes, I clean everything. I'm not upset at the dishes not getting done. I'm upset that you get so mad and attacking."

Terry, as listener, responded. "You aren't aiming for perfection. There's room for negotiation. You don't need me to be like your mother. Just communicate more calmly."

Sam smiled. "You got it." She handed Terry the heart stone.

Terry looked teary. "This is hard to say. I want to cook, not just clean, but I feel so inadequate and alone in both. You make choices. I feel I have no choice. In music, when I'm improvising there's an energetically 'finished' feeling when we reach the moment to end. It feels so satisfying. Maybe that's the feeling of 'right' I'm looking for with us."

Sam took Terry's hand. "I'd love for us to cook together—or you do stuff on your own. I know I can be opinionated, but I'll get better at biting my tongue."

Sam and Terry negotiated different systems of cooking and cleaning. They worked on noticing when they were hooked by judgments and used compassion to unhook. Sam understood Terry's need for her to stay closer and understood how she (Sam) was, like her mother, keeping safe through emotional distance. Terry understood how her anger and fear felt to Sam like an attack. When she had more compassion for herself, she was less reactive, and her shift in energy had an impact on the relationship. Sam was no longer judged "too far away and distant," and Terry was no longer judged "too angry and demanding." They enjoyed meals more—and each other.

The dynamics of a relationship radically change when we make the effort to be aware of our Full Spectrum and communicate it to others, then invite them to do the same. It's an effective alternative to believing that we're responsible for reading the other person's mind, or responsible for their interpretations and reactions. And it allows us to consider other interpretations that lead to other choices of action.

> The dynamics of a relationship radically change when we make the effort to be aware of our Full Spectrum and communicate it to others, then invite them to do the same.

A DECADE AFTER WE WERE in Montreal, Bill and I were in Mexico. He had done extensive and extremely useful research on what to do and where to eat. He had identified a restaurant rated "the best for lunch" and gave the Uber driver the address. Taxco is a town of steep, narrow, twisting, cobblestone streets, and we don't speak Spanish. We were dropped off, and

Bill proceeded to use the GPS on his phone to determine where to go. The address and street seemed to correspond, but there was no restaurant in sight. We asked several people if they knew the restaurant and got frowns and shaking heads. Bill's face and body language communicated what I understood to be frustration and discouragement. A man who spoke some English said he didn't know that restaurant, but there was another, just up the stairs, that was great and had a wonderful view. He turned to lead us there and I dutifully followed. Bill took up the rear. The small, empty restaurant did have a lovely view. The server smiled happily and handed us menus. I ordered what seemed simple, and Bill made a similar choice.

Choices. Bill was silent, and I experienced his energy as vibrating unhappiness. My old Sticky Belief was that he was mad at me. I'd done something wrong. His mood was my fault. I could silently choose to spin thoughts that supported that interpretation, dive into a shame spiral, and call for my Bodyguards to defend me in the imagined trial. Or, I could choose to be curious about his movie and ask, rather than assume. I asked.

He could have chosen to respond with denial—"It's fine!"—or hold me responsible for his feelings. Instead, he chose to examine his Full Spectrum and communicate that he was disappointed and frustrated that we didn't continue to look for the restaurant. He acknowledged that he could have spoken up, but instead went along with my actions and, along with his beer, was nursing the feeling of powerlessness and resentment.

I thanked him for sharing his movie and understood how that could happen. I explained that I wasn't trying to take over and control where we ate, but, in my movie, I was aware of his frustration and thought I was being adaptable and easing the situation. He could see how that was my perception. We successfully avoided calling in our Bodyguards. We admitted that increased communication would have given us more information about what we both were thinking and feeling, which we could have used to consider our choices. The tension vaporized. Neither of us had enjoyed or eaten much of our meal. "Why don't we still try and find the original restaurant?" I suggested.

And that's what we did. Around a few corners, hidden away, we found the sign and entered a magical place. The food was fabulous. The owner was a silversmith, and Bill pointed out a necklace that he thought I should try on. Bill thought it looked lovely, I looked lovely. We bought the necklace, befriended the artist, saw her herb garden and Airbnb, and returned the next day to have another meal. Each in our own movie, we made changes to our scripts. Those choices made all the difference.

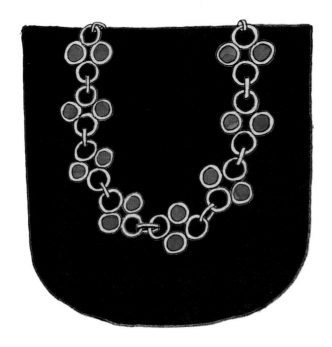

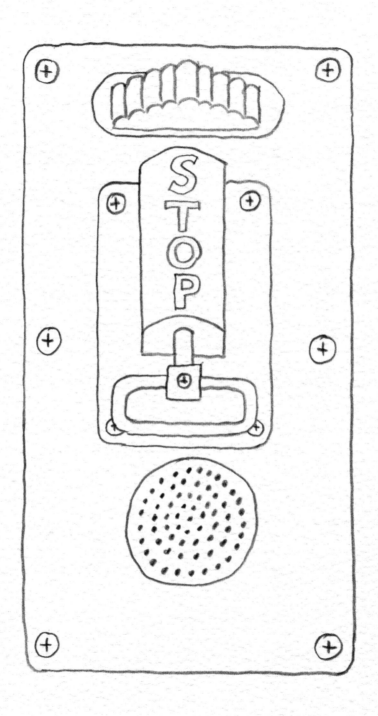

CHAPTER 10

Using the Pause When We See Red

R ed light . . . green light!" Remember the game we played as children? One person turned their back and hid their eyes while the rest of us got ready to run toward them while they called out, "Green light, green light." But when they called out, "Red light!" we had to stop, freeze in our tracks, and show no movement, or we were out. Red calls us to attention. Teachers use red pens to note mistakes and make comments on our school papers. A bull attacks the red cape of the matador, and a person "sees red" when they are angry. We can either heed the caution of the red sign or the red mark and adjust our actions, or react like the angry bull to a red cape.

Not all activation resolves so easily and calmly as our lunch moment in Mexico, even when we know and practice our mindfulness concepts and communication skills. Sometimes, when any of us is seeing red, we need to call "Red light!" and go through what we identify as seven steps for using a Pause before we are ready to do any kind of Speaker-Listener communication.

JEFF AND LINDA, A COUPLE we had worked with in the past, came in for an emergency session. They had been having horrendous fights in front of their two-year-old twin girls. Both felt very discouraged. Linda spoke about how her quick temper was impacting their relationship.

Jeff agreed. "You get so mean," he told her. "I feel like I'm being pummeled with accusations. I'm so hurt I just want to run away."

Linda crossed her arms and snapped, "You do run away. All the time." She turned to Bill. "I admit I get sarcastic and yell, but he checks out way before I start getting mean. I yell because he isn't listening, or is doing his 'yeah, but' and 'but you' thing, or he begins yessing me so I'll shut up and he can get on with what he was doing and ignore whatever I was saying. I feel like he has slammed the door in my face, so I start banging on it. Sometimes that actually happens."

I nodded. "Oh yes. We've done a lot of research on that conflict pattern!"

Bill explained. "Once, when Gretta and I were processing a particularly contentious conflict, Gretta suggested that when I felt slugged it meant she needed to be hugged. We laughed at the slogan 'slug means hug,' but it helped us understand more about the underlying dynamics. Something had stimulated a fear reaction in her, and she needed a reassuring hug, but I experienced her fear as an attack, not a request for reassurance. My defensive response—like Jeff's—is to shut down and go away, which only increases Gretta's fear of abandonment. Our defenses were perfectly suited to increase the other's fear and activation. It's difficult to engage in compassionately curious conversation when we both feel unsafe. That's why we began work on how to most effectively use a Pause."

"Unsafe," said Linda. "I never thought of it like that, but it might be true. It's hardest for me when Jeff comes home from work. I've had it, all day with the girls, none of my projects are done, the house is a mess, dinner is still cooking, and he wants to tell me about some big deal he's made. I don't want to hear it. Instead, I bring up things he hasn't done or needs to do. I've thought I was just being petty or jealous, but really, it feels more like fear."

"What are you afraid of?" asked Jeff. "We have a nice apartment, and the bills are paid. The girls are healthy except for the usual stuff, and I help—not as much as I could—but I always appreciate what you do. I tell everyone how great you are."

"At what?" snapped Linda. "Making mac and cheese? Organizing toys? You come home and start playing blocks with the girls, yapping about your day, and ask me when's dinner ready. I want to bite your head off. I get angry, but underneath, I'm scared."

Jeff shook his head. "I don't get it. Scared of what? You just seem pissed."

Linda looked ready to cry. Bill turned to Jeff and said, "Getting to the underlying meaning of the conflicts is one of the benefits of using a Pause, and I'm thinking that this would be a good time to show you the steps that will help you get the most out of taking a Pause."

Bill looked to see whether or not I agreed with this direction. I nodded, and he continued. "The first step is to recognize that you're activated and say so. Your defenses have been alerted. You can often feel it in your body first—muscles tightening, a knot forming in your stomach, a sense of systems firing up or shutting down. I can feel myself closing up, like a periwinkle sensing danger and shutting my shell. 'Oh! I'm activated,' I say to myself. And then I often have to ask myself, 'Now what am I supposed to do?' because when we're activated we lose access to our prefrontal cortex and its organizational skills. Then I remember. 'Say I am activated.' That's the first step."

I jumped in. "When two people are activated at the same time, sometimes one is more adamant about pursuing the heated discussion, getting the Something Important communicated and resolved, and the other is

Seven Steps for Using a Pause

1. Recognize you're activated and call for a Pause.

2. Listen to the story in your own head.

3. Describe the actions of the activating event.

4. Identify your pain points.

5. Look for associations to your pain points.

6. Relax and get grounded.

7. Get in touch with your curiosity.

more inclined to avoid confrontation. When an avoider calls for a Pause, the pursuer can feel frustrated and unfairly controlled. It's a problem if the pursuer has learned from experience that the avoider's 'I don't want to talk about this now' actually means, 'I don't want to talk about this ever.' You can guess what roles we each play in this dynamic. Humans prone to quick-triggered, high-intensity, pursuant activation and humans inclined to a shut-down, disappearing, avoidant activation need to work on different skills."

"So, if I call the Pause," Bill continued, "then I have to estimate how long it will take me to dial down my defenses, understand more about why I'm activated, and then get in a frame of mind where I'm truly curious about what was going on with Gretta. So I'll say something like, 'I'm getting really activated and I'd like to call a Pause, but I'll be ready to talk again in an hour. Does that work for you?'"

"Bill used to be the one to most often call for a Pause when he felt me getting upset, but as the years have gone by, I am more likely to declare, 'I'm getting activated and I'd like us to schedule a Speaker-Listener session.' A decade ago, we were having Speaker-Listener sessions a few times a week; now it's more like a few times a year. The work we have done during the Pause and Speaker-Listener has changed our actions, interpretations, and reactions."

Linda spoke up. "I can't even imagine what it would be like to only be activated a few times a year."

"Oh, our activation happens more often than that," I replied, "but with practice we've learned to make wiser choices about how we respond to our internal fire alarms. Using these steps has really changed our lives."

"How do each of you experience the energy shifting in your body when you get activated?" asked Bill.

"I feel it in my back," said Jeff. "My shoulders hunch. And I begin to feel spacey."

Linda put her hand on her chest. "I feel it here. But really, all over. Finger in a socket."

"Let's say the activation gets too intense to continue an effective dialogue, and one of you calls for a Pause," Bill continued. "The second step is to listen to the story in your own head." He turned to Linda. "What Sticky Beliefs are you supporting with your files of evidence? What's going on in your Full Spectrum when Jeff comes home?"

"Well, often he is later than he said, or he hasn't texted when he's coming home, or he forgot to buy milk or do something he said he would take care of. So, the Sticky Belief is he doesn't value me enough to even do the simplest things I've asked. And the evidence proves it: I'm not valued. My needs don't count. I'm not seen. It's all on me."

"And the fear?"

"I'm worthless. Unlovable. I'll end up alone and poor. We met at work. He was new and a shit negotiator before I taught him the ropes. The company gave him two weeks' paternity leave and me three months, but most of that was spent in the NICU because the twins were preemies. My getting preeclampsia was why they had to be delivered. My fault. I was having headaches and was tired, my feet and ankles were swollen, but I didn't rush to the doctor because our team was working on a big project. I was being responsible to my gang but not to myself and my babies. I wasn't paying attention. So, when I went back to work after three months, it didn't feel right. I couldn't pay attention to work and being a mom. Some people can, but I can't. I didn't want to make the same mistake I made when I was pregnant. I quit to stay home with the girls and develop my own consulting business. But that's really hard."

Bill summarized, "So those are the main outlines of your story: I'm not valued. My needs don't count. I'm not seen. But I'm responsible for everything. And alongside all that hurt is the fear that it's because, at your core, you're worthless and unlovable, and you'll end up poor and alone."

Linda nodded and wiped her eyes.

I prompted Jeff in a similar manner, and we learned about his story: his Sticky Belief that Linda would never be happy was amplified by the thoughts, "I'm never appreciated. What I do is never enough. I'm blamed for Linda's unhappiness, and that's not fair!"

Bill spoke. "In this second step you'll probably identify aspects of your story that you suspect are not entirely true. That's fine. We're not trying to establish their veracity; we're just trying to state the most powerful thoughts in their clearest terms. As you can see, it begins to explain why you each get so activated."

"We're doing this all together, today," I added, "so we can explain the steps. But when you actually call a Pause, you'll each be doing these steps on your own."

Bill continued. "Once you have a clear idea about your story—you could even write it down—you're ready for step three, which is to describe the events that led up to the big activation. The trick here is to leave as much interpretation out of the description as possible. Imagine that you're an extraterrestrial, newly arrived on Earth, and you're observing the Earthling critters interact. You don't know what any of the words or actions signify; you can only report what you see and hear."

"Let's start with you this time, Jeff," I said. "Describe the scene, trying not to interpret any of the behavior."

"I'll try," Jeff replied. "I open the door and throw my briefcase and coat on the chair. Then I look for the girls and join them drawing or coloring or playing with blocks on the floor. I'm kind of brain-dead, so that actually feels like a relief."

"We're trying to stick solely with observations right now," I reminded Jeff. "So, while how you're feeling at that moment is important information, we're omitting it from the description. What happens next?"

"I eventually notice that Linda has come into the room and is leaning against the doorway, watching us."

"And then?"

"After a while I get up and walk over to her. We start arguing almost immediately."

Linda's description of the event was similar, though, of course, it included only the actions she observed, including ten minutes of food preparation before she went looking for Jeff.

"That was the third step—describing the activating event. The fourth step is to identify the pain points. With your description in mind, tell us what feels like the most painful moment that you experienced over the course of this event."

"It's when I noticed she had come into the room," Jeff said immediately, hunching his shoulders. "My head started spinning, and I just knew we were going to get into it all again."

Linda spoke. "Mine came a little earlier, when I heard the three of them talking and laughing. That's when all those thoughts, the Sticky Beliefs came whooshing in. I'm sure Jeff could feel me vibrating."

"Okay. Good work!" Bill said. "Now you both have material for the fifth step, which is to gather associations to those pain points. Bring up the memory of that painful moment as vividly as possible. Are you able to do that?" Both Linda and Jeff nodded. "Now let your mind float back to earlier times, maybe even in your childhood, when you had similar thoughts and feelings. What's coming up for you?"

After a short silence, Linda grabbed a tissue, blew her nose, then laughed. "I was the oldest of four kids, which meant I had to look after them more than I wanted to. We kids picked names at Christmas, and my parents would help whoever picked my name to buy something I'd like. Except one Christmas, when I was ten, they forgot or something. All I know is that there was nothing for me. My parents praised me for being grown up and not making a fuss, but later I went to my room and cried." Linda laugh-sobbed. "And I can feel now how it's connected to all of the times I felt overlooked and undervalued by my parents and later by my friends and boyfriends. I work so hard to earn their respect, but it always turns out the same way. I get hurt and then I get mad."

Jeff reached for Linda's hand, and she let him hold it. "That's so sad," he said. "I had a memory from my childhood too, but I feel more sick about it than sad. My father was hardly ever home when I was a kid, he worked so much. I was an only child until I was eight, when my brother came along. My mother was very uncomfortable toward the end of her pregnancy, and she never really felt much better for a long time, maybe years."

"Postpartum depression, she told me," Linda offered.

"I suppose so. But by that time, I was a real bookworm. I just loved to find a corner to curl up in and read. I suppose I was hiding from her because I'd be so upset when she found me. And she'd always need me for something, or be reminding me of something I didn't do, and she just looked so unhappy all the time. I felt guilty, but nothing I ever did seemed to make a difference." Linda offered him the tissue box, and Jeff took one to blow his nose.

"This is the gold," Bill said. "This is the Something Important that needed to be communicated. Not just these stories, but how the beliefs connected to these stories suddenly came to feel truer than true and impossible to live with. The next two steps will help you prepare to share what you've learned about yourself with the other person. We're running out of time now, but here's what we recommend once you leave today." Bill nodded for me to explain the sixth step.

"Get grounded. Go for a walk, do some stretching, drink a cup of tea. Whatever it is, do it mindfully, paying attention to the present moment. After so much thinking and remembering, it helps to come back to the here and now, back to your body."

"And finally," Bill said, "see if you can connect with your curiosity about the other person's movie—especially about what beliefs the activating event stirred up and what emotions surfaced at the same time. Then, when you feel more settled, when you feel clearer about what happened when you became so activated, and when you're interested in learning about the other person's very different experience, use the Speaker-Listener format to share that information."

Jeff and Linda left that day committing to use the steps we'd outlined. They had many real challenges to address, but by using a Pause to stop destructive behavior and shifting their focus inward rather than outward, they were able to change their habitual conflicts, negotiate changes in behavior, and enjoy more satisfying connections.

CHAPTER 11

Yes — And

I had a habit of saying "No—but" in conversations when I meant "Yes—and." I didn't know why Bill would get so annoyed. In my mind, I was excitedly agreeing with what he was saying and feeling inspired to add to his concept. He, understandably, experienced my words as disagreeing, saying his idea was "wrong" and my alternative idea was "right." After several times tracing the hurt feelings and downward trajectory of our dialogue following my interjection of "No—but," I realized that other people might have a similar negative response to my habitual entrance into conversations. My unconscious figure of speech had unintended consequences. The words we use matter!

In my childhood home and in other social groups I have experienced, dialogue overlapped, with each person interrupting the other, no space in between. This was normal and not considered rude. Bill's experience with polite conversation is quite different. There are pauses and even long silences in between the units of speech. For me, silence in conversations, especially in groups, meant something was wrong, the conversation was lagging or boring, wilting on the vine, and it was my responsibility to fix it. I have reconsidered this as the only interpretation and adjusted my reactions.

Validating another person's reality before sharing your own makes for happier, healthier conversations. When others validate what we are thinking and feeling, our activation level gets dialed down. We may still be in a funk or feeling nervous, maybe angry, disappointed, or sad, but we are not alone in that self-state. Someone else is curious about the Full Spectrum of our inner reality and wants to understand what we are struggling to communicate. That effort changes our experience. Now, I not only strive to say "Yes—and," but I aim to repeat a version of what the other person said before I add my comment. This style creates fewer misunderstandings and hurt feelings. Validation is a useful skill for all humans.

Validating another person's reality before sharing your own makes for happier, healthier conversations.

The person respectfully struggling to understand what the other is communicating, while still holding on to their own interpretation and point of view, makes it easier to hold the paradox of both interpretations existing at the same time. This is the essence of validation. We act as alchemists and create a safe container, a cauldron of awareness, where we bring together dissimilar ideas, heat them with the fire of attention, and create the gold of understanding. "Yes—I am making the effort to understand your experience. And—I am communicating my experience in the hope you will make the effort to understand what it was like for me."

We act as alchemists and create a safe container, a cauldron of awareness, where we bring together dissimilar ideas, heat them with the fire of attention and create the gold of understanding.

Yes—And is also a well-known magic formula used by politicians, salespeople, and performers. It is even sometimes called the "power of agreement." In politics and sales jobs, the motivation might be manipulation, but the approach is effective because it employs the same human principle. Rather than arguing, "My idea is the right idea, and your idea is the wrong idea," the person using the concept of Yes—And first validates the other's point of view and then introduces their alternate point of view.

One summer I was the top door-to-door seller of encyclopedias in my district. From my earnings, I paid for that year's college expenses. I loved the books I was selling, and I was interested in the people I was selling to. I wanted their children to have the gift of stories and information I had valued as a child. In our training, one of the basic ideas was to avoid arguing with the customer. We were to listen carefully, agree with their reasons for not buying, and then offer an alternative way of looking at the situation. "Yes. We agree. The books are expensive. And a caring parent will make the investment." Successful salespeople at least create the illusion of a connection with the customer.

Yes—And is the core principle of improv. During improvisations, the first performer will declare a situation to be the reality. The next performer jumps in, validates that reality, and adds another element. "Yes—we are on a rocket ship. And—there is a giant space spider crawling around the outside of our ship." The next performer who jumps in says "Yes!" to those two realities and then adds yet another variable. The illusion would be broken if the next character said "No—we are not on a spaceship! We are on a New York City subway and a black backpack was left in the middle of the car." The audience would no longer be following the imagined realities.

The "Yes" part of our experience—especially if we're activated—feels obvious and truer than true. Yet if we attempt to share it with a curious and compassionate listener, we will often discover more: more details, more feelings, more associations, and eventually more interpretations—the "And" of our Yes—And, Full Spectrum view. Observation by others stimulates our own observing mind. An emotionally present, nonjudgmental witness strengthens our ability to describe and contemplate and helps us take our place in the center of our Full Spectrum circle.

In a connected, compassionate therapeutic relationship, the client processes experience and gains insights by communicating their inner thoughts and feelings. Even if silent, the therapist serves as witness, and the therapist's alternate reality is both imagined and felt. The therapist holds their own reality while expanding to hold the client's reality. Both people strive to understand. Curiosity and validation allow divergent realities to exist simultaneously. Both client and therapist are changed by the interaction. "Yes—I am attempting to understand your reality. And—I am not abandoning my own." We call this a Relationship Full Spectrum.

The Relationship Full Spectrum is created when we expand our awareness to include another person's reality. I am a different therapist with each client because the process is collaborative and each cocreated Relationship Full Spectrum is unique. When Bill and I work together with a couple, family, or individual, they get the Bill and Gretta Relationship Full Spectrum as well as our individual points of view. Bill has different training, has a different personality and history, and is another gender. We model the ability to comfortably hold dissimilar movies and invite clients to add yet more movies. A cineplex holds many movies, and we are interested in them all. When even shy, usually hidden, and seemingly shameful perspectives feel welcomed and safe, they emerge and unfold. "Yes—and yes and yes and yes!" With compassionate curiosity our hearts and minds expand.

When even shy, usually hidden and seemingly shameful perspectives feel welcomed and safe, they emerge, open and unfold.

BETTINA SUFFERED FROM ANXIETY AND panic attacks. She described how terrifying thoughts would take over and lead to physical reactions.

"I try and try to push away those bad thoughts. I feel as if I'm doing battle with them, but they keep coming, like in a movie where I lop off the heads of the monsters, but more keep coming. And then I feel even worse. I'm a failure. I can't stop the bad thoughts I logically know aren't true. What's wrong with me?!"

Over the course of our sessions, we identified many of the factors supporting the "Yes! There are reasons I am anxious!" Bettina's mother, as a child, had lost her father due to a fatal accident in the factory where he worked. As an adult, she self-medicated her chronic fears with alcohol and Valium, which led to unpredictable bouts of rage, weeping, or stupor.

Bettina never knew what state her mother would be in when she came home from school and felt responsible for the safety of her baby sister. In response, she developed the skill and defense of hypervigilance, becoming super aware of signs that an emotional explosion or dangerous situation was about to unfold. Bettina's father navigated life by ignoring the real problem of his wife's addictive behavior and either used work as an excuse not to be home or, when he was home, focused on the minutiae of household tasks that were not done to his notion of how things should be. Bettina had internalized the belief that life could explode at any minute and that it was her duty to relentlessly scan the horizon for approaching danger.

I suggested Bettina create an image of a Nurturing Parent who could understand and validate why she might be having an anxious thought, mentally give her a compassionate hug, and suggest that she focus elsewhere. Bettina instantly connected the thought of focusing elsewhere to her father's avoidance of how his wife's behavior was impacting his daughters.

"Everything in my being says that's dangerous!" cried Bettina. "If I take my attention off the potential for danger, then I will be caught off guard, and bad things will happen! My father didn't pay attention, and we were hurt."

I nodded. "Anxiety is our inner alarm system built into us to keep us safe. Traumatic experiences dial up the sensitivity of that alarm system. A super-sensitive alarm system can be passed down through generations and reinforced by additional traumatic experiences. Rather than telling ourselves or others, 'Stop being so sensitive!' we can use our compassion and communicate, 'Yes—I can understand why I am (or you are) reacting to a perceived possible threat or danger. And—it would be useful to self-soothe and expand our awareness to also consider interpretations leading to a gentler reaction.' Rather than fight with the thought of danger or try to ignore it, we accept it, understand it, and enlarge our vision to include other, more calming thoughts.

"If the smoke alarm is blaring, we want to make sure there really is no dangerous fire, just smoke from what we are cooking. If we take the battery out of the alarm, then we won't know if there really is a dangerous fire. If someone has heart palpitations that convince them they are going to die from a heart attack, then we suggest going to a cardiologist to make sure everything's okay and, if so, to give support to the idea that there are reasons for palpitations that are not signs of imminent death. 'Yes—I know they can feel scary. And—I know that I am okay,' rather than the certain belief, 'I am about to die!' We can acknowledge the thought, 'I am about to die,' with a 'Yes—I know why you are there.' And—invite other thoughts in our Full Spectrum to become visible. If and when the focus shifts back to the thought predicting danger, we can gently acknowledge that thought and shift our attention back to something less activating."

This ability to intentionally shift the focus of our attention is strengthened through mindfulness practice and meditation and can work in all kinds of situations. In meditation, we may realize we are lost in thought and are no longer focused on our breath or mantra. If we harshly judge ourselves for "doing it wrong," then we are strengthening our inner Judgmental Parent. However, if we respond with kindness and humor—"There I go again!"—and, like a loving parent taking our hand, lead our attention back to breath or mantra, then we are reinforcing a much more useful response.

As we do for our partner in the exercise of Speaker-Listener, we can say, "Yes—I understand why you might interpret the situation this way. And—I would like you to understand why I experience it quite differently." We learn to acknowledge and hold opposing and contradictory thoughts within ourselves and in a relationship. We let go of deciding who or what thought within us owns the truth.

"Yes—the plane may crash," I say to myself while I buckle my seatbelt. "And—it may not." On which thought do I want to focus? Have I done all I can to be aware of danger? Ultimately, I have to accept the results of my choice. We habitually think, "I need a guarantee that the outcome of my choice will be what I want before I can take action." But really, the only guarantee in life is that somehow, some day, we will die. Yes—that is a scary thought. And—holding that thought, I will choose to focus on all the ways I'm alive, while I am alive. Yes—I will die. And—right now I am being alive! Both are true.

We learn to acknowledge and hold opposing and contradictory thoughts within ourselves and in a relationship. We let go of deciding who or what thought within us owns the truth.

CHAPTER 12

Dictators of Reality

H e says I made him hit me, that I was attacking him first so it was self-defense. But I was just explaining why it wasn't okay that he took my car to go surfing. I needed it to run errands, and I let him use it all the time. He sometimes fills it with gas, for which I'm grateful, but he doesn't pay for insurance or repairs. I may have had a bit of a tone because I was annoyed. He was so insistent! But I didn't feel I was being mean or attacking. He said I pushed him, but I just grabbed his arm because he was walking away with the keys."

Kizzy was pleading with me to declare her not guilty, but she wouldn't really believe anything I said, not completely. A large part of her Full Spectrum of thoughts and feelings had been given over to this Dictator of Reality. Vlad, her boyfriend, had her remote, pushed the buttons, and controlled the radio station in her head, spewing the news that she—a selfish, stupid, sloppy bitch—was lucky to have Vlad in her life. Circumstances had left Kizzy insecure and vulnerable, easy prey for someone needing a worshipping, obedient acolyte for the cult of Vlad.

She had thought Vlad would be her salvation, the protector and nurturer she longed for so desperately. She adored him. Believed in him. Didn't want to lose him. If he left, everything he claimed about her would be proven right. She and Dylan would be all alone again because she wasn't worth the effort of a relationship. Damaged and worthless, she deserved to be discarded.

This wasn't the first time Vlad had physically expressed his anger. It was always somehow her fault and, according to her, "not that bad," never enough to report him to authorities. I considered contacting Child Protective Services, but she always maintained that she would deny it all, that Dylan was never hit, and that the abuse done to his mother was always out of sight. To Dylan, Vlad was the cool guy who took him surfing on the beaches of Long Island, fed him at McDonald's, and supported him when he didn't want to do his homework or chores.

Vlad could be charming and tell a convincing story with him as the good guy, injured party, and victim. "I try to talk about a problem, and by the end of the conversation, I end up apologizing, and then, later, don't know why," she explained.

During our sessions, Kizzy would halfheartedly acknowledge what I understood to be his carefully devised brainwashing techniques used to

dominate and gaslight, keeping her isolated and doubting her own thoughts and feelings. On some level, she realized that her Full Spectrum had become saturated with his interpretations of reality.

Control had been relinquished in return for connection. This exchange is common to human relationships. Connection to some kind of tribe, be it a family unit or a larger and more powerful entity, is embedded in our DNA as essential for survival. The question remains: How much of our own Full Spectrum—our perceptions, beliefs, and behaviors—are we willing to have dictated by others in order to be accepted by a much-needed person or community? The choice presents itself in many diverse situations.

Vlad was Kizzy's person, her man, and I was only her occasional therapist. Adherence to the tribe of Vlad, with all its dangers, seemed more immediately relevant to her overall sense of security. Our primitive brain is wired to know that a human alone is a human at risk. She came only intermittently, when something would happen. There was not much I could do other than to tend to a wounded rabbit seeking comfort. She knew I would give her that.

Kizzy first started coming to see me after the death of her husband, Quentin. She had supported and nursed him as the ALS destroyed him piece by piece. The condition was discovered soon after they were married. In response, she had switched from an English major at NYU to the nursing program at Hunter College and managed to become a registered nurse while caring for their young son and her dying husband.

Quentin had been her freshman English teacher and was married to someone else when he, as she described it, swept her off her feet. Her parents, strict Baptists from Kentucky, were horrified by the relationship, which became known with the announcement that Kizzy was pregnant and Quentin was leaving his wife to be with her. Their A-student, Sunday school–teacher daughter had followed her dream and a scholarship to NYU and now seemed lost to them forever. Her actions were incomprehensible and at odds with all they understood and believed.

There were the initial few years of complete silence, but after Quentin's death, they grudgingly accepted a visit when she brought Dylan to meet his grandparents. They maintained a minimal relationship with sporadic communication consisting of awkward phone conversations, initiated by Kizzy, and yearly birthday and Christmas cards with the obligatory small check sent along with prayers for her salvation.

In therapy, she mourned and raged and found her way to an independent life working as a nurse in oncology. She quit coming to therapy soon after she met Vlad. At first, I was happy for her, relieved she had found the partner she so desperately wanted. She was glowing. He seemed perfect. He was a handsome, attentive lover and great cook. He and Dylan hit it off immediately, playing and adventuring. They all had so much fun together! She couldn't remember a time in her life when she laughed so easily. Vlad played the guitar and wrote songs, and, as soon as he found the financial backing and his album came out, he'd be able to contribute to rent.

Kizzy believed Vlad's jealous, angry reaction to any attention she gave or received from others, male or female, was due to a hurtful betrayal in his previous relationship. That was why he always wanted just the three of them to be together. "Why do we need anyone else," he asked, "when we are everything to each other?"

It was a relief for Kizzy to believe she was so needed and loved. That was what mattered. Gradually the connections to friends dwindled and disappeared. The loss of friendships she had made since Quentin's death seemed less important than making Vlad happy, focusing on his needs, keeping things how he wanted.

Vlad did not like her going to therapy. Kizzy explained that ever since his childhood experience being sent to a psychiatrist, he knew all shrinks were brainwashers. Which of us was the brainwasher? Him or me? Kizzy was in the middle. Whose version of reality would be most useful for her? How could she claim her own Full Spectrum, know what she thought and felt? Vlad was smart and talented and knew so much about so many topics. He was so sure in his convictions. "Trust me," he said. And she did.

"I know what happens isn't okay, but my heart won't let him go," Kizzy told me. "I think of him as a hurt puppy that bites when it feels frightened but doesn't really mean to hurt. I know Vlad loves me and needs me. He sobs in my arms if I say I'm leaving. He can't help losing his temper. He just becomes his father. It isn't his real nature. I need him. Without him, I feel lost."

Kizzy didn't know his family or friends from the past. She told me he didn't want to talk about it, and so she believed his childhood had been hard. She would heal him with her love. She would never be mean, like the others she imagined.

I often wondered why he saw a psychiatrist when he was young. Why did he have no relationship with his family or really anyone from his past? What forces had formed Vlad and his conviction that the only reality he could safely consider was his own? What possible traumas or psychological limitations had led him to perfect his skill at inhabiting his own embellished reality and defending against all others? Those who, for a variety of reasons, have become convinced that any consideration of another reality is a threat to their existence tolerate only those therapists who mirror their perspective and support their point of view. Even soft-pedaled suggestions that there might be another way to look at a situation will result in a rupture or end of the relationship.

Periodically Kizzy would appear at my office and come for a few sessions. Sometimes it was that Vlad had been physically or verbally abusive, but other times it was that he had taken her car and not returned for several days, acting out the threat of abandonment. She would vow it was over. I would hope.

Then one day she came to say goodbye. She was leaving with him for Texas. She'd had enough being a do-gooder and part of the oppressive medical establishment. She avoided my eyes as she made her speech. It was as if Vlad was the ventriloquist speaking through her. Vlad was going to be part of a start-up company and make a lot of money. She had quit her job. He had a plan. "I'll be fine," she told me, attempting to convince herself.

I never saw her again. But I think of her often, and all the others who have passed through my doors, controlled by their Dictators of Reality. Vlad saw me as a rival. He was right. I was using my authority as a therapist to encourage her to question his authority.

IN MY ROLE AS A therapist, I am aware of how my perceptions can carry a certain weight. I strive to create an atmosphere of dialogue and collaboration in our sessions. In therapy, as in this book, I use stories of my own experiences, challenges, and fallibilities as a way to emphasize that my reality is not the only, or right, reality. My aim is to understand my clients' reality and their goals for our work together. I acknowledge that my ideas, perceptions, and interpretations are my own and not "the truth," and I encourage pushback and disagreement. Other teachers and therapists have certainly had an impact and influence on my reality but have left me room to do my own exploration. I hope to offer the same freedom to my clients.

Humans entrenched in their own realities are not necessarily malevolent, mean, or abusively controlling and violent. Was Vlad "being like his father"? Had he been shamed and abused, praised and indulged, or merely neglected? How do we distinguish between the biological and the psychological forces that lead someone to navigate life as such a dictator?

All of us at some times are completely oblivious to the realities of others, even those, and perhaps especially those, near and dear. How often have you heard about, or experienced, a sense of abandonment because a companion was focused on their smartphone? Or perhaps you were the one scrolling obliviously, down a rabbit hole of fantasy or fear. For most, that state of my-reality-is-the-only-reality is fleeting; for others, it can be a permanent perspective.

A full-time adherence to my-reality-is-the-only-reality can take many forms besides that of the controlling partner. Some Dictators of Reality are convinced—and convincing—that they are exceptional in their goodness, knowledge, and ability to care for others. Their seemingly selfless attitude

> *For most, that state of my-reality-is-the-only-reality is fleeting; for others, it can be a permanent perspective.*

and behavior can be a credible mask for their insatiable need to impart this certainty to others. Their Pride Identity insists that they are the next Mother Teresa or a knight in shining armor, and they expect recognition and appreciation. They supposedly understand another person's thoughts and behaviors better than that person knows and understands their own Full Spectrum.

High-minded justifications for their concepts prove difficult to debate: "You obviously don't understand me, or you would agree. I only want what's best for you." To argue can feel like slapping a saint or a savior. If you hold a different view, they are the altruistic victims and you are the wounding, unfeeling, morally deficient assailant. Any defense becomes proof that you are the aggressor and responsible for an unnecessary attack on the innocent. Those in relationships with these saintly dictators often carry around a belly full of guilt and a Sticky Belief that they are irrevocably selfish and mean spirited.

Adults in touch with their Child Self may have easy access to their sexuality, creativity, enthusiasm, and ability to play. Children and adults are often drawn to such childlike, creative, and charismatic individuals and happily follow where these Peter Pans and Pied Pipers may lead. Unfortunately, the position and perspective of a child might be where they are stuck. The self-absorption of such charmers might become an issue when another human requests that they participate in Adult-to-Adult dialogue or they are called on to take on the role of Nurturing Parent. Their inability to recognize and appropriately respond to the needs of someone else's reality can cause hurt, disappointment, frustration, and a host of other rupturing reactions. "If only I could make them understand what I'm feeling!" But they don't.

Humans raised by Dictators of Reality may have little experience with true dialogue. They might believe it is only fair for them to grow up and have their time as Dictator. Or they may unconsciously seek out another Dictator of Reality because that is what feels normal, feels like home. They are drawn to others who are in similar systems of relationship. Like attracts like. Addictive behaviors, also passed down through generations, enhance the human ability to remain happily ignorant of what they don't want to see or know. Dictators of Reality often use alcohol, drugs, video games, compulsive behaviors, and all-absorbing activities to maintain the belief that there is only one world and they are the ruler.

If the position of Dictator of Reality is absolute, nonnegotiable, and unimpeachable, then those others in the relationship must agree to the terms of the reign and remain permanent supporters of the Dictator of Reality's regime. When the Dictator of Reality also holds the financial power or is seen by society as in some way superior, then negotiating a new emotional contract can seem impossible. Do those under the rule of a Dictator of Reality accept the system, attempt to change the system, or leave and create a relationship based on a different system? Dictators with rigid, repressive regimes cause certain citizens to Flee, rebels to Fight, and the hopeless to comply.

WHEN THERE IS NO EFFORT put forth toward understanding the other person's experience, then there can be no satisfying circular exchange of energy. An intimacy of equals becomes impossible. Connection with a Dictator of Reality requires that the less dominant person be subsumed into the ruler's reality. To break from, or even to question, that reality is experienced as a threat to the connection, and the threat that love will be withdrawn can be very real.

My client, Clara, was in such a system. She explained that she was named for Clara Schumann, the famous pianist and child prodigy, "like I'm supposed to be. If I don't give up and let everyone down." Clara sighed and turned her face away. I knew she was holding back tears. She had learned to hold back most of what she really thought and felt. Clara had made it clear during her first session: "I don't cry," she had told me. Control was important. In our sessions, if something we were talking about brought up big emotions, she would get silent, not talk, and not answer.

"Where do you go?" I asked. "Is there an image?"

She paused before telling me, "My closet. Deep in, back behind the coats. I used to pile the shoes in front of my feet so even if someone looked, they didn't find me. Seems like since the hospital, I'm there a lot."

Clara had been diagnosed with bipolar disorder after a psychotic, manic episode landed her in the hospital. She had taken some edibles with a fellow student and had ended up in a fountain in Central Park, singing and flinging off her clothes. She believed she was starring in a movie and became hysterical when a police officer attempted to remove her. Her mother arrived the next day.

Her parents had divorced when Clara was five years old. Her father was a wealthy financier who lived most of the time with his third wife in Hong Kong or at his medieval chateau in France. His financial support was generous, his physical presence in Clara's life was minimal, and his emotional support was focused on pride in his daughter's musical accomplishments.

Clara grew up in Los Angeles, where her parents had met during an elaborate bash for the premiere of a film her father had helped bankroll. The story I eventually heard from Clara was that her stunningly beautiful mother had enchanted Clara's much older father with her tales of working as an assistant to the film's composer. They found they shared a common bond. Clara's father and mother both saw themselves as musicians for whom circumstances had led them away from the life of a professional performer. Nothing would stand in the way of their daughter's career. Clara came to New York to attend a prestigious music school. Her parents were adamant that she should remain in New York to pursue "her" dream.

There was a legacy to this dream. We did a genogram to unpack some of Clara's beliefs that would often dominate the sessions. I learned that Clara's great-grandfather, a famous pianist in Berlin during the 1930s, had died in a World War II concentration camp with his wife and eldest son. His daughter, Clara's grandmother, had been sent to London during the Kindertransport and eventually settled with a distant cousin in Los Angeles. She married and had one child, Clara's mother. Clara's grandmother was musically gifted, but her husband didn't approve of her having a career. Instead, she taught piano to private students.

Her dream was passed to Clara's mother, who showed promise as a pianist, but that dream was cut short in high school when her mother died of breast cancer and her father died soon after from a car crash on Sunset Boulevard when he'd had too much to drink. Clara's mother's ability to play and read music led her into a series of jobs in the recording industry. She never went to college. There was no time to practice. Money needed to be made and bills paid.

The psychiatrist supervising Clara's medication had suggested Clara see me when, once again, six months after the incident in the fountain, Clara had stopped practicing piano and was avoiding classes and social interaction. Clara's father, during a phone conversation held with me while he was on his private jet, was clear in his objectives. "You and that smart-ass psychiatrist need to do your jobs and fix my daughter. She was fine before she was given that street drug. You need to understand. She is losing precious time, which could impact her career!"

Clara's mother, still living in Los Angeles, would fly in to take her daughter on extravagant retail-therapy expeditions. Several times I suggested and held mother-daughter sessions during which I attempted to facilitate a Speaker-Listener dialogue. Clara's mother would interrupt Clara's attempts to share some of her experience and interject her own opinion of what really happened and what Clara needed to do about it. Her ability to deflect any of Clara's thoughts and feelings was similar to watching a kung fu master dodge an attack. Her hair, makeup, and attire demanded attention, and her energy obliterated any attempts at a different focus. There was the inevitable comment or two about Clara's appearance. Clara rarely wore the expensive outfits bought by her mother and usually came in sweatpants and an extra-large sweatshirt.

One time when her mother abruptly announced that she had to leave the session early due to a "previous commitment," Clara said softly, "The Queen has spoken, and the Queen has departed." On one hand, her parents wanted Clara fixed. On the other hand, they didn't believe that anything was really wrong. "She's fine!" proclaimed her mother. "She just needs more confidence in her gift. This is fear. Nothing else." Her mother maintained this stance even after Clara admitted that she had taken a handful of her medication in a suicide attempt, panicked, and made herself vomit.

Clara's father had set Clara up in her own apartment with a rented grand piano, a housekeeper, and plenty of money for takeout. The concept was for her to get back on her feet and continue with her musical career. From our work together, I gathered that Clara did have some talent, was able to spend hours and hours practicing when she was "in the zone," but was crippled by debilitating stage fright and panic attacks.

Since early adolescence, she had been secretly cutting, making tiny slits on her inner thighs, as a way to "feel something, do something" when the "Black Numb" descended. The Black Numb was filled with a continuous chatter of yelling voices telling her what she should be doing, what she should be saying, and how her body should look. She called the usual level of critical thoughts the "Gray Numb." The voices came from what she dubbed "the Screaming Meemie." Her self-conscious, inner, critical voices made social interactions a challenge.

Clara had therapy sessions with me twice a week, and those were sometimes the only days she left the apartment. A piano teacher came to work with her on the three days she didn't have therapy. Clara found it confusing that I had no agenda. She wanted to be told what to do in order to get fixed. She was the Captive Child reliant on two Judgmental Parents. Her piano teacher served as Judgmental Parent Number Three, and she expected me to be Judgmental Parent Number Four. I learned to balance the sessions between constructive problem-solving and offering a safe place for Clara to be curious about her Full Spectrum, out from under the jurisdiction of those who felt success was measured in advancements to her career.

Clara was curious and drawn to the shelves and baskets of miniatures and natural objects that I use for sandplay therapy. Sandplay is a powerful therapeutic method that allows the unconscious mind to communicate via the use of symbols and physical movement. Since early times, humans have used ritual and artistic expressions as a means of healing traumatic wounds. In my office, I have two large wooden trays, one filled with wet sand, the other with dry sand. The client is invited to interact with the sand, water, and objects. Their efforts manifest a felt and visible image of their internal experience. The boundary of the trays creates a *temenos*—a protected space, free from judgment, where the psyche's instinctual wisdom is allowed to express what is not easily communicated through words.

This technique is obviously useful with young children, but it's also useful for adults whose wounds are preverbal or nonverbal and are often repressed or unconscious. The modality allows a freedom of expression for those, like Clara, for whom verbal communication has been tightly entwined and controlled by the words and concepts of others. I invited Clara to engage with the objects and trays, but in the beginning she was concerned that sandplay was just "playing" and not serious work. Since her earliest days, her activities had been guided by an agenda, a purpose directed by others. I suspected she had hardly any experience with free play.

When she became more comfortable with the idea that I was not going to tell her what to do, think, or feel, she decided she could use a session to "play in the sand." Her first tray was revealing. The figures—animals and people—were lined up in orderly patterns. Only when Clara told me her imagined stories of the relationships between the different characters did she reveal her hilarious sense of humor and insight. Most of what was going on in the tray was not visible to anyone besides Clara.

To avoid the control of the dictators of her reality, Clara had learned to create a deeply secretive place. Her ongoing work in the sand allowed her to bring her secret place into the light. I was attentive to her work in the sand and interested in her associations and reactions. I did not tell her "the truth" about the meaning of the images in the tray. The meaning belonged to Clara.

She grew to trust that I was curious about what was going on inside of her, how she experienced her Inner Camera, not her performance for the Outer Camera. She began to tell me more about what had previously only existed in what we grew to call her "secret place." Clara began to laugh and even cry in sessions. A funny, quirky, enthusiastic young woman was slowly revealed. She returned to a few classes. Her favorite, "Genius, Madness, Vocation: The Artist as Eccentric," was taught by a psychologist. The piano was avoided except for lessons. She made friends with a group from the gym where she had gone to get back into shape.

She had not done any cutting for a while, but we spent time addressing how the pull toward her idea of perfection made her susceptible to other destructive and addictive behaviors. Disordered eating and obsession with appearance are usually rooted in the embedded belief that the only valuable self is the one seen by the Outer Camera. Any other way of being, besides a distorted and ultimately unattainable ideal, is unacceptable.

Clara was strikingly beautiful, with pronounced cheekbones, gray-green eyes, tan skin, and a mass of dark, curly brown hair, but she had never had a boyfriend and had gone on only a few dates. The reason she gave was she was "too busy," but gradually another reason emerged. She had made an internal vow to not be involved with anyone until she was "perfect"—the Clara she was supposed to be. When someone flirted with her, she only felt disdain. She believed they were attracted to her looks but would be repulsed (like she was) by all the ways in which she wasn't good enough, wasn't the perfect Clara who would fit her parents' idea of her reality.

Around that time, a counselor at the music school met with Clara and suggested that a liberal arts college might be a "better fit." Clara had been trying on that idea for a while. We had talked about it in sessions. But each time she imagined her father's explosive reaction and her mother's hysterical sobbing, she would retreat from that consideration. The only Clara worthy of her parents' love was Clara the beautiful and successful professional pianist. To relinquish the goal of a career as a musician would be to betray not only her parents but her grandmother and great-grandfather as well. The shame seemed unbearable.

After another disastrous semester, where the only class she passed was the one taught by the psychologist, the school sent Clara the letter. Clara conceded that the school's decision was humiliating, but also a relief. They made the decision. She didn't have to—at least not directly. She already had ideas of some other schools she might like to attend.

Clara was finding her own voice. There was still a long way to go, but she was getting used to the concept that having uncomfortable feelings and conversations, being afraid or confused, and not necessarily knowing how life would unfold, could all be part of her Full Spectrum. There could also be, at the same time, pie slices of hope, excitement, love, courage, and humor. All could be acceptable, workable.

That was the end of our work together. Clara was taken "home" to Los Angeles. Many months later, I got an email from Clara. She had taken the initiative and applied to several schools that were far from California. She had been accepted by her first choice, a school that she identified as one with "an interesting psychology department and some art classes that might be okay." She had even gone out several times with the same person. "We laugh a lot." That made my day. She was imagining who she could be, curious about her own Full Spectrum, and finding ways to explore and communicate her experience of reality to others. "I still play the piano," she wrote, "but just for me, not for anyone else."

CHAPTER 13

Trauma Land

Maria's friend recommended that she see me for her depression. Maria dismissed her friend's concerns as just her personality and the fact that life was hard. She came to see me to get practical advice on how to handle one of those hard things—her teenage daughter.

"I'm not a whiner," she told me. "But I get sad, worry. I want my daughter to succeed, have a happy life. Not make mistakes. I want us close, not always angry." At first Maria kept focusing on how her American daughter's behavior clashed with Maria's values, instilled from her deeply religious family and the traditions of their Mexican heritage.

It was six months before I found out about the rape. Humans hide sexual abuse, even from their therapists. This rape happened decades before. Maria thought she had buried the secret and shame long ago. She didn't realize how much the impact of that experience was still affecting her life, and her daughter's. The story came out in bits and pieces and, eventually, in horrific detail.

Humans hide sexual abuse, even from their therapists.

A clue to the past came from Maria's reactions in the present. We began to explore Maria's outsized expressions of self-loathing, her highly activated response to her daughter's blooming sexuality, and an intense focus and fear that she couldn't keep her daughter safe. Because, as Maria put it, "My daughter is just like me, naïve and careless, always making mistakes. Stupid!" A harsh, Judgmental Parent was a dominant voice in Maria's inner life, always ready to pounce on the slightest slipup—misplacing her keys, forgetting an item on a grocery list, or not remembering someone's name. All were evidence used to proclaim her guilty of being "Stupid!"

All the talk and rational understanding could not budge her toxic Sticky Beliefs that I suspected were rooted in some deep trauma. Finally, she told the story, reluctantly answering my question: "What happened in your life that left you so convinced you are 'stupid' when there is so much evidence that you are not?"

It started for Maria one night, as she walked home after a party. She was eighteen and a college freshman. Her roommate wanted to stay, but Maria had a test the next day in math, and she wanted to study. She had to keep her grades up, or she would lose her scholarship. The party was less than a mile from their apartment. Maria was used to walking, and it wasn't that late. Unfortunately, halfway home, the heel on her party shoe broke off. It was October. The ground was cold on her bare feet.

A car with three boys pulled over. They asked if she needed a ride. She didn't recognize them, but it was a big university, and Maria was a freshman. They seemed nice enough, her feet were freezing, and it was late. When she got into the back, the boy in the passenger seat surprisingly got out of the front and squeezed in next to her so she was seated between two boys with only the driver in front. The blonde one handed her a bottle of rum and asked if she wanted a drink. She declined and he pressed. While arguing with him, she realized they had passed her block. "Don't get weird," said the other boy in the red cap. "We just want to have some fun." Maria tried to climb over the boy and get to the car door. But they just laughed. That's when it got really scary. The driver turned around. He was holding a gun.

They drove for what seemed like hours, going deep into the woods that surrounded the town. As they led her into the woods, she was certain she would die. Maria tried pleading and then placating, then complied. The drunken rapes went on until dawn, mingled with discussion about ways to kill her. A bullet could be traced, so Red Cap favored a rock to the head. Blonde Boy suggested they fill her clothes with rocks and dump her in the quarry, but no one was exactly sure about how to find the quarry. Driver agreed with the rock idea. The coyotes and other animals would take care of the body.

Fighting or running away or just giving up didn't seem like options. So, she used her wit. From their conversation, she knew they had come to the college town "trawling for tail." They viewed university students as "wusses." She knew enough from her neighborhood about what it takes to survive, so she also ridiculed the college boys who she said didn't know how to "give a woman what she wants." She told them she was dropping out anyway and just wanted to have fun—with real men like them. Driver was more suspicious, but Blonde Boy and Red Cap took the bait.

They agreed to let her grab some clothes from her apartment as well as some promised pills and pot. They were all quite drunk and stoned. Perhaps that's why they agreed. Maybe they were afraid of actually committing murder. Whatever the reason, Maria ran upstairs. By the time the police arrived forty-five minutes later, they were gone. The car had been stolen. They were never found.

"I knew by the questions, the whispers, and looks that the police didn't believe me. I was the wrong color and I'd said the boys were white. One suggested they could take me to be examined, but I couldn't bear the thought of getting in the car with them, being poked, stared at, asked more questions. Besides, I knew. Rapists go free. Especially white ones. All I wanted was a stinging hot shower and lots of soap. Clean it all away, then sleep. But I couldn't sleep, not that night or nights after. I couldn't concentrate. I dropped out before the end of the semester and returned home.

"I told my family that college wasn't for me. My mother was battling a return of lupus and my father was busy working two jobs. My older brother was married with a new baby. No one thought much about my dropping out. I never told the real reason why. It became a secret that, if discovered, would explode everything. My mother was a devout Catholic. Virginity was important. I didn't want her seeing me as ruined. Instead, I was seen as the good daughter, earning money with a responsible job and caring for the household, my younger siblings, and Mama until she died. It felt meant to be, like it happened for a reason.

"Who did I think I was anyway? No one else in my family went to college. My high school guidance counselor was the one who encouraged me to apply for the scholarship. Said I could do it. Be a doctor. I had the grades, was always a good student. But after that night, I just felt dirty. Worthless. I blamed myself for being so stupid. Going to the party at all. Leaving by myself. Wearing those ridiculous shoes. Getting into the car. So dumb. I should have known."

Once the experience of the rape was revealed, Maria opened up about another, current source of humiliation. She had married an older, successful man who she thought would protect her and keep her safe. Instead, she found herself placating and complying with a husband who used her self-doubt and insecurities against her. Although never physically abusive, his constant put-downs, ridicule, and comments oozing disdain reinforced her own sense of worthlessness. They agreed: she was broken, damaged, and deserved no better. During her night of horror, she had learned how to separate from her body, how to smile and act friendly and be "fine,"

We are all wounded by life. How we interpret and respond to those wounds determines our reactions and experience.

when her heart and soul were anything but fine. She became adept at the art of Fawning.

WE ARE ALL WOUNDED BY life. How we interpret and respond to those wounds determines our reactions and experience. Our wounds can increase our defenses and make us rigid and judgmental in a misguided effort to stay safe. Or, our wounds—understood and tended—can expand our ability to maintain equanimity in the face of life's challenges and give us greater compassion for the wounds of others.

Some wound-making is chronic: put-downs; verbal and physical abuse; rejections and abandonments that happen over and over; hunger and material deprivations; physical pain; cognitive challenges; the emotional loss that hits hard and early, impacting all other relationships. Other traumas are sudden and dramatic. Sometimes not being "all there" is the only way to be in the here that is now. Dissociation, denial, and compartmentalization can be useful and even necessary for survival in the midst of an acute and terrifying life-changing psychological storm, or during day-to-day life in a chronically harsh environment. The Full Spectrum of possible responses offers whatever slice of the pie will get the person through the unfolding trauma.

But these special forces leave a residue of toxic Sticky Beliefs in their wake. Like oil from a damaged tanker, they coat our perceptions and change how we function.

From my own experience and from the traumatic experiences I have explored with my clients, I have imagined a protective process that operates something like this: our personal squadron of Bodyguards, using their standard defense strategies, are not equipped to handle rape at knifepoint, injuring car crash, or impending death by cancer. In those situations, our primitive brain creates a Survival Mind that brings in special forces (like dissociation, repression, or emotional numbing for example) to give us the means to deal with the crisis or chronic emotional or physical challenge. But these special forces leave a residue of toxic Sticky Beliefs in their wake. Like oil from a damaged tanker, they coat our perceptions and change how we function.

American psychologist Francine Shapiro discovered that bilateral stimulation of the brain imitates and initiates a natural path toward healing the psychological damage left by the mind's response to traumatic experiences. She devised a treatment protocol that uses visual focus on the therapist's finger as it moves right to left, back and forth, to create bilateral stimulation. Hence the name of the technique: eye movement desensitization and reprocessing, or EMDR. I'd heard from other therapists how effective EMDR could be when working with trauma, so I trained with Dr. Laurel Parnell at Omega Institute in Rhinebeck, New York, and became a certified EMDR practitioner.

In setting up the EMDR process, I give the client four choices of sounds, either clicks or tones heard through the headphones, that alternate between the right ear and left ear. In each hand they hold what are called tappers, small plastic discs that vibrate at the same pace as the sounds. This technique replaces the original approach that creates bilateral stimulation through eye movements.

In EMDR, a Sticky Belief or "negative cognition" is identified and transformed, allowing a more "positive cognition" to emerge. Our inherent wise self leads the way. During meditation, one's attention may wander off, following thoughts until it is intentionally returned to the breath, the present moment in time and space. This is similar to the process of EMDR, where the client's attention will toggle between imagined and remembered traumatic scenes and an awareness that they are also in the here and now.

Nurturer, Protector & Safe Place

Before ever going into processing the trauma, the client decides on and imagines a Safe Place, then uses the bilateral stimulation technique to vividly visualize being there. The Safe Place imagined by the client can be real and remembered or creatively constructed. We also create a Nurturer and Protector. The Nurturer is a figure, human or animal, that is able to embody compassion and comfort. Some clients choose a beloved pet turned huge or able to speak; others create an image of their wise self, a spiritual figure, or an idealized person from their past. Some choose characters from movies or books. This figure is often used in many ways, both in session and in the client's life, not just in the process of EMDR.

The Protector is usually fierce and strong, capable of fighting any foe or protecting against any threat. In my practice there have been samurai warriors, wolves, superheroes, and super-sized fluffy white poodles. These characters can be "called in" to the scenes of the trauma and impact the story. Through the experience, they become very real. This method has been researched extensively and found effective in treating all kinds of trauma, from 9/11 to car crashes and rape. I find it also useful for chronic mini-traumas where the person doesn't directly fear for their life, but their sense of self is threatened by experiences such as rejection, contempt, or shame. With access to their Nurturer and Protector and with me as therapist and witness, the client can utilize their wiser and older self to transform the original memory of the trauma and alter or eliminate the ensuing toxic Sticky Beliefs.

MARIA COULD NO LONGER IMAGINE anywhere as safe. We decided on a "safe-enough place." Through the EMDR process and several sand trays, Maria was able to identify and name a part of her untouched by the rape. In the sand tray she placed a red bead I had that was very old, supposedly from Africa. She called the fiery, alive part of herself "my Red Bead." Her Red Bead had talked her way out of being killed, took care of her dying mother, found a career as an administrator in a hospital, and survived an abusive marriage and an acrimonious divorce, all while trying to instill in her daughter the confidence she herself lacked.

In the process of EMDR, Maria was not only able to admire her strength and ability to survive as she observed the horrific scenes, but she was also able to finally fight back and say and do to her attackers all she had wanted to say and do then but could not. She reentered the scene several times, going toward the pain rather than choosing numbness and depression, and each time she emerged less afraid and more in touch with her Red Bead. My painted wooden Shiva figurine became her avatar, expressing her rage as a life force.

She was both in the trauma and in my office; and, with me as witness and support, she was not alone. One way to think of the process is that she was rewriting the experience of the actual trauma using the memory of "experiencing" the trauma in the protected space of my office. Her memory of the process of EMDR would now be associated with any memory of her trauma. The process was complete when she reported that her positive cognition—what she believed about herself—had replaced her negative cognition. The meaning of the trauma had changed.

"The shame kept me from knowing my Full Spectrum," she told me. "There was a big section of thoughts and feelings I kept walled off and out of consciousness. For years I wished I had an undo button, but now I accept my whole life with my complete color wheel and Red Bead in the center."

Maria was able to mourn the Should-Have-Been Maria, who would have gone to med school, become a doctor, and married someone who treated her with respect. Instead, she claimed As-Is Maria, who was thirty-two years old, smart, and powerful. She was able to give her daughter a mother in touch with her Red Bead. She was able to move into the next chapter of her life feeling her worth, not feeling like trash. Her relationship with her daughter changed for the better. Her reactivity to her daughter's increased independence was dialed down, and she was able to catch herself before she made the remarks that previously would have resulted in a heated exchange.

One day she told her daughter about the rape and how that experience had impacted her life. This helped them have more open discussions about relationships and sexuality. Maria become more aware of her harsh inner critic and realized how much that voice was often the voice she used with her daughter. Gradually, over time, she was able to speak to herself with greater understanding, compassion, and kindness. She achieved what she wanted from therapy, just not the way she had imagined.

Rape and sexual abuse are humans' dirty, not-so-little secrets. According to some statistics, fifteen out of sixteen rapists are never prosecuted, and since the majority of rapes and sexual abuse are never even reported, we know the statistics tell only a partial truth. In all the stories of rape and sexual abuse I have known through clients, family, friends, and my own history, not one of those perpetrators has been brought to trial. A few have been exposed, but there always seems to have been some legality that left them free. Most remain safely hidden, lurking in the shadows.

Shame and the fear of retaliation and judgment of others are powerful forces of control, reasons why abuse and rape are so often not reported, why the abused remains with the abuser. Our society has a long way to go before the beliefs that uphold the culture of rape are sufficiently transformed.

Life-changing events, wounds that leave indelible marks, are not always someone's fault and often not considered worthy of attention. People who live relatively happy, successful lives can still benefit from an exploration and adjustment to those Sticky Beliefs rooted in past traumas. When someone consistently has reactions revealing a sensitivity connected to a certain interpretation of an experience, it is useful to wonder what wounding event or ongoing indoctrinating attitude may have caused what we call a Sticky Belief.

Harsh judgments about oneself or others are often a reaction to a sense of vulnerability and fear of emotional pain. A sense that one of our Bodyguards has taken over and we are not connected to our whole, Full Spectrum self is a good indication that we are in what I call Trauma Land. Over the years, after a lot of psychotherapy, I learned to identify when I was in a fear reaction, emotionally hydroplaning with my wheels slightly above the ground, dissociating from the painful connection to an old distressing event or relationship dynamic.

Dissociation is a reaction that separates us from the pain of the moment but also disconnects us from our Full Spectrum of awareness. Physical pain tells where we need to pay attention and address a problem. Emotional pain points help lead us to our Sticky Beliefs about self, life, and others. Identifying the source of those Sticky Beliefs can lead us to the traumatizing events. Once we identify the origins of the trauma, we can use various methods, including EMDR and sandplay, to dial down and even deactivate the sensitivity and defensive response.

When Bill and I had to make an important financial decision that was tempting but perhaps a bit impulsive, I had a visceral fear/shame reaction. There was an uncomfortable physical sensation, and my reasoning alternated between thick fog and a racing montage of dire scenarios. I recognized that I was in Trauma Land and my emotional hydroplaning was preventing me from constructively discussing the issues. I got curious about possible connections to past events. The Sticky Belief emerged: "I'm being obliviously irresponsible."

I followed the feelings and went to a vivid memory of when I was in third grade and had been left in charge of my two much younger brothers. I had gotten to talking to my friend who lived down the block, and I wasn't paying attention to my brothers as they methodically smashed the wedding china on the street. The resulting beating by my father made clear that bad things happen when I focus on what I want to be doing and not what I should be doing.

The Sticky Belief that I am essentially, obliviously irresponsible led to my ingrained fear/shame reaction to certain situations and actually obstructed my ability to reason and act responsibly. It's as if I'm in a darkened theater, absorbed in a pleasurable movie, when suddenly a Fire Chief rushes in yelling, "Stop the film! Pay attention! You're at risk!" and I panic. Expanded, Full Spectrum awareness has helped me to recognize and name that Bodyguard and override the habitual response.

We all sometimes find ourselves in Trauma Land. We don't need to live there.

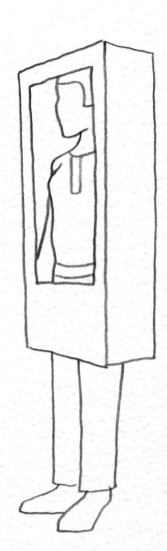

CHAPTER 14

The Should-Be Self

Should-Be Land is where everything is in place, the way it should be. Pain, worry, frustration, loss, disappointment—all those minor irritations and major hurts have no place in the imagined, happily-ever-after Should-Be Life. If only we could live in Should-Be Land! Instead, we find ourselves in As-Is Land, being our imperfect, As-Is Self, surrounded by all those other humans who are some version of crazy, lazy, or bad. As-Is Land is challenging.

This is true. There are many things in life that aren't okay and need to be addressed. There are dreams of what could be that require enormous effort and perseverance to achieve. Change and accomplishment happen in As-Is Land. This belief—that our happy, true life won't begin until we are that Should-Be Self living in Should-Be Land—deprives us of available emotional nourishment and distracts from our sense of purpose. It is by being present in As-Is Land, becoming more compassionately aware of our Full Spectrum, work-in-progress, As-Is Self, that we are able to appreciate who we are and all we could experience. By fixating on who we should be rather than getting to know more about our complicated Full Spectrum, As-Is Self, we lose the ability to function in As-Is Land, where dreams are realized.

> *This belief—that our happy, true life won't begin until we are that Should Be Self living in Should Be Land—deprives us of available emotional nourishment and distracts from our sense of purpose.*

PARENTS CAN HAVE STRONG OPINIONS or dreams about who their child should be. These ideas are attached to the parent's own identity and sense of worth. The child they imagine, the Should-Be Child, isn't necessarily aligned with the child's own experience and aspirations. There is no curiosity about their child's own Full Spectrum. A deep and long-lasting wound is formed in the child when a parent's love is affixed to their idea of the Should-Be Child rather than to the actual, As-Is Child. That love-seeking

A deep and long-lasting wound is formed in the child when a parent's love is affixed to their idea of the Should Be Child rather than to the actual As Is Child.

child, eventually a love-seeking adult, learns to perform for the Outer Camera, to perfect and project the desired image, and to ignore what their Inner Camera reveals.

Children taught to constantly perform for an all-seeing, always judging, real or imagined camera often become adults who are adept at playing characters and roles that win them success. We become addicted and dependent, longing for more of that sweet rush provided by the captivating and seductive praise of others as we strive to create their image of our Should-Be Self. Our actions become guided by the fear of losing what we believe is our only source of well-being. We no longer know and grow our own ways of feeling alive. Inner Cameras get turned off when what they transmit is at odds with what is required to please and appease the dominating ideas of others. Ignoring our own experience and needs, we never learn how to nourish our minds and spirits with inner satisfaction rather than others' praise.

KENNY WON THE APPLAUSE, BUT he was starving for something more. I first met Kenny in couples therapy. He and his wife, Hallie, were in their early thirties and were well known in some circles for their touring musical-comedy act that seemed poised to enter a new level of fame. Instead of rejoicing, they were on the brink of dissolving not only their marriage but also their professional relationship. Kenny and Hallie came to Bill and me to get more clarity about what they wanted and some help communicating their whirling Full Spectrums of thoughts and feelings. Hallie was definite that the marriage needed to end, but she hoped their friendship could continue. By the end of the first session, Kenny reluctantly agreed that he was powerless to change her mind about the marriage and agreed that he too hoped they could remain friends.

"It's what we are," said Hallie. "What we've always been. Friends—with benefits—but the benefits weren't ever really important to the relationship. In fact, for years, they've been hardly there. And that's on me as much as you."

"You're right. We weren't great in that department," Kenny admitted. "But I did try. Especially in the beginning. Bought us books, got the massage table."

"No need to apologize. That's why I began going to therapy, to sort out what happened with the neighbor when I was in third grade. Why I was so shut down. There were parts of me that were still that scared little girl. Our relationship felt safe to that little girl. Was safe."

"I hate that he hurt you. My love for you is so deep," added Kenny, choking slightly as he spoke. "I can't imagine you not in my life. We make magic together. People see that."

Hallie reached for his hand. She also was fighting back the tears. "We've had a good run. But we can't stay married. I believe we both need something else in a sexual partner." She paused. "And I don't want to keep performing as a couple. We've been too dependent on each other. I need to be on my own. I never was. Not really. It's time."

I found out much more of the story a few months later when Kenny began seeing me for individual therapy. We worked together on and off for a dozen years. There were many chapters on the way. He had become so used to pretending to be the Should-Be Kenny his parents or teachers or audience wanted him to be, it was hard to even know what *he* wanted, what *he* thought, what *he* felt. The idea that his Full Spectrum could include contradictory thoughts and feelings and be organic, fluid, complex, and changing meant he didn't need to pin himself down to one way of being, one character, one applauded, approved Should-Be Self.

His story came out in sessions filled with laughter, tears, and dramatic recounting. He and Hallie had met in the college theater department during their freshman year. Kenny was planning on becoming an electrical engineer like his father. But then his dorm roommate, who had seen Kenny play the piano in the student lounge and knew Kenny sang in his church choir, suggested Kenny try out for the role of L. M. in the school's production of *Pump Boys and Dinettes*. Kenny got the part, and his life radically changed—Hallie was one of the Dinettes.

It took him a year to confess to his family that he'd changed majors. He was used to keeping things hidden. A visiting friend blew the secret by raving about Kenny's latest performance. As soon as the friend left, Kenny's father went into a rage when Kenny revealed his change in major and plans for a career as a performer. Kenny recalled his father calling him a "lying, good-for-nothing waste of a human being, putting on makeup and airs, spouting drivel and bullshit!" or something to that effect. He threatened to pull Kenny out of school as Kenny's mother sobbed, "How could you do this to us! To me!"

Kenny reminded them that the school was paid with his student loans, and while he appreciated the money his parents gave him while in school, he was beginning to support himself, barely, with the money he was making as a performer. He didn't need their money, but he did hope for their love. His father told him to leave. Kenny left and never again lived at home. Only Should-Be Kenny deserved their love. His parents did come to his graduation, but their disapproval took years to unthaw, mainly through the efforts of Hallie.

This was not the first time his parents' love had felt conditional. The physical changes of puberty had made everything feel different, intense. Eighth grade had been difficult socially, but Kenny was funny, smart in school, and had a group of friends he'd known since kindergarten, so he was optimistic that the uncomfortable feelings would somehow sort themselves out. His feelings for Freddy, his new best friend at church camp, seemed so natural, so right.

"I was so naïve, or already good at compartmentalizing, not seeing what I didn't want to see, or maybe just too much in love, but, whatever the reason, I was completely unprepared for what happened."

A counselor found Kenny and Freddy cuddling in a zipped-together sleeping bag on an overnight camping trip. A youth pastor called the parents, and both boys were immediately sent home.

"My father came to pick me up. It was a five-hour drive back to our house. He didn't say a word after 'Get in.' My mother made up a story about me having mono, and I was not allowed out for the rest of the summer. I was in such shock and so ashamed that it never occurred to me to push back. I just accepted that I was disgusting and deserved the response. I was not, am not, who I should be. I don't know if I'll ever lose that feeling," he said, in one of our early sessions.

"My parents found a therapist who said he could save me from becoming homosexual because I hadn't yet been completely ruined. Luckily, they thought he was too expensive, so that didn't last long. I'd been in the children's chorus at church, and the choir director wanted me to join the adult choir and even do solos. My parents thought that church was a good influence, so okay. I shut down my feelings and focused on singing and being good. I became more serious about schoolwork and avoided social functions. My friends drifted away. I became a math geek, which got me into the university where I met Hallie.

"I realize now how much I was always performing, always acting as some character, imagining how they would respond, what they would say, what gestures they would use. I was terrified of being seen as feminine or told I was 'acting gay,' and so I modeled myself on the guys I thought were masculine but not too brutish. I wanted to be a suave gentleman." Kenny stopped and smiled. "I guess, that actually does feel like me. A suave, gay gentleman."

Kenny described sexually experimenting with a guy one drunken night in college when Hallie was visiting her parents. "I was terrified. It felt too good. Too right. A door opened and I finally felt real. Me being me. Thrilling, the sense of connection. Something. But the fear of shame was so great that when Hallie and I started becoming this fabulous performing, do-everything-together duo, I convinced myself that having that feeling wasn't worth destroying my life and becoming a pariah. Because that's what I believed. Being with Hallie was my ticket out of hell.

"On some level Hallie and I had both always known the truth. It was a relief to stop trying to cover it up. She was the brave one." After they separated, Kenny tried a solo act but wasn't that into it. The relationship had been what mattered. He stopped going to church and fell into a job at a community arts center, helping with their taxes. He began doing their books and eventually went back to school and got his MBA. He became a certified public accountant and won the spot as chief financial officer for a major arts organization. His parents were thrilled. "They still haven't really accepted that Dylan is my partner, but at least, in their eyes, I have a real job. You know, I always did truly enjoy math. And I keep performing!"

Along the way, Kenny found solace and support in a place he didn't expect it. He joined a new church. He had met the woman minister when he sang for Hallie's wedding to a close friend they'd both known for years.

"We talked about the concept of service, the meaning of life, values. She'd been active as a new, young minister during the AIDS epidemic, and she said it transformed her. The idea that God could love me, no matter what my identity was, made all the difference. As my therapist, you have to accept me." He laughed. "I pay you! But believing God loves and accepts me is something else. I believe there is the me that is connected to God—part of God, and God is part of everyone and so am I, connected to everyone, even the assholes who want to stone me to death. Now my outer identity is more aligned with who I am: As-Is Kenny, how I experience life, who and how I love, what I value." Kenny became an integral part of the church community, directing the children's plays and singing solos in the choir. Sometimes he even played the piano.

"I can't be a human in the world without people making up stories—interpretations—maybe harsh judgments about my life, my identity. And sometimes they hurt the part of me that wants the applause, the acceptance. But there is this other part, call it soul or spirit, that sees the identity stuff as part of the cosmic joke, the ridiculousness of our limited, Earthbound awareness. All my years of doing comedy, I realized that so much of what made people laugh was seeing the humor in humanity, making fun of all the stories we make up about others and ourselves. The clown knows how it works. Put on a red rubber nose and we are suddenly seen as something else. Clowns see the truth. Everyone is wearing red rubber noses and costumes. I've learned to look into eyes, not at the attire. The eyes reveal heaven." On our journey together, I taught Kenny many concepts and terms, and Kenny taught me much about how entrenched shame keeps our eyes lowered.

We hope to be seen.

We dread being seen.

SHAME IS A POWERFUL FILTER that clouds and distorts our perception, preventing us from seeing the light, the "heaven," in others' eyes, as we all make our way there. We become afraid to reveal ourselves, show our light. Those in power use shame as a brutal tactic to control those they wish to dominate. Control-by-shame can also be a subtle force used to direct the actions of others and is often habitually, unconsciously or consciously, used within ourselves.

Naked humans are vulnerable to shame. Outside the Garden of Eden, proper attire is required. There are reasons for those disturbingly familiar dreams where we are in front of a class or on stage or at a party serving hors d'oeuvres and suddenly realize we are stark naked. Our defenseless As-Is Self is exposed. The mask and protective layers are removed. We hope to be seen. We dread being seen.

During the process of therapy, we allow ourselves to be emotionally naked. Revealing ourselves to a therapist is practice for being less defended and more intimate with others. Held in the safety of the therapist's nonjudgmental gaze, we dare to communicate our inner landscape. We see and understand and therefore distinguish between our Should-Be Self and our As-Is Self. Step-by-step, in time and space, we move toward our Could-Be Self.

HUMANS WILL WORK HARD TO create the illusion of that state where there is no change. Like Never-Never Land, our Should-Be Land, inhabited with Should-Be People, will remain just the way we have fixed it in our minds. Peter Pan sings, "I won't grow up!" We understand. We are horrified, and yet we understand that urge to refuse to live here, in this ever-changing moment, in imperfect As-Is Land. We are intimately familiar with the primal wail of the Child Self that wants what it wants when it wants it and is angry when it can't be.

We relish the thought and anticipation of the Should-Be object or experience, which is outside the realm of change because it is outside the realm of birth and death. What is imagined can remain immutable. Once something is real, it is in time and space and therefore always changing. Once something is born, it is beginning to die.

"It's not fair! It's not right! This is not the way life should be!" we cry, angry at each rude awakening from whatever temporary dream womb we hoped was permanent. Each new birth into the present moment is an opportunity for increased growth and awareness. Instead, we scramble to find another womb.

> *Each new birth into the present moment is an opportunity for increased growth and awareness. Instead, we scramble to find another womb.*

Sometimes life simply feels too real, too threatening to inhabit, too out of sync with our family and culture's values and norms. So, we create a convincing alternate reality, a meticulously built identity that matches others' expectations of our Should-Be Life. Bit by bit, the protective façade, the mask we show to others, feels like all we are. We work hard to convince others and ourselves to accept the story of our identity that we want believed. We lose connection to our own thoughts and feelings, edit out all aspects of our Full Spectrum that don't agree with the fiction we become desperate to maintain. We fear that if we lose that identity, we lose ourselves. Nothing else is there. Or, what is there, we believe is too shameful to admit.

A PERCEIVED ATTACK ON OUR identity, a threat to our Should-Be Self, is often the hidden tripwire setting off an activation. Here is a story about an incident that happened not that long ago.

I am a huge fan of the *New York Times Cooking* blog. Every day, I read the newsletter and pick recipes I want Bill and me to try. I love to cook and take pride in all the wonderful meals we make together. There was an intriguing recipe for a leg of lamb, and I asked Bill to see if he could pick one up at the meat market. His mission was successful, and the next day I unwrapped the packaging to begin the slightly complicated recipe involving anchovies, garlic, fresh rosemary, and a lot of black pepper and lemon. I was shocked at the price he had paid. As I prepared the meat, I saw posted photos of my ex visiting our daughter and the grandson I had not been able to visit for a while. I had a reaction that slid into my unconscious.

Discussing how long the meat should cook, Bill suggested a longer cooking time than the recipe called for since the leg was slightly larger. Later, he felt we should take it out when the cooking thermometer registered that it was medium rare. I demurred to both suggestions, although I was worried that, like some other previous meals, it would become overcooked. When the thermometer read almost rare—the way I prefer lamb and beef—I wanted to insist we take it out then, but, again, I acquiesced to Bill's decision. Finally, the lamb was removed from the oven and sliced. It was well done. To the bone.

"It's ruined!" I wailed.

"I'm sure it will be fine," said Bill.

We served our plates with mashed potatoes, gravy, spinach, and the caponata I had also made. I was seething as I viewed the gray slab of meat and slathered it with gravy.

"Ruined," I muttered, as I resisted throwing my plate across the room and punching Bill.

"It's hard to enjoy this meal with you calling it 'ruined,'" said Bill.

I took a deep breath and struggled to voice a more useful response.

"I know I'm being judgmental. Your family ate and enjoyed meat that was more well done. Your experience is different from mine. I'm glad you can enjoy the meal. I had a different image of what it should be. For me, the experience is ruined."

We ate in silence. We watched a show. When it was time to go to bed I was still vibrating. Activation was a level 10.

I told Bill, "I am still having a big reaction, and I'm not exactly sure why. I'm so upset, I feel like I want to climb out of my skin, scream and cry, and wander the moors."

He took a deep breath, sat up in bed, and made a considered response. "Do you want to tell me about it?"

As I unpacked my thoughts and feelings, I found all the ways that my identity had felt threatened by attacks from a multitude of sources. The well-done lamb was proof I was not Should-Be Gretta! First and most prominent in my Full Spectrum was the judgment that I had been a wimpy woman, unassertive and acquiescing to Bill, a man. I accused myself of being subservient by not speaking up and advocating for what I wanted and what I thought.

Next, I identified the judgment that we had paid too much for this dinner that was not a special occasion. Should-Be Gretta would not have been so wasteful, greedy, extravagant, and bourgeois. There was also the lurking belief that if I was being who I should be, working toward saving the planet and caring for other sentient beings, then I would be vegan and refrain from eating any meat—and I would certainly not want it to be bloody.

I told all of this to Bill. He later told me that he had to work hard to overcome his own defensive response. He chose compassion instead of calling for his Bodyguards.

Encouraged that he was open to understanding my reaction, I allowed myself to access an even deeper wound. I became aware of a deeply hidden pain point setting off my high degree of activation. The well-done lamb connected me to the consistent shaming I experienced in my first marriage. My ex was always extremely critical of my cooking and found fault with anything I prepared (or did). I could imagine his remarks about the well-done lamb. Seeing his photo had brought him into my thoughts, and the old traumas of put-downs, criticism, ridicule, and disdain were reactivated. Judgment-judgment-judgment!

My intense activation was the result of multiple pain points directing me to feel shame for all the ways I was not my Should-Be Self!

Bill, in the role of Listener, offered a thoughtful paraphrase of all that I'd said, the tone of his voice conveying empathy and compassion.

"Yes! You get it!" I declared, feeling the tears well.

"Then I can understand why you were so upset," he said, and hugged me close.

Which story will I tell?

I felt all my activation dissolve, dissipate like mist in the sun. In his arms, feeling understood, I was able to be with my As-Is Self in the As-Is moment. I was able to let go of judgment and feel compassion for the two of us, doing our best, not exactly perfect, just being our As-Is—not Should-Be—Selves.

SOMETIMES THE IDEA OF WHO we should be is put on us by parents, peers, partners, and people we admire. But sometimes that idea of who we should be, what life should be, is something we create and believe in secret. Our own mission impossible.

Joe didn't want to die. But he was going to. In his early forties, he had stage IV lung cancer and was on his sixth round of chemotherapy. He first came to see me when he was in remission after his surgery and a seemingly successful first round of chemotherapy. He had returned to his job as a science teacher at the high school he had attended as a teenager.

"I don't want to be known as the nerdy nice guy with cancer," he told me. "I'm beating this thing and getting on with my life. I just need help building up my confidence."

Soon after Joe began working with me, he and his wife had decided to take the plunge and have a baby using the embryos they had made when they first discovered the cancer. They now had an active two-year-old son. Joe had taken a medical leave of absence in January after he began the third round of chemotherapy. His school hired another science teacher. They said it was temporary, just until Joe came back. But Joe knew he would never return.

"I know I should go and get my stuff, but that feels like admitting defeat. I've failed in every way. I'm letting everyone down. That's what keeps me up at night. My mother keeps praying her rosary, asking for miracles, telling me to not give up. You're the only one who will talk about death with me. Even my wife wants me to be positive. But she knows."

Over the years, in our sessions, we had worked on Joe's anxiety and low self-esteem. A source of pride was the early morning robot club he suggested and created that began winning state competitions. This required him to advocate and socially interact more than was natural or comfortable. He joked about creating a robot that could stand in for him and give the speeches. He did a few sand trays with the Tin Man as the central figure.

Joe was known within his circle of family and friends as shy and easy-going, a good guy, always ready to help, the mediator, never one to stir up conflict or argue. Joe's identity was all about never letting anyone down or causing anyone pain or discomfort. Those same qualities led him to retreat further into himself and distance himself from those he loved as the cancer and chemo sapped his strength. Early on in our sessions he had created a motivating mantra: "I'm being alive, while I'm alive!"

But as the cancer progressed, Joe began to focus on how his death was going to cause others immense emotional pain. The fact that he was powerless over the disease was not the point. "All I want to do is be alone, trying not to think, not feel. Being with Jemma and little Jimmy feels so hard, so sad, and I feel so ashamed."

Joe's father had been killed in a car accident that happened when he was driving Joe back to New Hampshire for the second semester of Joe's freshman year in college. His mother went into a deep depression and was unable to handle care for his ten-year-old sister and the legal battle with insurance. Joe transferred to Brooklyn College so he could live at home and help his mother and sister. He never left. He and Jemma and little Jimmy lived on the top two floors of the brownstone that Joe's parents had bought when Brooklyn real estate was cheap and Joe's father was a young, successful engineer with many dreams.

Joe clutched the pillow to his lap. "All the dreams of what we thought could be! I just keep imagining Jemma and Jimmy, my mom, my friends, all in such pain. I'm doing to them what my father's death did to my mother and little sister, and I won't be there to make it better!"

"You are not your father, and Jemma's not your mother," I told him. But Sticky Beliefs are not easily rationalized away. We decided to do an EMDR session about his father's death. Hunting for the negative cognition that seemed most relevant, Joe kept coming up with "I'm responsible. If I hadn't insisted on bringing up so much stuff, my father wouldn't have been driving in a snowstorm. I should have taken the bus."

We knew that was a huge weight that he carried on his shoulders, feeling responsible for everyone's feelings and well-being as well as his father's death. He decided that his positive cognition was "It's not all my responsibility."

Joe chose Sarge, the dog he had as a child, as both his Protector and Nurturer. His Safe Place was the fort he had made in a wooded area of the park. Joe and Sarge, the faithful mutt, went on their journey facing death. As we began the EMDR process, he was reliving the images of the crash: blinding snow; the skid to avoid the deer; the rolling, rolling over; the pain;

and the image of his father, eyes closed, his head bleeding before black unconsciousness enveloped Joe. But then the scene deviated from what actually happened, and a larger-than-life Sarge was magically pulling Joe and his dad from the car, and Joe was holding his father's head and telling him he loved him and his father was telling him, "It's not your fault! I love you!" Tears streamed down as Joe described seeing his father let go of life.

We paused, but Joe said, "I'm seeing me dying, but it's a different scene."

"Go there," I said. And he did. He imagined himself dying, in bed, at home, Sarge and Jimmy on the bed, Joe holding Jemma's hand. He told her he was really sorry. He didn't want to leave. He loved them. Jemma said she and Jimmy knew that. They'd be okay. "We love you and know you love us," they told him.

Then the scene switched to his mother. She was dying. He was seeing out through her eyes, having her memories. "She's okay," he whispered. "She is in the light, seeing her entire life. My father's death is there but just one part. There are happy scenes. She's okay. Sarge is licking her hand." Then he imagined Jimmy, grown, the age Joe was when he went to college.

Joe was sobbing. "I should be there to take him to school, to see him get married, to hold his babies. But I won't be."

"Go to your fort, with Sarge," I said softly.

Joe, eyes closed and holding the tappers in his hands, began taking long deep breaths. His face softened. He was quiet for a moment, then opened his eyes. I stopped the tappers.

Joe wiped his eyes. "Sarge always loved As-Is Joe. And that's how I want to love. I loved that fort and Sarge, but that time ended. And other times began. Like a death, I can't go back to that time. I wouldn't want to if it meant never knowing Jemma and Jimmy. I remember feelings, happiness, love. That's important. My father and I couldn't stop the accident. I can't stop the cancer, although I've tried. We do the best we can. Being alive, while we're alive."

Joe, believing he was responsible for his mother and sister, took on the mantle of Good Ol' Joe, to defend against the threat of being judged bad or irresponsible. Joe was naturally loving and aware of others. The crippling weight on his shoulders was the belief that if he caused any pain, did something "wrong" or even inconvenient to others, then he was "bad"—not who he should be. This led to choices, big and small, that were motivated by the need to maintain the identity of "Good Ol' Joe" and left him unable to choose options that might not have been what others wanted—not in line with Should-Be Joe. The need to avoid conflict and maintain this image left him often retreating behind a well-trained Bodyguard, his Tin Man, who could perform the tasks and maintain the communication with the appropriate cheerful demeanor.

Joe realized how his feeling responsible for making everyone happy left him powerless since he couldn't protect anyone from the pain they'd feel at his death. They would have to figure out their own path of healing. He couldn't do that for them. He set down the burden of the impossible task. There was enormous relief in accepting As-Is Joe and no longer striving to be Should-Be Joe. "I don't know how long I have, but only I can be in my life and my death. No one else can do it for me. And I can't do it for anyone else."

> There was enormous relief in accepting As Is Joe and no longer striving to be Should Be Joe.

Joe, miraculously, hung on for another year. He began coming to sessions with his portable oxygen tank; then all travel became too hard, and we changed to video sessions. When Joe knew the end was near, we arranged for me to come to his home. They had set up a hospital bed on the first floor. I sat on a chair I knew was usually occupied by others. There were framed photos crowded on a small table by the bed.

"That's me and Sarge," he said, pointing to a small photo. "I've been thinking a lot about that session we did, about my father's death. I figure, even when I get to the point I can't talk anymore, I can still be feeling love for my family and feel their love. I've been practicing focusing on that. That's one way I can still be alive, until the last minute I am alive."

And that's what he did. When Jemma called to tell me Joe died, she added, "His last words were, 'Thank you.' When he was gone, I realized his pinkie and pointer finger were up and the others closed. He was making the hand sign for I love you."

Being alive, while he was alive.

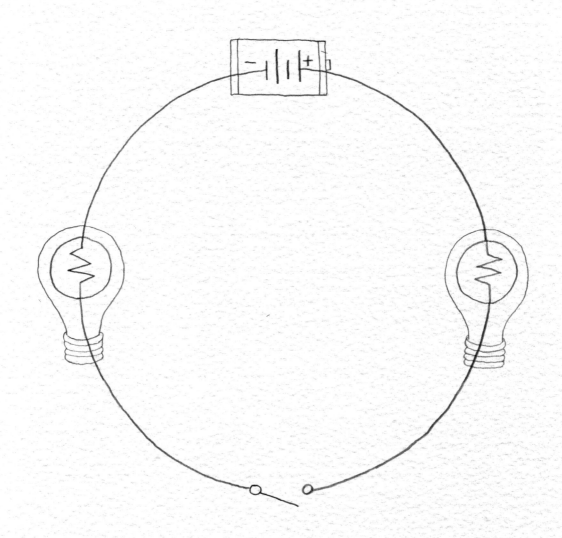

CHAPTER 15

Circles of Compassion

The exiled Tibetan Dalai Lama wrote, "When we are able to recognize and forgive ignorant actions of the past, we gain strength to constructively solve problems of the present"; "If you want to be happy, practice compassion. If you want others to be happy, practice compassion"; and "Compassion is the radicalism of our time."

Compassion, according to the Online Etymology Dictionary, is defined as "a feeling of sorrow or deep tenderness for one who is suffering or experiencing misfortune . . . literally a suffering with another . . . from *com*, 'with together,' and *pati,* 'to suffer.'"

There is a misconception that practicing compassion means that we no longer hold ourselves or others accountable and lose our ability to identify problems, address injury, and instigate change. Compassion is not passive acceptance and compliance. The practice of compassion requires genuine respect, greater accountability, and increased responsibility for one's actions, not less. Bill and I understand from experience how a lack of compassion keeps people stuck in destructive behaviors and unhappy patterns of relationship.

A client told me, "I can forgive others but not myself. I don't let myself off the hook, lower my standards. Fear of cock-ups and anger at myself when I screw up is what makes me successful." He was constantly comparing himself and others to some measure of worth. Those close to him were lashed with the same critical whip he used on himself. People he admired were idealized and put on a pedestal—until they fell off. Most others were secretly viewed as inferior, and he created an overly solicitous manner to disguise his patronizing pity and thinly veiled disdain. Relationships suffered, and many were lost. He couldn't forgive those he loved, and he couldn't love those he forgave.

It takes courage to expand our consciousness beyond our typical systems of interpretation and reaction and endure the shock of opening our heart to the inner experiences of other humans. We may need access to some extra wisdom and support from what I visualize as celestial energy, expanding our concepts of what it means to be human. Compassion connects and directs that energy and is the gateway to transformation.

A while ago, I desperately needed some extra help to make a radical change. I developed a practice I call Circles of Compassion to better navigate an important but difficult relationship.

I had two younger brothers, Bradford and Jason. Brad was born a year after my younger sister died at birth. Brad was a difficult pregnancy for my mother. At five years old, I was in charge of caring for her during the months of bed rest while my father was at work. My father, in his mid-twenties, was busy at his first real job as a teacher in the theater department of an elite girls' college in the Midwest. He was also the school's lighting, set, and costume designer and was at all the rehearsals and shows, often working late into the night. I brought my mother food and drink, helped her to the bathroom, and tried to draw her out of her gloom by getting her to draw and sing and tell stories. The role of therapist was forged early.

Brad was born with lots of problems. Early on he was diagnosed as "brain damaged," a catch-all phrase used in the late fifties. A year after Brad's birth, my brother Jason was born. My mother, diagnosed with rheumatoid arthritis at the age of six, had been told she should never have children. Her arms were permanently bent at a ninety-degree angle, she walked with a limp, and she was in chronic pain. On bad days, when she was having an attack, she hardly left the couch. She had her hands full, and I often needed to help with one or both of my baby brothers.

I changed diapers, wiped snotty noses, and was their bossy big sister and babysitter until I left for college. My responsibility did not end there. After I left home, my parents went through an acrimonious divorce. My father was living with the woman he eventually married. After college and a series of adventures, I moved to Atlanta, where I was getting my MFA in printmaking and working as a preschool teacher.

Both Brad and Jason left New York and showed up on my doorstep within months of graduating high school. While attempting to manage my own emotional and psychological hurricanes, I was in that thankless role of being responsible for them but having no power to control their actions. There was no parental financial support for any of us after we graduated from high school. That was made clear.

In the early years, we three Keene children were a tiny flock of odd ducks. I had grossly deformed teeth, so buck that my lips couldn't close, and the gap in my front teeth was large enough for me to stick my pencil in. I wore elaborate braces until I was in college. Brad had no chin and a large, bulbous nose that continually leaked thick streams of yellow mucus, which he would habitually lick. His perpetual drool sprouted warts over the lower part of his face. In his teenage years, a doctor determined that he was allergic to his own mucus. His nose dripped his entire life. For years, I wiped it. When he was older, I just handed him tissues. He was skeletal, rib-showing skinny, until his thirties, when his diet of beer and pretzels resulted in an enormous belly protruding below his concave chest. Jason, the chubby one, got the flaming red hair and large freckles that covered his body. He weighed 250 pounds in middle school. When I was away at college, he grew a foot taller and lost the weight, emerging as a cool and talented musician, spending the next decade living the gypsy life as a member of various bands.

Over the years, I would attempt to get Brad presentably groomed, sell employers on his sweet nature and useful qualities, and then deal with the subsequent spiraling into failure of each attempt. He had gone to a technical high school and learned to run a printing press, which he adored. Unfortunately, that industry disappeared when he was in his twenties. There were certain physical jobs he could do and enjoyed doing, but his cognitive deficiencies, social awkwardness, and odd appearance, combined with the world's transition to increased automation, meant that employment for Brad was a lifelong challenge. There were times when I set him up in his own apartment, but that situation would never last long and would end in some kind of disaster. Brad lived with me, my brother Jason, or my mother for most of his life. Friendly but socially awkward and physically challenged, he never once had a proper date he didn't pay for and was often the target of unscrupulous characters who took advantage of his need and naivete.

Brad's cognitive abilities were difficult to diagnose and therefore difficult to address. He could astonish everyone with his knowledge of obscure facts and surprising visual memory yet not understand what seemed incredibly simple. He could drive, although he destroyed the brakes on every car, left one abandoned in a ditch, and used them all as giant containers of treasures and trash. He could cook simple meals, but cleanliness—for self or abode—was never his thing. Over the decades, I hired lawyers and fought with the system to get him benefits, got him into job training programs, and arranged psychotherapy evaluations and treatment. I helped him move more times than I want to remember and did the best I could to keep him off the streets. During several periods when he was attempting to live on his own, I discovered him homeless, sleeping in his car or in laundromats. He hadn't wanted to tell me that the job was lost and his possessions had been thrown out by eviction or stolen by those he unwittingly trusted.

When I married my first husband, Brad, Jason, and my mother all followed me to Los Angeles. Brad and Mom became an inseparable duo and an almost daily part of my household; they needed support in all areas, and I was it. As my mother's physical and mental health deteriorated, Brad took on all the driving and shopping and cooked simple meals. After her dramatic death a few years after I moved back to New York, Brad returned to living with me.

Several years later, when Bill and I moved to Brooklyn, Brad chose to stay upstate and remain close to Sara, his angel of a case worker. He developed a paranoid fear of the city, and all in-person interactions had to be on his turf. I set up systems to manage his finances and housekeepers to help with laundry and clean and relied on Sara to oversee many of the details involved in keeping Brad afloat. He hated doctors and refused to go to dentists. Sara had him in a state program where he did piecework with other disabled adults for less than minimum wage. Brad, with his extensive CD collection, became the unofficial director of music as they worked. He loved having a role to play and was cheerful, reliably punctual, and friendly.

That did not translate into having friends. He was caught in the cracks, too intelligent to want to hang out with those with obvious cognitive difficulties and too uncomfortable to join in other social interactions. My lifelong attempts to get him connected to people and activities and provide helpful hints about how to manage the essentials of life were usually met with his strong-willed, insurmountable resistance and a resolute, often angry, "No."

Communication between us became increasingly difficult and fraught with tension. His calls usually meant there was something that needed to be bought or fixed. I made efforts to call him just to chat, but the dialogue would soon become me asking questions and him avoiding answers, getting annoyed, and calling me "Mom." My tone would become increasingly agitated and angry.

I'd get off the phone feeling dreadful, seesawing between blaming him for being so difficult and me for being such a bitchy big sister. Our interactions were getting worse, and it had to be someone's fault—his or mine. If I kept in touch, I felt bad. If I didn't stay in touch, I felt bad. What was wrong? I was there for my clients. Why couldn't I be there for my own brother?

Circles of Compassion became the answer. As long as I was blaming myself or blaming Brad, we were caught in the toxicity of judgment. Bill and I were working on recognizing and converting our habits of judgment into habits of compassion. The more we practiced compassion in our lives together, the more we felt the radical shift in both our experience and behavior. Our work as therapists also began to evolve, and we saw the results in our clients' lives.

I vowed to myself that I would practice what I preached and practice compassion with my brother. Then it hit me. All my life, I had worked at having what I thought of as compassion for my brother. But it was really pity. Pity required me to view him as inferior and me as superior. If I was superior, I deserved no pity, which I had confused with compassion.

Through the lens of judgment, I was deemed "the responsible one" and Brad was "the irresponsible one." And that left me feeling angry. My inner child screamed, "I don't like always being the responsible one!" Then I imagined Brad crying, "I don't like always being the irresponsible one!" I recognized our common denominator. Our roles and experience in family and in life were difficult for both of us. We were each disappointed in ourselves and in each other. I was never the Should-Be sister he wanted, and he was never the Should-Be brother I wanted. We both lived in As-Is Land. Life had presented both of us with challenges. Different? Yes! But when comparison is eliminated, judgment dissipates and compassion has room to grow.

> When comparison is eliminated, judgment dissipates and compassion has room to grow.

Practicing compassion began to shift the relationship. When we would talk on the phone or meet, I would imagine the light-filled energy of compassion soothing my heart. "You are doing something hard," I would silently acknowledge to myself in the voice of a nurturing parent. "Your Full Spectrum is spinning with so many contradictory thoughts and big feelings. You are doing the best you can. You are human, not perfect. You are aware of his suffering, and it hurts. It's hard to hear about the latest problem. You keep trying to save him, make his life better, but it's his life; he makes choices. It's not all your responsibility."

I would then focus on the common denominator that felt most accurate in the moment. "We both can feel disappointed in life, others, ourselves. We make choices that don't go how we planned. We are human, not perfect. He gets annoyed at me, and I get annoyed at him. We wish everything was easier. Neither of us knows what to talk about that isn't a problem."

Then I would imagine the light-filled energy of compassion traveling across the connection of our common denominator, going from my heart to his heart, and I would feel compassion, not pity, for him. I would imagine his thoughts: "She probably will scold me, judge me, see me as not doing it right. This is hard for me. I'm uncomfortable. I feel ashamed telling her I need help. I wish it was easier. I wish I was different."

As we talked, I would keep visualizing, without so much thought, compassion for myself, compassion for Brad, our common denominator

> I would imagine the light-filled energy of compassion traveling across the connection of our common denominator, going from my heart to his heart.

making us equals—not one of us superior or one of us more deserving of compassion. We both needed it. The light-filled energy would seem to circle around us, and I would feel myself loving and loved, Brad as loving and loved. Human. Imperfect. Doing our lives as best we could. Playing the hand each of us was dealt.

Bill noticed the difference immediately. There was more laughter and less tension in the conversations I had with Brad. I was lighter after an exchange. There were just as many problems to face and solve, but the required actions weren't soaked in depleting, poisonous judgment—or seething resentment—toward myself and Brad. It was still hard, but it was okay. Compassion filled me with the love that judgment took away.

Compassion filled me with the love that judgment took away.

Brad's life got harder. He got sicker. I took him to a specialist who said his diabetes was destroying his kidneys and he needed to go on dialysis. Brad refused. "Never!" There was no convincing him. Then one day he called, scared. He couldn't get out of his recliner. I called an ambulance and jumped in my car. By the time I got to the hospital, he was in a coma. They did dialysis, and he was saved. My brother Jason flew from LA, and we all supported the doctor who said, "You can refuse dialysis, but you will be dead in a few weeks." Brad finally agreed. He went three times a week and began to form friendly relationships with the nurses. The doctor recommended I take him for kidney transplant evaluation. It was a long day of tests that made clear that Brad was not a candidate.

The circulation in his feet became a problem. There were operations and special shoes, but gangrene set in, and it was determined his leg needed to be amputated. That meant he couldn't stay in his apartment. It wasn't wheelchair accessible. Our country house was a rabbit warren on five levels, and we were only there half the week. I worked at finding an appropriate place nearby where at least I would be regularly close and have a place to stay when I was dealing with emergencies. Life was changing.

His experience those six months in the hospital and the rehab center was a nightmare. He got infectious, chronic diarrhea and a skin condition that covered his body with itchy, flaky scales. The care he received was abominable. Every spare minute, I was on the phone pleading with administration, doctors, and social workers and getting increasingly discouraged trying to find an appropriate and affordable place for him to live.

Finally, a place was chosen that was twenty minutes away from our house, and Bill and I began the gargantuan and unpleasant task of cleaning out his apartment. Gruesome details were uncovered in the process that will forever remain an aspect of my remembered experience. Circles of Compassion became increasingly necessary. Breathe in, breathe out, compassion for me and compassion for Brad was the way I navigated through the high waves of intense emotions and high stakes problem-solving.

The day came when he was well enough to move. He had helped me pick out a new couch, bed, and bedspread, plus details like a shower curtain featuring an antique racing car and red towels to go with it. I had scrubbed and scoured, placed favorite objects, hung his posters and framed photos, and arranged his clothes. Bill and I took him out to eat his favorite meal, fish and chips, on our way to his new place. I had told the office when we would arrive, but they had left without making accessible the call button he was supposed to wear around his neck. He had his cell phone, and we agreed he could get the button when I came to bring him to breakfast the next morning. We made sure he could maneuver the toilet, television, and new recliner. Photos were snapped, and I said I would be giving him a wake-up call before I arrived in the morning.

Morning came. He didn't answer my call, and I realized there were distressed messages from the night before because he couldn't get the stereo to work. I reprimanded myself for not hearing his call and hurried to get there to help him get ready in time for breakfast introductions. I opened the door and the smell hit me. Around the corner, I found Brad, naked and unconscious with a path of diarrhea from his bed to where he lay sprawled on the bathroom floor.

The 911 operator told me to go into the hall and scream for help, and then she talked me through giving Brad CPR until the paramedics arrived. He was warm, seemed alive, but as I held his nose and filled his lungs with my air, I felt no response. The act felt incredibly intimate. I was touching my naked brother in a way that recalled early days when I was changing his diaper or chasing a skinny, naked boy who didn't want to get into his pajamas.

Bill and my daughter arrived soon after the medics took over and were there when they told me that Brad was gone. I became hysterical, howling. I had killed my brother, I had let him down, I wasn't there when he needed me most. That was the first felt pie slice of my Full Spectrum. Over the next hours, days, and months, Circles of Compassion enabled me to move to a place of compassion for myself and compassion for Brad. But mourning and healing take time.

Recently, my cardiologist, observing discrepancies in my lab results, asked me if there were any emotional reasons for why I might be ignoring aspects of stress-relieving self-care. We were speaking as colleagues as well as doctor to patient.

She said, "Is there something about yourself that you haven't forgiven?"

Tears sprang to my eyes, and I knew the answer: Brad.

My doctor explained how she had used the Hawaiian practice of Ho'oponopono during a stressful period in her life. The mantra of "I'm sorry. Forgive me. I love you. Thank you" is repeated over and over. We were heading to the Adirondacks for two weeks of kayaking, and I used the mantra throughout each day whenever I had a moment of repose. I was first saying it to me and then to Brad, and then I felt Brad saying it to me. As with Circles of Compassion, I could feel something shifting. Then one night, Brad came to me in a dream. It felt like a long visit. We were both much younger, healthier, and we were going about a day, shopping, doing chores, engaging in comfortable, loving, easy sibling banter. "It's okay," I felt him telling me. "We shared so much. We were together my whole life. We did the best we could. We love each other. There's nothing to forgive."

Yes. And thank you.

I'm sorry. Forgive me. I love you. Thank you.

How to Use Circles of Compassion

Acknowledge you're activated, and bring mindful awareness to the dynamics of the relationship.

Take responsibility for your actions.

Think: In what ways are we similar?

Maybe: I don't like what they're saying and doing, and they don't like what I'm saying and doing.

Invite compassion— this is really hard!

Extend compassion to the other person along your Common Denominator.

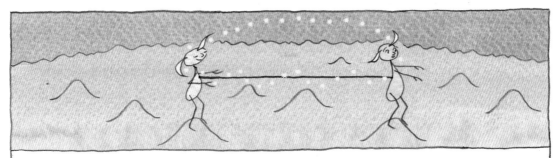

Connect with the Light of the Universe in a circular flow of healing energy.

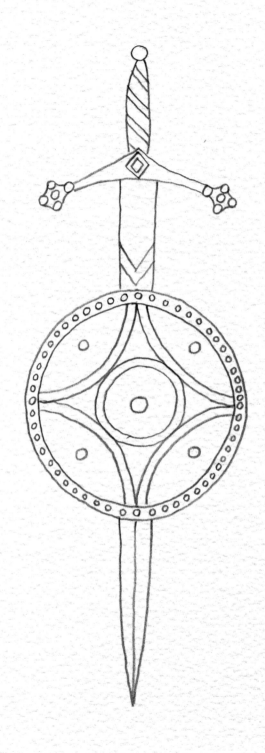

CHAPTER 16

The Courage to Lay Down
Our Sword and Shield

Our species developed our ingrained behaviors to ensure survival, back when we were small tribes roaming a turbulent planet with vast areas uninhabited by humans. Our lizard-brain Bodyguards make quick decisions of safe or not safe, a necessary response in times of crisis. Deep-rooted Sticky Beliefs perpetuate ancient indoctrinations meant to ensure tribal unity. They persuade us that a relentless stance of suspicious, self-righteous blame and bitterness toward those identified as a threat will promote survival. Deviation from tribal norms often merited harsh punishment. Our ancient, internalized authority figures, those powerful Judgmental Parents, assert that self-flagellation is what we deserve when we stumble or stray, and that shame and threat of banishment will mold us into who we should be.

Traditional cultures teach us to hold tight to our shields of anger and swords of hate. It takes courage to lay down our weapons of judgment and defense and instead choose compassionate curiosity, communication, and collaboration. Changing defensive behaviors of retaliation and resentment isn't easy and certainly isn't instantaneous. The practice of compassion helps us rewire our embedded habits of response.

> It takes courage to lay down our weapons of judgment and defense and instead choose compassionate curiosity, communication and collaboration.

Brené Brown makes the point in her book *I Thought It Was Just Me: Women Reclaiming Power and Courage in a Culture of Shame*: "I don't believe that compassion is our default response. I think our first response to pain—ours and everyone else's—is to self-protect. We protect ourselves by looking for someone or something to blame." She also wrote in *The Gifts of Imperfection: Let Go of Who You Think You Should Be and Embrace Who You Are*, "When we practice generating compassion, we can expect to experience the fear of our pain. Compassion practice is daring. It involves learning to relax and allow ourselves to move gently toward what scares us." There is so much in life that scares us.

A young couple, Cynthia and Henry, began therapy to see if they could heal their relationship. They had been together since high school and engaged since college but discovered that they both had been secretly having sexual affairs with others. An elaborate wedding had been scheduled and planned, but now all was on hold. Should they call the whole thing off?

Different people have different definitions of what constitutes an affair. The meaning of an affair and how to respond is also not the same for everyone. Cynthia had had what she thought of as "an intense brain blip," a fling that happened at a four-day conference with someone she hadn't known before and intended to never see again. "I liked the attention and the compliments. I've always been the 'serious, good girl,' and this was giving me a chance to rebel without anyone knowing. I felt like I was outside my real life and so it didn't matter. Until I got home and realized it did. Memories stick. They don't stay put in the past."

Henry's affair was emotional. An older girl he'd had a preteen crush on when he was at camp contacted him through social media. What began as friendly chat became flirtatious, and eventually they arranged to meet. "We made out—although we never did anything where she could get pregnant," he vehemently declared. "But I became a bit obsessed, and I hid the contact from Cynthia. Even if it didn't cross certain physical boundaries, it still messed with our relationship. I realized that the idea of being married scared me. It felt like I was becoming old, turning into my parents. I wanted to hold on to the me I was at camp when my biggest concern was whether or not I'd strike out when it was my turn at bat."

They both worked at being curious about what led to each of the affairs, not just blaming and judging the other as bad. They each took responsibility for how the actions they had taken affected the other person. Expressed remorse and repeated efforts for understanding made way for renewed intimacy and connection. In sessions, they repeatedly came back to their strong feelings of love, shared values, and dreams of a future together. They chose to view the affairs as a wake-up call to address issues they had ignored and to create a better foundation for a marriage, rather than a sign that they should break apart in an emotional storm of accusation and resentment. Next came the hard process of healing.

There are many kinds of relationships and rules regarding those relationships. Some rules are governed by legal, religious, or cultural authorities. Other rules reside within an individual and can be both conscious and unconscious. No two affairs are exactly alike, and the impact of all those affected by what becomes identified as an affair can also be vastly different. The meaning of an affair for each person is generated by their personal experience as well as the values and cultural norms of their community. Healing requires an understanding of what the affair meant for each person involved and a willingness to address the defensive behavior activated in response to that meaning or Sticky Belief.

Cynthia and Henry both confessed to persistent, uncomfortable moments when the Bodyguards took over. Unspoken and secret, the fears would grow and grow—expanding balloons of fear in their chests—inflated with thoughts of "How do I know I'm safe?" and "What do I do to make it feel better?"

Cynthia would think, "How can I be aware of all his actions so he can never again surprise me with betrayal?" Her Bodyguard prodded her to remain hypervigilant, constantly checking his phone and email, searching for damning evidence. Her mind would spin, endlessly imagining all the possible unhappy scenarios playing out in a future together. She wanted guarantees that none of them would ever happen.

Henry was more inclined to push all bad thoughts and feelings out of consciousness and focus on actions he believed would convince Cynthia of his love and his ability to be the perfect man he thought she wanted him to be. His overly solicitous, anxious, and eager actions began to irritate Cynthia.

"When you bring me flowers, text me hearts every hour, and fold my underwear, I think it's all an act and you won't keep it up. It feels like a demand that I love you and promise I'll never get mad!" she told him using Speaker-Listener.

Henry began to see how his habitual avoidance of any confrontation and distancing from his own thoughts and feelings were his ways of feeling safe. But these defenses were also what led to the compartmentalization of relationships and the affair. His main Bodyguard, whom he dubbed "Happy Hank," preferred the defense of Fawning and demanded he focus on doing, rather than thinking and feeling. His Bodyguard was protecting him from thinking and feeling, since that led into the dangerous territory of uncomfortable memories and judgments, which in turn threw him into a swirling whirlpool of shame.

He relied on his skill at creating the image of Should-Be Henry (aka Happy Hank), a mask that he had crafted early on in life to escape the wrath and verbal whip of his real and internalized Judgmental Parent. Fear of Judgment left him emotionally frozen and unable to examine, understand, and thereby change the impulses that led to the affair. It took courage to show up each week in therapy and uncover the confusing, uncomfortable, and sometimes contradictory thoughts and feelings of his complex and changeable Full Spectrum. He also needed courage to stay present in the emotional discussions he and Cynthia had in their apartment.

Cynthia and Henry spent many months in individual therapy, exploring all that led them to make the choice to have an affair, as well as understanding and shifting other problematic habitual behaviors. Cynthia and I used Circles of Compassion on her frightened thoughts. Instead of either banishing her fears by judging her thoughts as wrong or fueling fears by replaying scenes and judging Henry as wrong, we held and softened her fears with love and understanding. She imagined the light from Circles of Compassion healing the pain and wounds created by her need to be perfect and Henry's need to be perfect and the pressure they both felt to be the ideal couple in the perfect marriage. Judgment derives from fear and an effort to stay safe. Compassion requires us to have courage and override our habitual judgment and defensive response.

Cynthia imagined the light coming from her heart to Henry's heart, healing the hurts created by that need for perfection. The light of compassion flowed toward her imagined Bodyguard, a vigilant detective, "Suspicious Cynthia," keeping her safe by constantly investigating and judging. She spun the Circles of Compassion out toward members of her family who had honed her use of judgment, and she spun Circles of Compassion toward all those who felt judged by her and all those who judged her in an effort to keep themselves safe.

In a couple's session, Bill asked Cynthia to describe the monster of fear that required her Bodyguard to be continually patrolling the grounds around her fortress.

"I imagine Henry attracted to another woman, and I think I'll never recover! I'll be wounded to my core! Our relationship would be over!" Cynthia declared, acknowledging her intrusive, looping, fear-inducing thoughts.

I asked Henry if he had thoughts like that, and he visibly recoiled and vehemently denied he ever had thoughts that they might not be together.

"I would never let myself picture something like that!" he replied. He believed that to allow a scary thought or feeling would magically make it happen.

Since Henry's Bodyguard preferred to use avoidance and compartmentalization to keep Henry safe and Cynthia's Bodyguard preferred hypervigilance and strict rules of right and wrong to keep her safe, it was usually Cynthia who instigated heated, marathon discussions. In the system of their relationship, Cynthia was in charge of having the scary thoughts and Henry was in charge of doing all he could to sweep the scary thoughts away. His style of sweeping was the use of actions rather than words. Henry's special breakfasts, eager running of errands, and many gifts were symbolic acts he hoped Cynthia would experience as evidence of his love and faithfulness to distract her from focusing on his shortcomings.

Bill invited Henry to consider what it might be like to quit his striving to always present as cheerful, positive, helpful, and good. "What would it be like if you gave up trying to manage Cynthia's emotional state by only showing her a small part of your experience?"

Henry realized how much he had been formed by his family culture. "If you can't say something nice, say nothing at all" was the family motto. Appearances were emphasized, and all were ruled by the real and imagined judgments of each person's ever watchful Outer Camera. Henry was a Captive Child ruled by the verdicts of others and his own internalized Judgmental Parent. The affair felt outside of normal existence and therefore beyond all probing eyes. His ability to compartmentalize was derived from his need to find relief from perpetually probing, accusing, and shaming authority figures. His fear of failure and the ensuing mortifying humiliation made him reluctant to dare anything where he might not immediately succeed.

He and Cynthia began to understand how her habits of hypervigilance and need to control

Henry attracted to another woman

In the system of their relationship, Cynthia was in charge of having the scary thoughts and Henry was in charge of doing all he could to sweep the scary thoughts away.

played into his fear of judgment. She had been raised in a family where one parent held rigid views of what was right and wrong, good and bad, acceptable and unacceptable, and the other kept the peace by not voicing their opinion and spending a lot of time outside the household. They recognized the common denominator that was part of the attraction. Both were driven by the need to appear perfect and never make what could be judged as a mistake.

"We don't want to repeat the cultures we grew up in!" declared Cynthia. "I want a marriage where we can be our true selves, where we aren't so afraid to reveal what is uncomfortable or confusing, where we can have the courage to be vulnerable and honest with each other, not just performing in some show we present as a 'happy family.'"

They both worked at not relying so much on judgment to navigate their actions and reactions. They began to replace judgment with compassion, for themselves and others. Gradually, they became more used to checking in with their own thoughts and feelings and really talking, communicating more of their Full Spectrum to each other.

Henry revealed that when he saw Cynthia texting or talking on the phone, he became worried that she had found someone more attractive as a possible mate. He confessed that he would then counter that thought by doing something he thought she would like.

"I'm so glad to know you have those thoughts too!" Cynthia exclaimed. "If you tell me you worry about me leaving, then I don't feel I have to worry so much about you leaving!" She described her anxiety barometer as going from a 9 to a 4.

Henry was quite pleased and admitted that he felt more comfortable when able to tell her thoughts that weren't just hopeful. He would often tell her "I love you," and she would question if that were true. It was both counterintuitive and confusing to voice worries, rather than "I love you and everything is fine," and to have those "bad thoughts" create a closeness.

I told them of a book I had read about a World War II German soldier and his relationship with a French woman resistance fighter. They courageously opened their hearts to have compassion for both their enemy and themselves. They realized that the roles they played in the horrors of war were spawned in real fear created by truly powerful Dictators of Reality. When the soldier and resistance fighter related as individuals, they found they had much in common. They could relate as equals with a shared humanity. They were using what we could see as Circles of Compassion, giving them the courage to lay down their swords and shields of attack and defense.

When we are activated, the other person becomes the enemy, and our self-righteous rage and resentment feels like the only truth. We make the other person into a two-dimensional caricature instead of seeing them as a whole, complicated being such as ourselves. The judgmental portions of our Full Spectrum, with rigid interpretations of who is right and who is wrong and who is at fault and who is not, take over our awareness and push all other interpretations into tiny, imperceptible slices. We lose touch with our Wise Whole Self who knows all aspects of our Full Spectrum, preventing us from calling up the wise warrior within us who has the courage to face extreme fear with Circles of Compassion.

Henry was intrigued by the concept that facing real pain or painful thoughts could be a warrior's act of bravery and love. He revealed a thought he'd had that morning and never would have said out loud.

"I saw a posting about breast cancer, and I thought that if you had cancer and both of your breasts were cut off, I wouldn't love you any less. I pictured caring for you and actually treasuring you more. I imagined using Circles of Compassion for both of us."

Cynthia was amazed. To say such a thing was very unlike Henry. It took courage. She put her hand on his knee. "You have told me two things this session that you thought you should push away, ignore, and certainly not say. Yet both those things leave me feeling closer to you—not further away. When you're not afraid to show me the real Full Spectrum you, I'm less afraid to show you the real Full Spectrum me."

Cynthia added, "I think my fears have lately increased because we have been talking about having a house and children, and I keep thinking that I can't until I completely trust you."

Bill asked what she meant by "complete trust."

Cynthia answered, "Knowing it will never happen again." Then she heard what she said. "But that's not possible, is it? Things can happen. I never would have imagined I would do what I did. I had my rationalizations and stayed in those thoughts and feelings. I didn't let myself be aware of the other parts."

Bill said, "Trust is going forward in spite of uncertainty, not because there is certainty. Trust, like courage, is choosing the possibility of pain because that means you are choosing to be in life. Courage comes from *cor*, the Latin word for 'heart,' which was regarded as the source of emotions. In this case we could say that courage means speaking your mind by telling your heart."

Henry took Cynthia's hand. "I'm ready to be a warrior, a knight winning your hand by having the courage to speak my heart."

Cynthia smiled. "So, I guess I can have the courage to put down my sword and shield. Most of the time. Except when I really feel I need it!"

We all laughed. How true. We are all a work in progress. Sometimes, when we are activated, we don't even realize that we have already grabbed our shield and are about to start swinging our sword. Those are the moments where we also need compassion, an internalized Nurturing Parent who can see we are frightened and upset, lovingly take our hand, help us to put down the sword, and encourage us to face our fears without shield in hand.

I imagine Circles of Compassion for myself and all other humans who get scared and choose judgment over compassion, who weren't able to take a Pause when they saw red. We need the courage to go toward the compassionate awareness that enables us to change.

We need an internalized Nurturing Parent who can see we are frightened and upset, lovingly take our hand, help us to put down the sword and encourage us to face our fears without shield in hand.

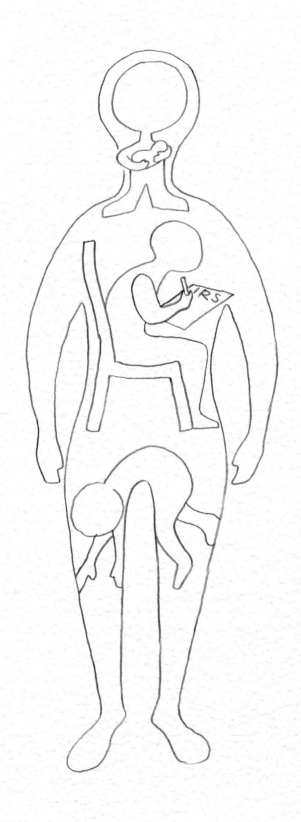

CHAPTER 17

Parent, Adult, or Child?

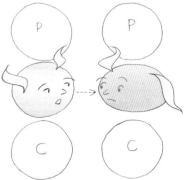

Did you remember to mail the check?

Sometimes in a relationship, two adults find themselves falling into the roles of Judgmental Parent and Captive Child. In some relationships, those roles stay fairly consistent. In other relationships, there can become an ongoing tussle over who is in the role of Judgmental Parent and holds the power over the Captive Child. They may occasionally share pleasure and fun in a Free Child–to–Free Child interaction, or be pulled by the obligations of life into an Adult-to-Adult discussion, or work together, Parent to Parent, caring for another being. Then, something will cause one or both to become activated, and they retreat into the habitual roles of Judgmental Parent and Captive Child.

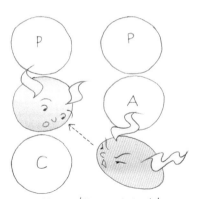

Don't blame me! You never told me to!

Roger was in his early fifties, and Christy was in her early forties. They had attended the same elementary school but met in later years through Christy's older brother who had stayed in their hometown, just outside Milwaukee. Roger's first marriage happened right out of high school, the result of an unexpected pregnancy. The marriage lasted only five years, but Roger had stayed involved in the raising of his two daughters and was close to his grandkids.

Christy moved to New York for college and career. She'd never been married and wanted a child. Roger was ready to retire. Over the years, Roger had turned his one-man cleaning service into a company with a small fleet of trucks. After a lucrative sale of his company and a quick long-distance courtship, Roger married Christy and moved from Wisconsin to New York. Christy was pregnant within a month.

They lived in Christy's house, and Roger stayed home with their son, Ryan, while Christy continued her career. They both had definite ideas about the way things should be. In Roger's family, his father was the boss. In Christy's family, her mother held that role.

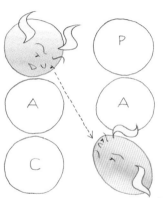

Right. I forgot—I'm responsible for everything!

Roger was clear about what he wanted. "I spent too long on the job. Now is my time to be social." He liked to cook and invited people over for impromptu dinners and barbecues. He joined a softball league, played poker with the guys, and knew all the shopkeepers and moms and nannies at the playground.

Christy, before marriage and parenthood, was used to having a clean and quiet sanctuary where she could unwind after work, listen to relaxing music, knit, do crosswords, and read. She had suffered from postpartum depression during the first six months of Ryan's life, and Roger had willingly stepped into the role of primary parent. For Christy, finding peaceful alone time was hard enough with a small child. Roger's big energy and obliviousness to the finer details of housekeeping added to Christy's unhappiness. Roger felt perpetually criticized and unappreciated. After a loud and vitriolic verbal battle that left three-year-old Ryan in tears, they decided they needed some help.

Within relationships, the different roles each person plays—including the ones played by our Bodyguards—are all part of a system. In chapter 3, I introduced Eric Berne's concept of transactional analysis, emphasizing the Nurturing Parent. The theory can be used in many ways, and it is helpful to review. Berne identified Parent, Adult, and Child as three different roles, or self-states, of our personality that take shape early and are part of us, in some form, during all of life's stages.

In Berne's model, the Parent role can be either compassionate and nurturing or critical and judging.

The Adult is the one who takes care of business. A child, in the role of Adult, picks up toys, does homework, and figures out how to climb onto the counter and reach the cookies on the top shelf. The grown-up version pays the bills, takes out the garbage, and books airline tickets.

The Child is conceived of as the aspect of our personality that is playful, spontaneous, dreaming, sensual, creative, and passionate. These qualities flourish in the presence of a Nurturing Parent.

When a child is trained to always look to a parent or other authority figures for a verdict on the success or failure of their actions and the assigning of a Shame or Pride Identity, we conceive of those dyads as a Judgmental Parent and Captive Child relationship.

Relationships work best when all involved are encouraged to inhabit all three roles and relate to each other, Child to Child, Adult to Adult, and Parent to Parent. The actual parent playfully engages the Child part of their Full Spectrum with the Child aspect of their actual child. Then, when it is time to clean up, the actual adult engages the Adult aspect of the child as they pick up the toys. They join as Parent to Parent as they care for the dog, stuffed animal, or younger sibling. Of course, there will often be times when the child is in the Child position and the parent is in the Parent role. It is useful to identify the different kinds of interactions. No matter the role, there is mutual respect and an acknowledgment that each have their own point of view.

Adults also feel in sync and more connected when relating to the same aspect in each other. They may at times enter the Parent-to-Parent realm, working together, nurturing people and pets and other elements of a shared environment. They can get down to business together, Adult to Adult, and plan a trip, make a meal, or problem solve the latest challenge. And they can happily join Child to Child, having fun, being sexual, and engaging in dreams about the future and adventures they might have. Communication and collaboration became habitual and skillful.

Roger and Christy often found themselves in battles over dominance.

Christy admitted, "I come home to a disaster zone, a chaotic mess with toys everywhere and dishes in the sink. I become a raging lunatic. I can't help it. He's a lazy slob."

Roger had strong opinions about how Ryan should be parented that were often ignored by Christy. "She's either on her phone, gossiping, shopping, or scrolling social media. Or she's busy cleaning when she's supposed to be interacting with Ryan. She puts him in front of some device and feeds him crap rather than taking the time to make him something decent."

Each would at times become the Judgmental Parent, letting fly with name-calling and a list of all the things the other did wrong. This would prompt a reaction from the other person, in the role of the obstinate Captive Child—usually a sarcastic "Who made you the boss?" or a direct attack. They would fight, retreat, and then come together with the roles reversed.

Sometimes they could both identify and focus on pie slices of their Full Spectrum that aligned with their Adult perspective. But soon one of them would slide into their critical Judgmental Parent personality, and the other would relapse into defiant Captive Child. Only when they both were able to be together, Child to Child, in their playful personalities could they truly enjoy their interactions and connect.

In the past, they would critically discuss what they saw as other peoples' ridiculous or shameful actions, Judgmental Parent to Judgmental Parent. But that activity, which we identify as Joining in Judgment and Eric Berne called playing "Ain't it Awful," was becoming less satisfying. Roger began to criticize Christy for "always being negative," and Christy criticized Roger for being too sensitive and "acting high and mighty." He was judging her judging, and she was judging his judging of her judging.

Christy's parents used ridicule and disapproval of others as a way of feeling both more in control and superior to the recipient of their disdain. The habit of seeing the world through the lens of toxic judgment connected her family to the tribe of Us-Versus-Unworthy-Others. Christy's well-trodden path of connection, confidence, and identity became a contentious place of discord and disconnection as Roger rejected that all-too-familiar mode of communication and refused to play "Ain't it Awful."

In sessions, Bill and I helped them to see how criticism and ridicule were familiar actions that both Christy and Roger associated with being with family. Roger experienced Christy's comments as being like his caustic, sharp-tongued mother, while Christy felt that what she thought of as

Parent-to-Parent

Adult-to-Adult

Child-to-Child

her useful suggestions and perceptions of others were being either ignored or dismissed.

Vulnerable and defensive, they slowly came to understand the origins of each other's Sticky Beliefs and ingrained behaviors and began to choose which habitual actions and reactions were useful to their family system and which were not. Much curiosity and compassion were needed to accept their differences. Circles of Compassion helped them focus on what they had in common and replace the internalized voice of the Judgmental Parent with the more comforting and understanding words of a Nurturing Parent bestowing compassion on their wounded souls. They began to recognize when they were falling into a Parent-Child dynamic and got better at moving into an Adult perspective.

Christy came to realize how much she suffered under the constant barrage of criticism she directed at herself as well as others. Self-righteousness felt empowering when in the flame of a big reaction but left her burnt out and depleted and did nothing to improve her connection to Roger or Ryan. Roger realized how much his take-charge attitude, disparaging remarks, and impromptu lectures on how to parent fed into Christy's shame and insecurity around her parental role. They made a commitment, Adult to Adult, to a weekly Speaker-Listener check-in to better understand their own history and present experience and to learn more about the other person's perspective.

Christy became able to identify when Roger was moving into a parental role and speaking in a tone that Christy experienced as patronizing and "mansplaining." Rather than respond with sarcasm or her own sharp barbs, she was able to communicate how she was experiencing his comment, saying her version of "I feel like we are moving away from having an Adult-to-Adult conversation. I am interested in your suggestions. We are partners. Can we have a redo on that last bit?"

When they got overly activated, one of them—usually Roger—would call for a Pause. They would each work on understanding more about their own reaction to the moment of conflict rather than focus on all the reasons what the other did was wrong and caused the problem. Rather than "You always do this thing that makes me so angry!" they learned to formulate the problem as "When you do this, I interpret it this way and have this reaction."

They practiced giving themselves compassion for how hard it was to change habitual ways of perceiving and responding to stressful situations. They reluctantly accepted that all change is a process over time, and they both were going to have to spend many uncomfortable moments in Stage Two (of the Four Stages of Change), Consciously Incompetent, and Stage Three, Consciously Competent, before new skills and concepts became the natural fit of Stage Four, Unconsciously Competent.

The couple's habitual judgmental approach to life, where all was firmly labeled either this or that, slowly transformed into a more open stance due to their adoption of descriptive, open-ended language and their newfound compassionate curiosity. They moved toward greater awareness about their systems of interaction and a better understanding and consideration of each other's experience.

"Yes—I have this interpretation and reaction. And—I am going to struggle to understand your interpretation and reaction," as well as, "Yes—I am aware of my habitual defensive reaction, supporting old beliefs. And—I can respond by choosing to do something different."

They used playtime with their son to be more playful with each other. In session, we focused on ways to enhance their Child-to-Child experience, and satisfying sex came back into their lives.

The circles of blame, vying for who owned the role of Critical Parent, became less toxic and less frequent. Ryan was able to be a child with two loving, playful parents who were both capable of being in the roles of Parent, Adult, and Child.

Vulnerable and defensive, they slowly came to understand the origins of each other's Sticky Beliefs and ingrained behaviors and began to choose which habitual actions and reactions were useful to their family system and which were not.

CHAPTER 18

Circularity and Vital Play

When we say we feel a connection to an action, person, place, or thing, we are describing what I imagine as a circular current of energy going from us toward the object of our attention and from the object toward us. This energetic circularity can be a fire hose of passion or a trickle of mild interest. Focused, mindful attention both increases our awareness of those connections and guides the flow. We sense our aliveness when we're in the flow of an all-engrossing activity or an emotionally charged interaction. An environment may evoke a strong reaction, or we may see or hold some item we either value or scorn. When the flow is shut down in one direction, it will often find another, sometimes destructive, pathway. Melancholy and depression seep in when nothing can hold our interest and we feel disconnected from life.

Our Child Self is conceived of as the aspect of our being that is inquisitive, impulsive, pleasure seeking, and playful. These early energetic pathways are usually firmly directed into categories of appropriate or inappropriate—or are even completely shut down—by those in authority and the surrounding culture. A Judgmental Parent can inadvertently crush some of the life force in their Captive Child through their effort to improve conformity and success within the prevailing environment. A Nurturing Parent attempts to encourage the Free Child's intrinsic vitality while still guiding them toward acceptable, generative, and useful behaviors. It is often a fine line dividing the two, and, as a parent and as a child, I have experienced both dynamics.

> A Judgmental Parent can inadvertently crush some of the life force in their Captive Child through their effort to improve conformity and success within the prevailing environment.

Grown-ups still want to have fun. We want to experience that connection to our original sense of aliveness. In the model we use, adults in a

Experiencing the circular energy of mind, heart and body

Child-to-Child interaction engage those qualities associated with a not yet fully indoctrinated human. Playful, pleasurable, creative, and improvised exchanges, including sexual intimacy, are conceived of as Child-to-Child interactions. We feel connected, in the circular energy flow. Recognizing and developing these conduits of energy—a dynamic we call Vital Play—is essential to being alive, while we're alive.

Vital Play creates and reinforces connection, stretches our awareness, and can process emotions that are ineffable, unconscious, or not easily put into words. Sandplay is a therapy technique that is not reliant on words and engages deep symbolic knowing for both adults and children. I have been profoundly changed by my experience doing sandplay as an adult, and I have witnessed remarkable transformations in children. "Malika" was one of those cases. In our work together, I served in the role of Nurturing Parent as well as playmate in the magical realm of Child to Child.

> Vital Play creates and reinforces connection, stretches our awareness and can process emotions that are ineffable, unconscious or not easily put into words.

WE HAD BOTH LOST OUR mothers. My mother's dramatic death in the chaos of New York City during 9/11 was still recent. Something would happen and I'd think, "I have to tell Mom about this," or the phone would ring and I'd think, "Maybe it's Mom." Perhaps that is why I so readily accepted the assignment to work twice a week with a preschool child whose mother had recently died. Malika was acting out and had used adult scissors to attack an assistant. She had Something Important she wanted addressed.

Malika and her father had been living in homeless shelters for most of Malika's young life and had only recently moved to their own apartment after her mother's death the month before. Malika's mother already had a five-year-old daughter with another father and was on chemotherapy while she was pregnant with Malika. Overwhelmed by the demands of cancer treatment and parenting, she asked Malika's father to take Malika. At the same time that Malika's mother was dying, Malika's father entered a program to become a registered nurse. Malika was then left in day care from 8:00 a.m. to 6:00 p.m. Malika would visit on her mother's better days.

Before we were introduced, I observed Malika in the classroom. When rest time was finished, Malika did not want to leave her bed and hung on to her cot until the assistant wrenched it away. Malika responded by throwing blocks into the middle of the room. No one noticed. I thought about how many times Malika's bed had been taken away from her. When could Malika ever really safely rest? Malika remained separate while the other children were gathered in a group to sing. She negotiated to have time to make something for her father. With great determination and creativity, she made a piñata out of folded paper and a toilet paper roll and several colored pipe cleaners. She worked intensely, problem-solving and adding artistic flair. She showed the finished elaborate piñata to the teacher and sat on her lap. She chose a book on fire engines and happily turned the pages that showed a big fire in a city apartment and the firefighters who put the fire out. Everyone was saved.

I was struck by the symbols. I imagined a blindfolded Malika desperately flailing about with a stick, attempting to hit and break open a piñata and be rewarded with a glorious rain of goodies. When she threw the blocks, she seemed to be hoping someone would notice. Was she always flailing her stick, hoping to break open the piñata and get at the goodies of human attention and interaction? Would I help her get to some goodies, or would I be hit? Malika was described as always "exploding." I imagined Malika's emotional house bursting into flames.

After book time, Malika took my arm and pulled me into her fantasy play in the block corner. She explained she was making "beds for princesses" out of blocks. Beds in myths, fairy tales, and children's literature are often vehicles for transportation into another world. I gave her an invisible magic stone. Malika grinned and took the magic stone, examined it in her hand, then put it in her pocket to "keep it safe."

Malika put a skirt on her head. She announced that she was Rapunzel and pulled me into a small storage room where she told me her version of the story as we huddled together: the witch, the prince, and Rapunzel's mother and father, all climbed up the long hair to visit the princess imprisoned in her tower.

I asked, "Was Rapunzel glad to have them come join her in her tower?"
Malika vigorously nodded.
"So, she wasn't alone, all by herself?" I added.
Malika smiled and touched my long hair. I said I would like to hear more princess stories when I saw her next week. She took my hand as we went back into the classroom. I had been welcomed into Malika's tower.

In our first official sandplay session, Malika told me to hide all the scary animals. She excitedly put a miniature toilet in the sandtray, then added beds. She laid the princess in the white dress on a bed and told me, "She is dead."

A grandmother figure put blankets on the ducks that were her "babies." Then Malika became the mother, and I was told to be the daughter. As a mother, Malika cuddled baby dolls while watching herself in the mirror. She made a garden out of silk flowers for the house in the sand. As we were about to leave, Malika asked me to put the silk flowers in her hair. I did.

At one point she told me her mother was dead and asked if I had a mommy at home. I answered, "No. My mommy is gone. She died too."

She asked, "Was she sick?"

I answered, "Yes. She was sick for a long time."

She asked, "Did she go to the hospital?"

"Yes," I replied. "She went to the hospital many times. I was sad when she died."

Malika nodded and we were both silent. The feelings were close. We were in sacred space. I did not want to force culturally expected responses onto her authentic, complicated, Full Spectrum experience of her mother's death. I let that be expressed and processed by her, through the play.

After a month, we moved to another room with an elaborate castle. The first day, Malika discovered long white gloves in a costume box. She carefully put on the gloves, smoothing them over her hands and arms. Oddly, a forgotten, dead hermit crab sat motionless in a small terrarium. There was also a large red plush hermit crab. Malika swaddled the red crab in a blanket and then sat in the rocking chair, whispering and hugging "her" as she rocked.

Putting on the white gloves and greeting and hugging the baby girl hermit crab became part of a ritual performed at the beginning of each session. In the full-length mirror, she would look at herself with the white gloves holding the baby hermit crab.

There was intense dramatic play using the queen, the king, and two princesses. The queen often ruled the castle, defended by her soldiers. She would fly into rages with Malika growling and roaring commands as she acted out being the queen. The queen would inevitably demand that the king "Leave!" or she would kill him. Malika often buried the queen and princess figures in the sand. She had me hunt for them using tiny hats as clues. Was the only way the daughters could now be close to their mother was to also be buried?

The queen sometimes morphed into the princess-daughter, and the daughter would hide in the sand so "no one can find me." Sometimes she would begin screaming, "Stay asleep!" and would howl, "Leave me alone!" In a dramatic session, the buried queen figure repeatedly flew up from her sand grave and out of the sand tray, so the searching figures—directed by Malika, acted by me—couldn't find her. The last time Malika had the figure spring from her sand grave, she called out over and over, "I'm in heaven! I'm in heaven!" Malika was smiling. There was a visceral feeling in the room of release. Malika never used those figures again.

We had a team review including her family case worker, the day care director, the head teacher, the classroom assistant, a psychologist brought in to do testing, and the aide who now served as a "shadow" for portions of the long day. The teacher remarked that Malika was much calmer and more compliant on days that she was with me. The social worker explained that Malika's mother had on long white gloves in the coffin and Malika had been told her mother was "asleep." She also said that the mother's rages were quite extreme and often resulted in Malika and her father being told to "Get out!"

I saw Malika's ritualized wearing of the white gloves as a way to bring her mother's death into the room. The act of putting on the white gloves created a connection to her mother. Malika was both her mother and the little girl who had lost her mother. Malika was able to put the gloves on and take the gloves off. She touched the emotional connection to her mother without being overwhelmed by the feelings of longing and loss.

As our sessions progressed, Malika began to costume both of us. With a veil, she made me "a bride." Sometimes we were "twins" and went dancing. She put red scarves on both our arms where we were "hurt," hers on the right and mine on the left—mirror image wounds.

Mother and daughter were both wounded by the mother's death. Malika and I were both mother and daughter. Malika connected to her mother by wearing the gloves; I was connected to her mother by wearing the veil. As in other deep therapies, the memory of our time together became internalized with her memories of her mother. She was no longer as alone in the experience.

When Malika searched for the buried princess, I saw that as her searching for her buried mother, as well as searching for herself. She was buried with the events in her past, and she needed to be found. The princess screamed, "Keep out! Get away or I will kill you!" to the king figure, but Malika had him keep coming back. The princess in the sand wanted to be discovered, unburied, and released. The hermit crab wanted to be taken out of her shell and cuddled and rocked. Two "pretty girls" in front of a mirror wanted to go to a party and dance. Life would go on. Malika enacted many rituals placing me in different roles. After five months, Malika was admitted to a specialized school and our time was over.

During our last session, Malika put on the white gloves and touched the sand. She reverently smoothed the sand with her white-gloved fingers as if performing a sacred ceremony. Then she removed the gloves and listlessly looked around the room. She spied the terrarium with the dead hermit crab. She wanted me to hold it. I did not really want to touch the slightly smelly dead crab, but I did. She tenderly stroked its shell. "We need to get it food," she announced, running out of the room and off to the kitchen with me racing behind her.

She asked the cooks in the school kitchen if she could have some food. They gave her cheese and apple slices. She told them the food was for the hermit crab, "not to eat—because he's dead—but to make him safe." Malika arranged the food around the crab and then decided we had to show it to the day care director who was in her office.

"How nice," said the director, when shown the dead crab surrounded by scattered food. Malika pointed to a tin cookie box on the director's desk. "He needs a better house." The blue tin was given, and Malika poured crab, sand, shells, apple slices, and cheese into it. She asked for a few colorful stickers, which were added to the collection.

"You need to get the school a new crab, one that is alive," she told the director.

"I will," the director promised.

As we were returning to our room, a friendly teacher's aide passed by, and Malika showed her the dead hermit crab surrounded by food.

"Is that for him to eat?" asked the aide. Malika was indignant.

"No! The food makes him feel safe! He can't eat it. He's dead!" She contemplated the crab, then found silk flowers similar to the ones I had put in her hair after our first session. She tenderly arranged the flowers around the dead crab.

"He needs water." Malika got a cup of water and carefully poured the water over the crab.

Then she looked at me and, with great import, went to the sand tray with her cup and scooped some sand. She had always followed the rules and kept the sand in the tray. I smiled and nodded. She covered the dead hermit crab with the sand.

"Now he's safe," she said. "Goodbye, crab." She placed the lid on the blue tin box. She kissed the box. "I love you," she said. She handed me the box. "Now you do it."

I kissed the box and said, "I love you."

"You keep him for me," she said. In exchange, I gave her silk flowers and a book of fairy tales with some of the stories we had reenacted together. We hugged goodbye.

The sessions with Malika brought me in touch with my relationship to my mother and feelings I had not yet processed concerning her recent death. My mother had been in and out of hospitals since she was six years old and had had her first serious attack of rheumatoid arthritis. The frequency of this-is-it moments greatly increased during the last two decades of her pain-filled life. The trips to the emergency room, ICU, or rehab; endless conferences with her doctors; and episodes where she vented to me or others her frustration, fury, and confusion became a constant in my Full Spectrum of experience. I saw or spoke to her every day and was her fierce advocate as she increasingly lost physical and mental capacity. I tried, as best as I could, to be the mother she'd lost when she was thirteen. She had worked hard to be a mother and grandmother. But there remained in me a residue of searing memories and lingering resentment.

I had certainly spent many hours in my own years of therapy, talking about my relationship with my mother. I don't know how I would have coped without my therapists' perspectives, understanding, and support. But after my work with Malika, I knew there was still work to be done. With another sandplay therapist, I did a series of trays that were specifically about my mother. The last one still brings a lump to my throat.

The instructions are minimal for someone doing a sand tray. "Have a soft focus. Let go of planning and trying to make something specific. As much as possible, allow your unconscious to choose and place the objects."

I was surprised by what I was putting in the tray. The items felt like the choices of a child hungry for life. The tray held many small happy scenes. There were trees, birds, flowers, and baby animals on a tiny sand hill and another area with a bed, a book, and doll-like figures. There was an exotic oasis with a palm tree, chalice, and treasure chest. I realized I was imagining myself as my mother when she was still young, still hopeful, not yet beaten down and scarred by all the pain and loss that was yet to come. I began to weep as I felt one with my mother's Child Self, felt her yearning to be fully, excitedly alive. In the tray there was also a wall surrounding a castle and giant black spider in a corner, representing the fears and suffering that held her back.

I hadn't yet developed the practice of Circles of Compassion, but in doing that tray I felt moved by intense compassion for our young Child selves, two little girls bubbling with optimistic curiosity, ready for adventure, eager to greet life. Using the ritual and symbols of sandplay, I felt the circle of energy, the love, flowing from my mother to me and from me to my mother. Mother to child, child to mother, our roles interchanged, and all felt one, all was okay, in this sacred realm of Vital Play.

I was with my mother when she died on September 13 in a New York City emergency room as smoke still rose from the crumbled Twin Towers and sirens constantly blared. My mother was alert and resolute, demanding morphine and refusing more efforts to keep her alive. The daughter who I had almost lost during the period when my mother went into cardiac arrest and coma was with me. We sat on either side of her hospital bed holding her hands, three generations, mothers and daughters.

"I'm done," announced the lifelong news junkie and politico. "You're on your own. The world will have to deal with this mess without me."

My mother's darks were dark, but her laugh was loud and infectious, and her enthusiasm and resilience were legendary. On her deathbed, she asked for her head to be raised so she could feel the light from the window. I read her the Twenty-Third Psalm and began to weep, telling her how much I loved her and how much she meant to me.

"I know all that," she said, her oxygen face mask jauntily perched on her head. "You can stop talking now. This is my death."

She placed the mask over her nose and mouth and squeezed our hands. We watched as she looked straight ahead. Her breath became ragged and weak and then, eventually, stopped, as I imagined her leaping into the abyss.

For many years, over a decade, I kept my mother's ashes on a shelf surrounded by the books she loved. Finally, one summer not long ago, Bill and I kayaked out into the New England ocean she adored and released her ashes in a small cove, next to a large rock near Irony Island. We sang "We Shall Overcome" and "You Are My Sunshine." I spoke words she said to me after a particularly difficult moment in our relationship: "No matter what happens, what gets said, we love each other—so much—like Niagara Falls."

By then, I'd become a strong and more confident kayaker. Much had changed in my life since my mother's death. I was older than she was when her heart stopped for six minutes and she almost died. If only I knew then, in those years long gone, what I know now. But life doesn't work that way. I have compassion for her and compassion for me, doing the best we could with who we were and what we knew then. I hold my mother's Potato Rock and feel her courage, her choice to be alive, and like Malika, engage with life that, like a potato, is good enough.

MENU

Choices

Starters

	Yes	No
Take music lessons	☐	☐
Stand up to the bully	☐	☐
Pick a school far from home	☐	☐
Introduce yourself & suggest coffee	☐	☐

Mains

	Yes	No
Say, "I do."	☐	☐
Change careers	☐	☐
Try for #2	☐	☐
Blow it all on an RV	☐	☐
Try rehab	☐	☐

Endings

	Yes	No
File for divorce	☐	☐
Hand in your notice	☐	☐
Reach a compromise	☐	☐
Have one for the road	☐	☐

CHAPTER 19

Owning Our Choices

Decades before I ever kayaked, I would have dreams and images of myself lost at sea in a vast ocean of water, desperate for an island to appear where I could rest and find nourishment. Other times I would feel like I was on a river being pulled by the current toward a roaring waterfall. Life can feel that way. As if we have no choice. The current directs our route, and we are merely floating bodies, squeezed tight into our inner tubes, watching life on shore as we drift by. When kayaking, we are influenced by weather and water conditions, but every stroke requires a decision. We are responsible for how we respond to life—the As Is, not the Should Be.

The year before we began kayaking, the As Is of our lives was pretty brutal. We had coped with life-threatening illness (Bill's colon cancer), gruesome treatments, and other drastic life changes. By August we were exhausted, vulnerable, and just beginning to slowly emerge from the altered state of intense crisis. We decided to go to Nova Scotia for some very needed R & R. We saw a flyer and, on a whim, decided to book a kayak rental for our last day in Cape Breton. Neither one of us had ever been kayaking.

The morning arrived and rain was beating against the windows. "Maybe the weather will let up by the time we get there," Bill suggested. The dark gray sky did not look encouraging. Neither of us wanted to spend our last day holed up in a cabin. Every moment seemed precious. We knew from Bill's brush with death that we were lucky to have any moments at all. How we were going to spend our days on Earth had new meaning.

The woman who ran the kayak rental from her home was surprised to see us. She lent us waterproof pants and fitted us with kayak skirts to attach to the kayak. She handed us paddles and led us to the double-seater kayak. "Have fun!" she called as she fled back to the warmth of her house. The rain was coming down so hard it was difficult to see.

"Are we crazy?" asked Bill.

"Yes," I replied. "But when has that stopped us?" The images from the past year's illness and treatment were intense. We had survived. We had learned to be in As-Is Land, not clinging to Should-Be Land. There had been a lot of rain, not much sun. Oh well.

Coordinating our paddling in a double kayak provided many laughable moments. I was in the front with Bill in the back. Sticking close to the shore, we approached a massive lodge and spied an astonished beaver. An eagle took off from a low branch a few feet away. A great blue heron snapped up a fish. Humans were not expected in such weather! The rain gave us a glimpse into a world not as visible on a sunny, boat-busy day. The torrent turned to drizzle. A narrow inlet led to the open ocean. The tide was coming in, so the water was rushing toward us.

"Waves would be fun," said Bill. Yes. But not easy. Our frantic paddling reminded me of cartoon figures in a blur of motion yet not moving forward. Slowly and steadily, we made our way through the rushing water, and then whoosh—we were bobbing in the sea, feeling the power of ocean swells! Hints of blue began to push through the gray sky. We eventually returned to shore exhilarated and in love—with life, each other, and kayaking. Our lives were forever changed by the choice to keep going with our plan in spite of the rainy weather.

Every decision, every turn leads us to yet another choice of turns. Every day presents us with crossroads and roundabouts. If you could download a map of your life that recorded every action, every moment of your life, there would be obvious, big decisions involving such things as money, moving, or marriage, but the seemingly inconsequential acts—an understanding look, an avoided conversation—would also show their cumulative impact on the terrain traversed. Each moment, each "now" involves an action or inaction that creates a cause leading to an effect.

Some choices are conscious and well thought out, with definite plans as to where the decision will lead. Other choices are impulsive, with only a vague notion of how the subsequent path may meander. Some choices are unconscious, and we don't even realize we have made them. Sometimes life or others make choices for us and activate the belief that we are powerless and have no say in any choice. Judgments involving our identity distort our perceptions and influence how we choose to act and how we tell the story of those actions.

When we saw the brochure for kayaking, I could have gone with my belief that I was not athletic and my joints too creaky and said, "No. I'm not fit enough to go kayaking."

Bill could have chosen to go kayaking without me, or to stay with me but regret the choice. If he had gone alone, I could have been resentful, activated by old Sticky Beliefs that my feelings didn't matter and I would always be abandoned. When he returned, I could have been cranky and chosen to pick a fight, accused him of being self-centered and insensitive. He might have chosen to counter with his own defensive accusation that I was impossible to please, leading to my own sense of hopelessness and despair about the relationship and another Sticky Belief—that the conflict was all my fault for not being either gracious or more athletic. Or, I could have chosen to be comfortable with our divergent decisions and enjoyed the day walking along the shore collecting rocks and taking pictures. We didn't bring a camera kayaking, and we could have stayed frustrated that we did not get a picture of the beaver, eagle, or heron. Instead, we decided to be in the moment and focus on our Inner Camera experience.

We could have Joined in Judgment and complained about the kayak owner's general indifference or reacted to our difficulty coordinating strokes with annoyance or disdain. We chose to laugh instead.

Each of those choices would have led both of us down different trajectories. Both the way we experience a moment and the way we make sense of that moment influence our choices, which then, in turn, create the next story.

We all have images of the way things should be in Should-Be Land. The brochure in our mind has pictures of sunny days and smiling people. Life in As-Is Land can look very different. Even if we get the perfect brochure shot, the pictures not taken or shown might hint at other stories, and any words, images, or sounds can only suggest, not truly convey, our feelings. There is no record of that day. We only have the experience and the experiences that evolved from that fateful "Yes!"

The Yes! Let's go in spite of the rain, in spite of being still weak from treatments, in spite of not knowing how to do it perfectly, became a Yes! to life, a Yes! to going toward what is difficult and unknown.

As our sign says, "You can't choose the weather, but you can choose your response." That choice makes all the difference.

LIFE CAN BE JOYFUL. LIFE can be scary. There are many dangers and much pain. Horrible things happen all the time. The Something Important pushing the button of activation may be the real possibility of death. But we also have choice when we are coping with the really big challenges.

Many decades ago, long before I ever even thought of becoming a therapist, I discovered a place inside my awareness where immense joy and pain were joined, residing at the same time in my heart and in my experience, to the point of being almost undifferentiated, all part of this energy called love. It was my first inkling of what I now conceive of as my Full Spectrum of thoughts and feelings.

When my second daughter was not yet two, I was told that my elder, almost four-year-old daughter had been born malrotated, internally deformed; she would never digest properly, would suffer, and would probably die before she was ten. Finally, there was a diagnosis. This was why, as an infant, my daughter projectile vomited across the room and didn't gain weight. This was why she threw up if she drank juice too fast. This was why for a week in another hospital she had tubes draining her stomach through her nose to stop the relentless vomiting. The doctors had said it was a very bad virus. Now we knew what was really going on.

There were years with hospitalizations and operations, semipermanent catheters for IV solutions, drawing blood and feeding her thick, white nutrients from a bag. There were radioactive X-rays, drugs, and many, many doctors. When she was in the hospital, my nights were spent on a cot beside her bed in a crowded double room. Before cell phones, there were calls to be made from phone booths. Before Google, there were healing alternatives to research and office appointments all around the city. At home, there was her catheter to clean every day in a strict and complicated procedure with instructions stating in bold letters, CARELESS ACTIONS CAUSE INFECTION AND DEATH!

Fear cannot protect us from death. I had to ignore the Sticky Belief that my carelessness, lack of responsibility, and obliviousness would kill my daughter. I had to ignore the hurt I was inflicting on her as I pulled off bandages and put stinging solutions on the wound surrounding the catheter. She would get teary, but she rarely complained. She had been with the much sicker kids, the ones who died.

During that period, I had a steady meditation practice, prayed for others, and went to services in a beautiful garden that surrounded a lake with swans. I was trying to be good to keep away the bad. As I struggled through the avalanche of challenges, I felt betrayed by the Higher Power I imagined marking my life report card. None of what was happening was fair.

I deserved better. Life was definitely not being what I thought it should be. Yet courage meant going toward pain, staying awake in spite of fear, in spite of the impact on identity, and in spite of the desire to be safe. I asked a spiritual mentor for advice on how to navigate this scary time.

"Think of one thing that, during the day in the hospital, brought you some joy."

I answered with a touch of sarcasm, "Well the cafeteria has real lemonade made from fresh lemons."

She answered, "Yes. That's it. Your way in. Focus on the lemonade. Really taste it. Appreciate it. Acknowledge its cooling nourishment. Whenever you are in challenging moments, there is always something like lemonade where you can choose to put your focus, touch joy. Always look for those opportunities."

I did. She was right. The day was sunny and not too hot. My daughter and I desperately longed to be outside, away from medical smells and sounds. There was a small but beautiful garden on the hospital grounds. The nurses got us a wheelchair with an attached IV stand for all the necessary fluids. We promised to return in an hour. We were free! Early California spring gave us fragrant jasmine, mock orange, exotic silk trees, and lavender petals falling from tall jacarandas. My daughter and I breathed in sweet life while holding the possibility of death.

We both remember that moment, the center of the storm where all was calm and still. Golden light and immense love poured into our cracked-open hearts. I momentarily let go of fear. We were in the garden, feeling love—for each other, the beauty of the world, the wonder of life. Whatever happened, including her death and my death, this immutable something, the spirit manifesting this magical moment would remain.

I came to know this feeling place of love and spirit, pain and joy, fear and hope. I envisioned it as a light-filled, rainbow-hued, spinning wheel planted deep in my heart and connected to a universal source of energy. My Full Spectrum. Where contradictory thoughts and feelings reside together, connected by a common denominator. All are aspects of being alive. Choosing to become more aware of and in touch with our Full Spectrum is how we become fully alive, while we are alive. Where in our Full Spectrum is the lemonade, the sun, the flowers?

In that moment in the garden, my daughter was alive, and we would be fully alive in whatever time we had together. We said goodbye to the garden and wheeled back to her hospital room with the stuffed animals, balloons, walls covered in pictures, and stack of Little House on the Prairie books.

THROUGH THE YEARS OF CRISIS, I became more aware of my Full Spectrum of thoughts and feelings. Greater awareness of my multifaceted inner workings gave me more choice in how I perceived and responded to life's challenges. Amid the emotional swirl of sickness, pain, and loss, I found the still and powerful place inside myself where fear dissolves and pain and joy exist together. In that place of grace, I feel held by spirit, connected to an energy of aware aliveness. Fearful stories of past hurts and possible future hurts become like books on a shelf. There is only now. Breathe in, breathe out; I am in the air, and the air is within me.

But, like in meditation, the specifics of each now moment drift into view. Today my right hip is aching. I think about the difficult emails I need to write. I'm annoyed that the squirrel is swinging from the bird feeder. Ukulele the poodle puppy is under the table, his head resting on my foot. I have a wave of sadness remembering a friend who recently died. I'm looking forward to the fruit salad for lunch. And, of course, those stories tied to painful memories and real fears appear, like email alerts on your phone you can choose not to read.

Carl Jung wrote, "Your vision will become clear only when you look into your heart. Who looks outside, dreams. Who looks inside, awakens." Inside? Our heart? Not really. That would be a bloody mess. We create metaphors to communicate the ineffable. What do I mean by "a place inside myself where pain and joy exist together?"

One image I have is of an island of plastic floating on the ocean, representing all the stuff that holds our attention until some other stuff becomes our focus. This flotsam and jetsam of life is what we see on the surface that creates the story of our experience. If we dive down below the realm of objects and activities, we are in the realm of emotions such as sadness, satisfaction, confusion, creativity, longing, desire, anger, and grief. Sometimes we have a wave of emotion, and we aren't really sure what event, what surface stuff, gave rise to the surge. When we dive deeper still, we reach the realm where the emotions become undifferentiated. We are aware of feelings, powerful feelings, like tears in meditation, both joy and sorrow, our birth containing our death, a beginning that is part of an end. All one.

I have experienced that place many times, but sometimes in the chaos of life I forget how to get there, even though I know it exists. In another metaphor, that place of grace is a secret, light-filled garden hidden behind a tiny door in a narrow, nameless alley, in a bustling city, always there, just sometimes hard to find. Each time I find my way, I remember more about the route. And when all seems dark and hopeless and I am surrounded by fears, I remember that place. I know it exists. I can choose to inhabit the memory if I cannot access the space.

When we love, we invite the pain of loss. While we live, we head toward death. One cannot exist without the other. If we choose to bring home a puppy and love that puppy, we choose to feel the pain when the puppy, someday old, will die. We hope we die before our children, but one of us will die first and the other will feel pain. But pain also holds joy, for pain holds the recognition that our aliveness is a tiny, finite spark tethered to a vast and awesome universe. Expanding awareness, having the courage to open our heart to love and fully experience the joys and pains of our multifaceted aliveness, connects us to the energy of stars and beyond. We feel, in some ineffable way, home, whole.

EACH PERSON'S SUFFERING IS BOTH unique and shared, as is our fear of suffering. Rituals, both religious and secular, remind us of our common humanity. We are not alone in our pain or our love. A lit candle accompanied by prayer is one of many candles on the altar. A quilt representing a loved one who died of AIDS is one of thousands. A name on the Vietnam

Veterans Memorial is surrounded by the other names of those who died. The Buddhist prayer of loving-kindness asks, "May all those who are suffering, as I am suffering, find peace and happiness and release from their suffering."

My daughter lived, and as an adult she uses her profound experiences facing pain and death to inform her work as an artist, healer, spiritual guide, and mother. Time has passed.

I have come to take responsibility for my choices. I'm still learning how to turn judgment about those choices into compassion and description. I draw up a mental contract with myself where I remember who I was and what I knew (and didn't know) and what I was experiencing when I made that decision, that choice. I practice compassion for that past Gretta, rather than judge her for those choices. I may feel remorse for some of those choices, sad and disappointed and sometimes ashamed, but I own them. They were what I did then, when I was who I was then, doing the best I could with what I knew. I did not know, when I made my choices, what I know now. And I don't know now what I will know in the future.

So, my contract states that my future self will not judge my present self for choices made now, and my present self will forgive the choices made by my past self for choices made then. This reprieve from judgment allows more aliveness and joy in the present. The looming fear of future judgment dissipates. The Nurturing Parent within me will love me, no matter how my choices unfold.

A friend asked me what gives me the ability to go toward fear. I am not really sure. I think that in ways I have always been afraid, never really felt safe. If I had waited until things felt certain and secure before I proceeded with my life, then I would have waited forever. There has always been enough to sustain me if I look up to the stars and into my heart. In the center of an inner garden, I am held in golden light. The stories I call my life will change, transmute, and swirl around. In the center of my Full Spectrum, joy and pain are connected, part of the whole. All is one. Courage guides my choice to be fully alive, while I am alive.

In another metaphor, that place of grace is a secret, light-filled garden hidden behind a tiny door in a narrow, nameless alley, in a bustling city, always there, just hard sometimes to find. Each time I find my way, I remember more about the route. And when all seems dark and hopeless and I am surrounded by fears, I remember that place. I know it exists. I can choose to inhabit the memory if I cannot access the space.

CHAPTER 20

Your Way There

What is your current *there*? We are always headed somewhere, always wanting to reach one more goal. Our *there* can be specific and immediate, or more long term and general. For me, one stormy day, my *there* was the shore I hoped to reach without capsizing my kayak. Or, when I was younger, my *there* was the two-wheel bike I desperately wanted, and the knowledge of how to ride it so I could join my best friend who already had a bike. Our age and circumstances determine which *there* is in focus.

An early and lifelong *there* is a special someone we hope to find. As children, we long for the BFF who will sit with us at lunch and pass us notes in class. We grow older and long for that special someone, a partner to be with us on the way to each new *there*. And then life happens and, with that someone, our *there* may become the wish to change the pattern of bickering and judgment to regain the closeness we somehow lost. Our *there* might be to adjust our appearance or to find acceptance for the way we look. Culture and circumstance influence each *there* we dare to imagine. We have thoughts tied to identity and accomplishment: "If only I were there! If only I could achieve this goal!" Usually the "I want to be there" thoughts are tied to feeling safe, feeling loved, believing we have value. We may want to find the reason and courage to keep on living or to find a way to peacefully die.

The paths we take to get to each emerging *there*—and our experience on those paths—create our life. Our resumes and then our obituaries list the facts of what we did from birth to death—records of each achieved *there* that is deemed particularly worthy of note. Our experience of our life is something else. That is our *way*.

I imagine our *way* as a trajectory of energy that can manifest in many forms. Like a multiplex theater moving through time and space with different movies unfolding simultaneously and continuously, creating experience lanes on our own personal, nobody-else-knows highway. As we hurtle through life, we change experience lanes, adjust our interpretation and behavior, switch the movie, and make choices about the way we want to travel to each new *there*.

These experience lanes correspond to various slices of our Full

TO CHANGE YOUR EXPERIENCE
CHANGE YOUR LANE

Spectrum of thoughts and feelings. Sometimes, inspired and optimistic, we sail along on lanes paved with confidence and enthusiasm. Our favorite music is the soundtrack as we pass by images of beautiful landscapes. Other times we may slide back onto the familiar, bumpy, potholed lanes of Sticky Beliefs, full of doubts, judgments, resentments, old stories, ingrained defenses, and trauma residue. The soundtrack is annoying, the weather is awful, and our windshield wipers don't work. Or, circumstances may be like big, speeding semis that threaten to push us off the road, and we clutch the wheel as we drive on experience lanes full of fear and uncertainty.

With attention to our Full Spectrum, we gain awareness of the different available ways we can interpret and respond to a situation. We can then ease ourselves into a nearby experience lane that validates the fears, adds compassion for our past wounds and challenges, engages our courage, and reminds us that patience is necessary for every expedition into new territory. Maybe we invite our Nurturing Parent to sit in the passenger seat and serve as navigator. Our life is the journey, not the destination. Awareness of our Full Spectrum enables us to have more choice in how we travel, as well as the impact we have on people and things we meet on our voyage.

In the Four Stages of Change, Stages Two and Three are where we are most of the time. In Stage Two we realize we are in or have drifted back into the lane of experience that is full of habitual perspectives and behaviors. We are in the realm of Consciously Incompetent. Resisting the urge to judge ourselves or be discouraged, we can instead gently turn the wheel to ease ourselves into a lane of Conscious Competence, encouraging our vulnerable self to choose more useful interpretations and behaviors. Courage (having heart) joined with compassion (the ability to be with suffering, love, and intense aliveness) serve as our key. The Nurturing Parent we develop within us cheers us on while lovingly pointing out where we need to direct our awareness. Greater awareness enables us to confidently sit in the driver's seat and take responsibility for the lanes we choose to drive in.

Here we are, creatures on a planet we call Earth, doing this thing known as life. I get dizzy when I go to planetariums and get a glimpse of the awesome and incomprehensible reality of our solar system orbiting around our dear, heat-, light-, and energy-spewing sun, nestled in our spectacular Milky Way galaxy, part of a vast, expanding universe composed of unfathomably small and powerful atoms with their neutrons and protons and spinning electrons (not to mention quarks, leptons, gluons, and Higgs bosons)!

We humans are complicated critters made of flesh and bones, guided by information emanating from gray matter and sent along neural pathways—all composed of those same mighty atoms and speeding electrons that form suns and planets—making our hearts pump and our lungs breathe and all our senses do their "I'm alive!" dance. Waves of energy connect us. Our ancestors recognized the power generated by the sun, experienced the energy of lava and lightning, harnessed waves and wind, and eventually learned to direct the energy of fire, electricity, radio waves, microwaves, X-rays, and nuclear power.

I have only vague notions about how my phone, computer, and television deliver their messages, but I'm glad they do. We get frustrated when we are unintentionally disconnected from that power, that energy. There is tangible evidence of the disruption of that energy connection when our video chat freezes during an important conversation, we are out of range for cell phone service, or our battery dies. But what about the disruptions of our energy connections that are not so obvious, even though they are more important to our experiential journey?

When we are choosing an experience lane, the one we decide will be best suited to take us on our *way* to any *there*, I find it useful to consider the energy connections. There might not be a visual cue of energy bars displaying the strength of our connection to a certain person, and we may lack an old-fashioned clap-o-meter measuring our enthusiasm for the content of what is being said, but we can feel it in our bones. We know when we are doing a task that creates excitement, stimulation, and pleasure versus one that is mind-numbingly boring and deeply unsatisfying. We know the difference between losing a favorite, beloved, and sentimental object and having the same thing happen to something we regard as having no emotional value.

When we visit a place that holds powerful memories, full of connections to people or experiences we have had in the past, we feel the energy. Since ancient times, humans have traveled long distances to stand in spots that have historical significance, feeling the connection to that past energy exchange. We say that an idea resonates with us or that we feel connected to a person, place, or object.

Our bodies hold an electrical charge when we are alive that is gone when we are dead. To be fully alive, we need to be fully charged and connected to people, actions, places, and things where our energy can flow. Scanners take pictures of our brain as it lights up when our bodies are brought into physical contact with another human. A blood pressure monitor can show the change that happens when we lovingly stroke our dog or cat or focus our minds with meditation.

We all have ideas about the meaning of life and how to live it. These ideas can be vague or specific, fluid or rigid, gradually formed or early and emphatically taught. The concepts I use daily and have presented in this book are all ultimately about different paths of energy connection. How do we connect with our inner experience? What are the ways in which we connect to the tasks and events that form the history of our life? With whom do we feel those strong emotional connections we call love? What is it about those connections that leaves us feeling fully alive—or not so much?

One slice of my Full Spectrum holds this concept: In the beginning we are enwombed in the wholeness of our mother/universe. Then we are born. Subjective consciousness slowly emerges, as separation from the primordial union is comprehended. Existence is no longer child-within-mother, tethered to the universe in a perfect symbiotic dyad. The cord is cut, and the child experiences the mother and the rest of the universe as other. But the longing for the return to wholeness remains. We seek certain people, things, and experiences in order to feel connected to that life force, not realizing that we are intrinsically connected to everything and everyone all the time. The portal is within us.

Humans use sacred and beloved objects—relics—to remind us of the wholeness we feel when connected to that universal energy we describe in many ways such as "spirit" or "divine love." We tell stories of other humans—how they both embodied and were a conduit to others of that awesome force. Religious objects are obviously meant to produce links to those departed humans identified as filled with that spirit, love, and wisdom. But a T-shirt with Bugs Bunny as a conductor, a rock shaped like a potato, a red bead, a dead hermit crab, or a cup of fresh-squeezed lemonade from a hospital cafeteria can also hold such power. They are no longer just objects but symbols, emanating energy and meaning—a felt aspect of connection that is sensed, yet impossible to completely define.

In ancient Greek, one of the meanings of the word *symbolon* is "token." People parting would cut an object—such as a coin—in two, and each person would retain half and perhaps pass it on through generations. Like a signet ring or a personal seal on a letter, the return and matching of the severed parts established the connection of the bearers of each half to one another. Even though the bearers of the matching *symbolon* may never have met, they are not aliens; they share a connection.

A Symbolon

A circle symbolizes wholeness. The word *mandala* comes from Sanskrit, with meanings of "magic circle" and "from the essence." This connection to wholeness is why I envision our Full Spectrum of thoughts and emotions as a circle with our wise, observing self in the center.

Tibetan monks create elaborate mandalas with colored sand. Native Americans have a medicine wheel. Labyrinths, used as a form of meditation, are circular mazes that spiral in toward the center, then spiral back to the circumference. The dark and light opposites of Yin and Yang are enclosed in a circle. Wedding rings are circles. When humans sit in circles, hold hands, or join arms, they become connected as a whole, no one first or last. Cycles are circles. Birthdays, holidays, and anniversaries mark the return of a day that is the same, but not the same, and yet somehow still conveys some sense of wholeness. The parent births a child who becomes a parent as we ride the circle of life.

Electricity runs in a circle when it forms a circuit. We are aware of our aliveness when we feel an energetic connection to someone, some action, some place, or some thing. There is a sense of simultaneously giving and getting, a circularity of flowing aliveness. Energetic circularity manifests in many forms. When we mindfully connect to our tasks and others, we create a powerful circular energetic connection. We feel whole.

Will we make our way through life on experience lanes offering aliveness, full of connections to people and actions where we feel that nourishing wholeness? Or are we simply moving forward, stuck in lanes that are familiar but full of broken, feeble, or painful connections, leaving us depleted, hungry, and yearning for something else? We have a choice in what lanes we travel. What *way* will we go from here to *there?* The destinations, the focus of our attention, will continually change. Awareness of our Full Spectrum provides a map to help us determine our way there. With greater awareness, we can make choices about our energy connections. We will need to have courage for our journey, as well as compassion and curiosity. We humans are capable of making radical changes in how we live our lives. I know. I have made those changes and watched as others have changed as well. You can do it too.

My hope is that the concepts I have learned from others, expanded and honed through my connection to others, will connect with you and be of use as you identify how you want to be fully alive, while you are alive—and find *Your Way There*.

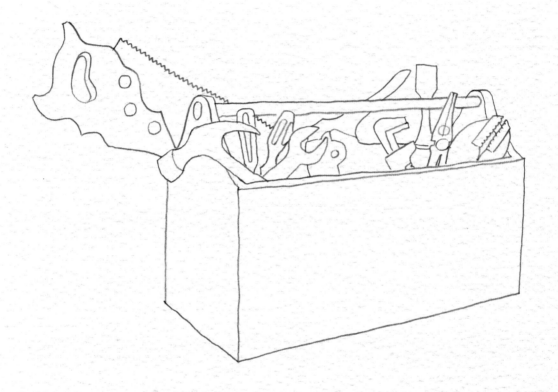

CHAPTER 21

The Toolbox

This section is a review of the concepts presented in each chapter. Some may want to read the Toolbox after each chapter, and some may want to read the whole book and then review with the Toolbox. The questions are to help integrate the ideas into your experience and make them your own. They are designed to stimulate thoughts and feelings and conversation. The Toolbox can be used by an individual as part of a meditation practice, or as a way to stimulate dialogue in a relationship. Groups could also use the Toolbox as a guide for discussions. Perhaps the questions will lead you to ideas that you will pass on to others. My hope is that these tools will be of benefit for you, on your way.

....

CHAPTER 1

A Double Rainbow

"Breathe!" The moment when I focused on my breath was the moment things began to turn around. I was able to get out of the stories in my head and focus on the present moment. This focusing on my breath is related to my practice of meditation.

1. Here are simple instructions for meditation:
    a. Set a timer for how long you intend to meditate.
    b. Sit comfortably with your back, neck, and head straight and your hands resting on your thighs. Eyes are open, with a soft, slightly downward glance.
    c. Focus on your breath as it leaves your body.
    d. What are the bodily sensations and sounds that you notice?
    e. There is a pause as your body takes in more air.
    f. Then comes another release of the observed out-breath.
    g. Repeat.

2. Thoughts will come up. In fact, you may find you have been lost in thought for just a moment or for a while.
    a. Say to yourself "thinking" and return to focusing on the out breath. There is no wrong. Simply spend the allotted time sit-

ting and focusing on your breath, noticing passing thoughts and feelings, returning to your breath.

b. Each time you return to your breath, you are in the present moment. In that moment you are awakened.

c. Practicing kindness and patience with ourselves is as important as successfully focusing on our breath.

d. Is our inner voice shaming, harsh, and critical, or is it gentle, soothing, and encouraging, with a hearty sense of humor?

e. Meditation develops patience and self-compassion and gives us needed practice in letting go of judgment.

f. There are many different approaches to meditation. Find one that works for you.

....

CHAPTER 2

A Full Spectrum Perspective

The concept of a Full Spectrum perspective is key to the other concepts presented in this book. Creating a mental model that encourages us to acknowledge contradictory, hidden, and perhaps surprising thoughts and feelings gives us more choice in how we experience a situation and how we choose to react and proceed.

1. Make a map of your Full Spectrum of the present moment.
    a. Draw a circle almost as large as a piece of paper.
    b. On the side, make a list of all the thoughts you are aware of in this moment. They may be something like: "This feels silly," "I want to do it right," "I'm a lousy drawer," "I wish this was being done for me in a session," and "I like having clear directions and specific things to do."
    c. Then add a list of emotions, one-word descriptions that connect to those thoughts. These could be words like uncomfortable, hopeful, discouraged, longing, and confident.
    d. There may be associations like school, math class, games, puzzles, and online quizzes or a specific memory.
    e. Looking at what you have written, from a dot in the center of the circle, draw two lines creating a pie piece for the thought, emotion, or association that stands out as what you are most aware of at the moment.
    f. Fill in the circle with other pie slices of varying sizes, roughly comparable to the proportion of your awareness that they currently occupy.

     g.   You may slide in a few slivers for some additions that didn't make it onto the original list. I often squeeze the words into the pie slices, but there can also be arrows connecting the pie slice to the descriptor.

2.   Repeat this exercise using a recent activated interaction. You may find yourself adjusting the proportions as you run through the incident in your memory.

     a.   Are you focusing on how you remember that first moment of activation?

     b.   Or is it how you view the incident now that some time has passed?

     c.   What would be different if the other person in the interaction were to do a Full Spectrum diagram of what (they believe) you were thinking and feeling at the moment of activation?

     d.   How do you envision they would draw their own Full Spectrum perspective of the moment of activation?

     e.   I suspect you have several quite different diagrams of the situation!

....

CHAPTER 3

Nurturing Parent or Judging Parent?

Our parents, and those who were in positions of authority in our childhood, serve as role models and can become the basis for that ever-present voice in our head. There are multiple factors and many ways to conceive of what forms our inner dialogue and sense of self. This is one model.

1.   Here are the four basic types of parents in this model.

     a.   A praising Judging Parent usually declares the object of focus as "the best, the smartest, the most beautiful, talented, amazing, handsome, and incredibly wonderful." This type of Judgmental Parent doles out compliments as a way of establishing and ensuring connection, showing love and winning acceptance. They use praise as a way to guide behavior and reward success. They often fear that any criticism will be wounding and avoid confrontation.

     b.   A shaming Judging Parent usually has something critical to say about everything and everyone. Nothing and no one are up to their high standards. They initiate and strengthen connections by getting others to join with them in judgment. There is often an attitude of "us versus them," and a high value is put on loyalty. This Judging Parent uses criticism to control behavior and reinforce their position of power and authority. They believe the threat of shame is what produces the desired achievement. "Spare the rod and spoil the child" is often the motto. They often see themselves as either victims or victors.

c. A Nurturing Parent who tends to utilize encouragement acts like a benevolent coach by pointing out strengths and accomplishments and reinforcing an awareness of self-satisfaction. They acknowledge that life can be difficult and emphasize that the experience of patience, persistence, willpower, and hard work is its own reward. Opportunities for growth are valued and provided, with the parents often actively involved. The child's process is recognized and validated as much as the product. They cheer for the game played, not just the winning score.

d. Another style of Nurturing Parent is one who values self-reliance and leans toward an attitude of compassionate, non-judgmental curiosity. They convey love by showing interest, asking questions, paying attention, and engaging in activities that create connection. They want to know more about the child's experience and appear more neutral in their reactions. These parents tend to let a child learn through trial and error and support the child's inclinations toward areas where they want to focus. These parents restrain from doing tasks for the child, encouraging a child's sense of agency and self-satisfaction, while recognizing and celebrating the child's accomplishments and offering help when needed.

2. Make a list of all those who were in the parental role or were an authority figure when you were young. This can include influential peers.
   a. As you remember each relationship, think about what kind of "parent" would best describe them.
   b. Sometimes a person, for a variety of reasons, can seem to have several distinct personalities and is experienced as being one kind of parent and then suddenly another kind of parent. Include this fluctuation in your description.

3. Spend a day or two tracking the thoughts and comments you make about yourself or others that you don't say out loud, or perhaps only under your breath.

    a. How does the voice in your head correspond to the voice of your parents or those in a position of authority?

    b. Is your inner voice harsh and critical or compassionate and encouraging?

    c. Were your parents satisfied with life? Why or why not?

    d. What are moments when you have felt satisfaction? Why?

    e. What would you change about the voice in your head?

    f. What would you change about how you get to a feeling of satisfaction?

4. Children raised by either kind of Judgmental Parent are more likely to be in the Captive Child position even as adults, always looking to those in positions of authority to determine the worth of what they do and who they are.

    a. Do you rely on others to determine your current worth?

    b. Are you always comparing yourself to others?

    c. Were the authority figures in your life judgmental of themselves?

    d. Did you rebel against authority figures? Are you still rebelling?

    e. Did you seek the approval of authority figures? Are you still seeking approval?

5. A Nurturing Parent works to encourage a child's sense of agency and an ability to determine for themselves what they think and feel about their actions, while also considering the impact of their actions on others.

    a. How were you taught to evaluate your actions?

    b. Can you feel satisfaction when only you know what you did?

    c. What are areas where you generally feel frustrated?

    d. What are areas where you generally feel satisfied?

    e. How often are your inner thoughts imagining others' experience?

6. Both Judgmental and Nurturing Parents are most likely communicating love and care in the way it was shown to them.

    a. How was love and care shown by your family when you were a child?

    b. How was love and care shown to the people who raised you?

    c. How was love and care shown by other people in your life?

    d. How do you generally show love and care?

CHAPTER 4
How Interpretation Directs Our Path

It is not the action that directs our reaction, it is our interpretation of that action. When we become more aware of our Full Spectrum of thoughts and feelings, we have access to other interpretations that might not be our first or most prominent interpretation.

1. When we are curious about other people's interpretations of an action, we further expand our own choices for interpretation and thus open ourselves to more possible reactions.
    a. Identify an experience from your past that still has emotional impact.
    b. List the different characters who either were involved in the event or know about the event, and note how they are related.
    c. Write how you imagine each person interpreted the event.
    d. How did each person's interpretation direct their subsequent behavior, interactions with others, and ultimately the story they believe about what happened and why?

2. Traumatic events change our interpretation of experience.
    a. Can you think of an event or long-term experience that changed your perspective?
    b. How would you describe the change?
    c. Did it change how you view yourself?
    d. Did it change how you view others?
    e. Did it change how you view life?

3. Identifying the beliefs that support our interpretations enables us to stretch into greater compassion and take actions that are more useful and aligned with our goals and values.
    a. What beliefs and values were an important aspect of your family culture?
    b. What beliefs dominated your peer culture as a child, teenager, and young adult?
    c. What beliefs were influenced by organized religion or political perspectives?
    d. What beliefs have changed over the years? Why?

4. When we change our interpretation of an experience, it often changes our feelings about ourselves and the other people involved.

a. Write about the event or relationship as if it were a story told in third person from your point of view when it happened. "Gretta was upset by his decision to . . ."

b. Write about the event from the point of view of another person involved.

c. Write a new version of the event told from your point of view but incorporating other interpretations and other possible reactions.

....

CHAPTER 5

Inner Camera or Outer Camera?

We all have what I dub Inner and Outer Cameras. They serve different functions. It is helpful to pay attention to which camera we are more likely to use and practice shifting our view from one to the other. It is good to know we have a choice!

1. What I call our Outer Camera is a view of our life that evaluates actions in judgmental terms: praise or criticism, good or bad, right or wrong, pride or shame.

    a. Our Outer Camera informs our sense of identity and how we believe we are seen by a specific character — a parent, older sibling, authority figure, or figure identified with a specific belief system.

    b. Our Outer Camera is what usually produces the images we present on social media. It can also be the part of us we experience as our editor, coach, evaluator, or rule enforcer.

    c. Who we conceive of as a Captive Child, raised by either a praising or shaming Judgmental Parent, is someone more likely to rely on their Outer Camera to inform what they believe about themselves, another person, a place, an object, or a situation.

    d. We can "Join in Judgment" with others who are seeing through their Outer Cameras as a way of feeling connected by way of our strongly held interpretations, verdicts, and beliefs.

    e. We are most likely viewing life through our Outer Camera when we are feeling self-righteous, defending our interpretation as the one that is right, and judging ourselves as the one who is good.

    f. When we feel that someone is viewing us through their Outer Camera, we feel judged and often become self-conscious and defensive.

2. What I call our Inner Camera is the perspective I identify with an open-hearted and compassionate perspective, focusing on our experience of a situation and interested in understanding the experience of others.

    a. With our Inner Camera we can "see" more of our Full Spectrum and discern whether we are feeling frustrated, challenged, confused, satisfied, sad, or joyful.

    b. With our Inner Camera we can work to validate our experience and be curious about the experience of others.

    c. Our Inner Camera creates and informs us about our emotional and energetic connection to ourselves and to others.

    d. Who we call a "Free Child" is someone raised by a Nurturing Parent who encouraged the child to find satisfaction in their effort and not just rely on the judgment of others. A Free Child adult is more able to see life through their Inner Camera.

    e. When we experience someone viewing us with compassion and empathy, through their Inner Camera, we are more likely to feel safe enough to expose our own vulnerabilities and not simply try to present an image we think will win approval.

3. Think of a recent situation, with other people present, where you felt at least slightly self-conscious and wondered how others were judging you.

    a. Describe yourself with your Outer Camera using judgmental terms. Are you harsh or complimentary or a mixture of both?

    b. Now shift the focus to your heart and your Inner Camera. Describe what you were feeling in that same situation. (Emotions are generally able to be described using just one word: satisfied, curious, scared, frustrated, happy, worried, excited, etc.)

4. Pretend you're an extraterrestrial with a camera. You have no concept of judgment or emotion and can only observe and describe. Remember an activated situation.

    a. What do you notice about yourself?

    b. What do you notice about the others involved?

    c. Practice communicating your extraterrestrial perspective as a starting place when you are engaged in a Speaker-Listener exploration of an activation.

5. Changing our focus from Outer Camera to Inner Camera can change our experience and how we interpret and remember a situation.

    a. When you realize you are looking through your Outer Camera lens, try switching to your Inner Camera.

    b. What is the difference in your feelings, interpretations, and reactions?

6. When you are in conversation, imagine the other person's point of view.
    a. Does it seem like they are looking through an Outer or Inner Camera?
    b. Can you feel the difference in a conversation that feels Inner Camera to Inner Camera versus one that feels more like it is Outer Camera to Outer Camera?
    c. Have you experienced a situation where you were speaking from the perspective of your Inner Camera and the person listening kept responding from what felt like their Outer Camera?

....

CHAPTER 6
Activation! Do We Fight, Flee, Freeze, or Fawn?

When we are activated there is Something Important that we want recognized and understood that may or may not be totally conscious. That Something Important sparks feelings ranging from mild to extreme discomfort. There is often a connection to a past experience where we felt hurt physically or emotionally. What feels like an attack on our identity can also be the match that sets off our activation. Our defenses serve to protect us from pain and threat. Unfortunately, the focus is often diverted from uncovering and exploring the Something Important to arguing about the nature of the defense.

1. Some defenses are difficult to categorize.
    a. Sarcasm, eye-rolling, ridicule, verbal flooding, or intellectual bullying fit the category of Fight even though that person may not have raised their voice or displayed an angry, aggressive demeanor. Who, among the people you know, tends to use that style of defense?
    b. A person who retreats into work, sports, or some absorbing activity, such as scrolling through social media, could be engaged in a kind of emotional Fleeing. Is that a defense that seems familiar?
    c. Procrastination is sometimes connected to a kind of emotional Freezing resulting from a fear that what needs to be done will be viewed as inadequate, wrong, and/or revealing incompetence or lack of intelligence or skill. Have there been times when you have felt trapped in that defense?
    d. Someone who is always focused on the needs of others, continually complimenting, or acting flirtatious, could be using

Fawning as a way to feel accepted and therefore safe. This is a tricky one. The behavior can look the same in two different people but not be experienced in the same way, or it can serve some other unconscious function.

2. Write examples of when you reacted with different kinds of defenses.
    a. Which defense is the most comfortable?
    b. Which is the one you use most often?
    c. Which brings the most shame?
    d. Which one do you believe is the most hidden or unconscious?

3. How would you describe the common style of defense used by those in your childhood?
    a. Different members of your family?
    b. Friends and peers?
    c. Authority figures?

4. What defenses do you believe are used by others in your life at present?
    a. Those you consider family?
    b. Friends?
    c. Colleagues?

5. Think of situations where you or someone close is more apt to get activated. Here are some common factors that can spark activation:
    a. Stress caused by pressure to perform tasks; a high expectation put on the fulfillment of the task; a time pressure on the task; a task that is unfamiliar or a known challenge.
    b. Physical conditions such as exhaustion; lack of sleep; transition of place or activity; hunger; or caffeine, nicotine, alcohol, or other mood-altering substances.
    c. An unrelated event creates an intense shift in mood just before the activating conversation or interaction. This could be an upsetting phone call, a message with disturbing news, or even an exciting win that creates a sense of elation that is not shared or understood by the other person.
    d. The activating event is either consciously or unconsciously related to a previous traumatic experience and an entrenched Sticky Belief.

6. When we recognize that we are in conditions that make activation more likely for ourselves or another person, we can raise awareness, engage our tools, communicate our concerns, and/or change the situation.

    a.   What conditions can you identify as ripe for disaster?

    b.   What could you change about the situation?

    c.   How could you adjust your reactions?

    d.   How could you or the other person effectively communicate that you are possibly entering a danger zone?

7.   If the train has left the station and activation has already begun, we can pull the emergency cord by calling for a Pause, or just get off at the next station and take the train back toward your original destination. You don't need to stay on the train just because you got on it! Use your words and communicate where you went and where you would prefer to go. No judgment, no shame. We all sometimes jump on that train!

....

CHAPTER 7
Bodyguards to the Rescue!

We find it useful to get to know more about our defenses by imagining them as personalities and giving them names. This enables us to have a sense of compassion for the part of us that is attempting to protect us from some perceived threat, is limited to one rigid interpretation of the moment, acts impulsively, and often makes the situation worse. When we think of them as misguided aspects of our personality, our wiser self can have a conversation with them and inform them that their services are no longer needed. Suggest they retire.

1.   Here are examples of some identified Bodyguards:

    a.   Poor Pitiful Pearl goes "belly up" when she feels threatened by someone seen as more powerful and in authority. She emphasizes her position as victim, apologizes and takes the blame, ingratiates with compliments, and acts subservient and needy in an attempt to avoid aggression or abandonment. This can be understood as a Fawning defense.

    b.   Ms. Suffragette is a fighter, full of self-righteousness. She believes she is fighting against oppression and aggression and for justice. She gets loud, rolls her eyes, is sarcastic, and will interrupt and monopolize a conversation using her overflowing collected files of evidence. She comes out when she feels silenced, misinterpreted, or treated with disregard or disdain, especially by males.

    c.   The Fire Chief is hypervigilant and probably doesn't think of himself as a fighter, but can be perceived by others as aggressive. Freud would have identified him as part of the antilibidinal ego—an aspect of the personality that feels the self is in danger when attention is absorbed by an activity that is pleasurable, creative, and all-engrossing. The Fire Chief comes into the movie theater, turns on all the lights, and inspects the smoke detectors.

d. The Doc is a similar character. She focuses on what could be wrong physically as a way of avoiding focusing on other challenges. Attention on possible physical ailments can create reasons why there can be no change to a situation that needs changing. In a way, she is frozen, with the attention on ailments acting as cover.

e. Buddha Boy believes he is being "the calm one" when others are angry or upset. He gets quiet or speaks in controlled tones that appear highly rational and persuasive, usually preaching that his interpretation of the situation is the Truth.

f. Fantasy Fran is always fleeing from whatever might be uncomfortable. She hides from distressing feelings and interactions by focusing on imagined realities. These can be her own fantasies or an immersion into fantasies created by others. She retreats into shows, films, books, podcasts, and social media.

g. Dan the Doer uses work in the way Fantasy Fran uses fantasy. He retreats into a role that is familiar and comfortable, keeping his focus on doing what he knows how to do and avoiding exchanges that feel emotional and vulnerable.

2. Describe your habitual defenses:
   a. What does it look like when you Fight?
   b. What does it look like when you Flee?
   c. What does it look like when you Freeze?
   d. What does it look like when you Fawn?
   e. Which do you do often and which hardly ever?

3. Can you picture the defensive parts of your personality as Bodyguards?
   a. What do they look like?
   b. How do they behave?
   c. What are their names?

4. When you notice one of your Bodyguards taking over a situation, can your wiser self have a conversation with the part that believes you are threatened?
   a. Ask what called them into action.

    b.   What do they believe about the situation? What is the threat? What is the solution?

5.   Does someone in your family—childhood or present—have a similar Bodyguard?

    a.   What would you name the Bodyguards you encounter in other people?

    b.   Can you dialogue with them?

Be sure to thank the Bodyguards, even if their behavior is destructive. They believe they are needed and serve a purpose. Be grateful for their desire to protect, and tell them, "I've got this." Maybe buy them a bus ticket to Florida.

....

CHAPTER 8

Sticky Beliefs

Sticky Beliefs can be about specific tasks ("I can't do insurance forms, drive a car, speak in public") or broader in scope ("people always reject and abandon me, I'm too intense, I'm unlovable, I'm a loser"). They can be about us or others or life in general. They feel true. They are a combination of thoughts and feelings that are always hovering. The Judgmental Parent within us loves to find evidence to support our Sticky Beliefs.

1.   Sticky Beliefs can become embedded through repeated comments by people in your life who are in some kind of position of authority: "You're irresponsible, lazy, sloppy, stupid, fat, smarter than everyone else, clumsy, pretty, talented, a show-off, damaged, bad, too much, ugly, needy, special, disrespectful, sinful, weak, strong, a klutz," etc.

    a.   What people in your life have influenced your Sticky Beliefs?

    b.   Were you or they influenced by a certain doctrine or norms of the family culture?

    c.   What influences in your life have been at odds with previously accepted beliefs?

2.   Sticky Beliefs are often formed and solidified due to a traumatic event or relationship: "I'm powerless, never safe, all alone, permanently damaged, broken, sick, incompetent, unlucky, a failure." They are the negative cognitions that, after a traumatic event, feel irrevocably true.

    a.   Can you identify Sticky Beliefs that were the result of a specific traumatic event?

    b. Can you identify Sticky Beliefs that were the result of traumatic relationships—perhaps involving psychological, physical, or emotional abuse—or a traumatic situation that continued over a period of time?

3. Sticky Beliefs impact your interpretations and actions and are often what spark activation and keep it going.
    a. Can you think of a Sticky Belief that impacts a specific, internal reaction?
    b. What familiar Sticky Beliefs are present in activated situations with others?
    c. How do you imagine a situation would unfold differently if you or the other person did not have your Sticky Beliefs?
    d. What Sticky Beliefs have you changed through greater awareness and compassion?

....

CHAPTER 9
How Do We Communicate When We Are in Different Movies?

The Speaker-Listener approach to communication may feel artificial and clunky at first, but the strict rules actually make a space for meaningful dialogue by slowing down the exchange, prohibiting destructive elements like name-calling, and ensuring that each person is deeply heard. Eventually, this pattern will become the template for how you normally communicate.

Begin by choosing one person to be the Speaker. The other person will have an opportunity to be the Speaker in a few minutes, so it doesn't matter who goes first. It helps at first for the Speaker to hold something (like a rock or special object) to signify that they "have the floor," in order to reinforce the Speaker-Listener structure of the dialogue.

The Speaker begins by using "I" statements (e.g., "I feel lonely when you're out in the evening" rather than "You always leave me alone at night"). The Speaker speaks in "bite-size chunks"—no more than a few simple sentences—so the Listener can remember what was said and paraphrase it back to the Speaker. The Listener should not make comments that defend, clarify, or correct. The Listener's goal is to repeat what the Speaker just said in such a way that the Speaker responds, "Yes, that's exactly what I meant."

This continues until the Speaker has explained one concern. Then the chosen object is handed over, and the roles switch. With this exercise, you are both on the same team working toward achieving the goal of getting the Speaker's reality understood.

RULES FOR THE SPEAKER:

1. Speak for yourself. Use "I" statements and talk about your feelings.
2. Replace "You make me feel" with "When you do/say _____, I feel _____."
3. To help the Listener, keep your statements brief—i.e., speak in bite-size chunks. Cover only one point at a time.
4. Stop and let the Listener paraphrase. Allow the Listener to say in their own words what they think they've heard.
5. If the paraphrase was not quite accurate, politely restate what was not heard the way it was intended to be heard. Your goal is to help the Listener understand your point of view.

RULES FOR THE LISTENER:

1. Focus on the Speaker's message. Don't rebut. In the Listener's role, you may not offer your opinion or thoughts. Wait until you are the Speaker to make your response. As the Listener, your job is to speak only in the service of understanding your partner.
2. Make sure that you understand what was said. If you need to, ask the Speaker to repeat what was said. Feel free to ask, "Did I get that right?" Your goal is to have the Speaker be able to say, "Yes! That's exactly what I meant."
3. Paraphrase what you hear. Briefly repeat back what you heard the Speaker say using your own words (or the Speaker's words, if they seem more powerful).
4. Ask, "Did I get that right?"

....

CHAPTER 10

Using the Pause When We See Red

We all get activated. We always will. What we do when we are activated is where we have some choice. Greater awareness of our Full Spectrum and practices that strengthen our patience, compassion, and curiosity about the experience of others will help us make more useful choices that are better aligned with our values.

When activated, ask yourself: "What do I really want in this situation? What is the Something Important I want understood? How do I best achieve my goals? What responses are most aligned with my values?"

When we choose to be responsible for our actions and our reactions, we move out of shaming, blaming, and co-dependent relationships. We learn to tolerate, understand, and manage our uncomfortable thoughts and feelings rather than reflexively call for our Bodyguards. It is also important to do the same for others' reactions that may feel distressing, confusing, or unjustified. Considering the other person's reactions to our actions is not the same as being responsible for their reactions. We need to own our choices and respect that others are making their own choices, which may or may not be in sync with what we expect or want. It takes courage and awareness to mindfully navigate through uncomfortable feelings.

DIRECTIONS FOR THE PAUSE:

1. Acknowledge you are activated. Tell yourself, "I'm activated." If another person is involved then it is also useful to tell them, "I'm becoming activated and would like to have a Pause" rather than "You're making me mad!"
2. Listen to the story in your head. Are there Sticky Beliefs about yourself or the other person? Does it feel like you are the victim in the situation? Or, do you feel that you are being seen as the villain?
3. Describe the scene of the activation as if you were an extraterrestrial and had no ability to interpret meaning or identify emotions. What were the actual actions as you perceived and now remember them?
4. What moments of the incident were especially painful?
5. What previous events are associated with those pain points?
6. Relax and get grounded. What helps you be in touch with the center of your Full Spectrum where you have access to your other possible interpretations and reactions?
7. Are you ready to be curious about the other person's experience? Are you ready to share your interpretations and associations via Speaker-Listener?

....

CHAPTER 11

Yes—And

The ability to acknowledge that we have contradictory thoughts, contrasting emotions, and more than one way to interpret an experience is an important concept of Full Spectrum awareness. Greater awareness gives us greater control over our choices.

1. The practice of Yes—And strengthens our ability to look for the often many other feelings hidden beneath our first reaction. "Yes—I am angry. And—I am also confused and scared, disappointed and/or sad."

    a. Describe some instances where you felt angry but after consideration found other emotions that were driving the anger. Yes—I felt angry when . . . And—I also felt . . .

    b. Describe instances where you felt scared and also excited.

    c. Describe instances where you felt sadness and also relief.

    d. Describe instances where you felt frustrated and satisfied.

2. The practice of Yes—And reinforces our ability to take responsibility for our choices and also to invite exploration of why we had such a reaction to the situation.

    a. Describe a situation where you want to blame and understand.

        "Yes—I want to blame you for the situation and insist you made me feel a certain way. And—I also realize that my interpretation, based on associations to past events, led to such feelings."

    b. Describe a situation from both your Bodyguard's and wiser self's point of view.

        "Yes—my Bodyguard believed . . . And—my wiser self understood that . . ."

    c. Describe a situation where you made a choice that you later regretted, and you now want to blame your former self for not being able to anticipate the future.

        "Yes—I'm angry at myself for making what I now view as a mistake. And—I have compassion for my past self when I remember who I was then, what I knew, and what I believed to be true."

3. The practice of Yes—And can remind us that we all are in different movies.

    a. Describe in detail a situation where you and another person were in very different movies.

    b. Validate the other person's point of view before you tell your own.

> "Yes—I understand that the actions and the ensuing exchanges meant something quite different to you than to me. And—I want you to understand how I experienced the situation that led to my feelings and reactions."

    c. What other perspectives and reactions are most difficult for you to validate?

    d. Describe a situation where you and the other person argued about the truth of one interpretation over the other. "Yes—this is what I believe is true. And—I realize you believe the other interpretation is true."

    e. Describe a situation where you or the other person felt strongly that one action or reaction was right and the other wrong.

4.   The practice of Yes—And can remind us of our Should-Be beliefs.

    a. Describe a situation where you thought the experience would be different.

> "Yes—I imagined what our vacation would be like in Should-Be Land. And—I will focus on what I can appreciate on this vacation in As-Is Land."

    b. Describe a person's actions that were not what you thought they should be.

> "Yes—if you were the Should-Be person I expected and wanted you to be, you would have behaved this other way. And—I understand (and accept?) that you are your As-Is self and not the Should-Be self I imagined."

    c. Describe a situation where you didn't behave the way you believe would have been more useful or effective. Can you understand and have compassion for your As-Is self?

....

CHAPTER 12
Dictators of Reality

We all are ego-centric Dictators of Reality when we begin our lives as humans. Our ability to get others to focus on us and attend to our needs determines our ability to survive. Experience during the early days of this most essential mission directs our perceptions and actions, forming and solidifying what we think of as reality.

The ability to be attuned to another being's emotional experience can begin before speech. How the adults in a child's life respond to the child's actions impacts the expectations and behaviors of the emerging person. We can encourage and refine actions in ourselves and others that successfully communicate empathy and a consideration of others.

Nature and nurture and circumstance all contribute to how a person navigates through life. Our immediate family, as well as the generations before them, taught the belief systems that form our interpretations and guide our reactions to everything that happens. Forces outside the home can have a significant impact, but those early, internalized systems still hold power.

Genograms create a basic map of the nature, nurture, and circumstances impacting a family culture. It is useful to understand the forces that shaped you and any significant other.

1. Draw out your family tree. Go back at least three generations. Traditionally, circles represent females and squares represent males. Lines are drawn to show relationships. The names are put inside the circle or square.

2. Think about who you were when you were around seven years old and describe the people in your family as you knew them then. This gives information about what you internalized as a child. Descriptions are written in the vicinity of each name. Just like life, the resulting diagram can seem a bit chaotic.

3. After that first layer of impressions, you can add changes in behavior, facts known, and interpretations from your adult perspective.

4. Now add stories you have heard about the people in your family you never met or did not know well.

5. Here are some questions to ask about each person in the genogram:

How would you describe them—first impressions?
Physical attributes? Athletic? Affectionate?
Were they emotionally responsive or more removed?
Would you describe them as verbal? Monologue or dialogue?
Academically and/or professionally focused? Competitive?
Artistic and creative? Religious? Spiritual? What did they value?
Did they have inflexible beliefs about many topics and other people? What views?

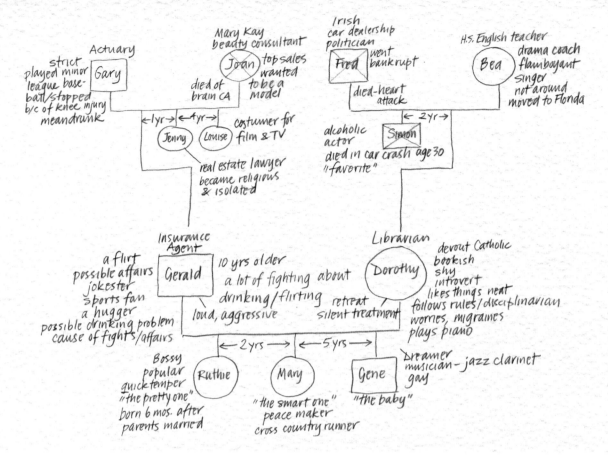

Were they compassionate and empathetic, curious about many topics and other people?

Did they prefer to be with others or alone?

Were they passive and easygoing, or did they prefer to be in charge?

Were they teasing, ridiculing, or shaming? Violent? Did others feel bullied by them?

Evidence of addictions? Mental illness? Cognitive difficulties?

How would you describe their Bodyguards?

Were they seductive? Flirtatious? In what way?

Did they experience traumatic events?

What was their role in their family of origin? Relationship to siblings? Birth order?

Did they view themselves as a success or failure?

Were people drawn to them, uncomfortable, or fearful?

Did they have many close friends? Long term? What were the connections?

Did they see themselves as unlucky or a victim? Confident? Happy?

Were they casual, chaotic, or controlling in how they maintained their environment?

Was their reality the only reality that mattered?

Were they curious and open to understanding another person's reality?

Was there a story or something they said or did that represents how you think of them?

6. What beliefs, values, defenses, habits of interpretation, and patterns of behavior have you internalized?

7. Which ones do you want to keep, and which ones do you want to change?

....

CHAPTER 13

Trauma Land

When we experience a dramatic event that is traumatic or we are in a relationship that is chronically physically, emotionally, and/or psychologically abusive, we internalize Sticky Beliefs that impact our sense of self and how we interpret and react to future situations.

1. It is helpful to be able to identify when we are in Trauma Land—the feeling that we are back experiencing the original trauma.
    a. Old traumas can become a filter impacting how we interpret and experience the current moment.
    b. Our rational mind may suspect that our present situation is not actually placing us in the same position of powerlessness and peril; however, certain familiar characteristics resembling the original trauma lead us to disregard the evidence and react as if we were experiencing the same original traumatizing threat.
    c. New traumatic experiences join with old traumatic experiences, increasing the intensity of our response and reinforcing the associated Sticky Beliefs.

2. How do we recognize we are in Trauma Land?
    a. All other possible interpretations disappear and only one pie slice becomes visible.
    b. It feels like the traumatic reality has always been so, was never different, and leaves no hope of change.
    c. A Bodyguard takes over. We are activated.
    d. There is Something Important that needs to be understood, and the Sticky Belief feels like the only option.

3. Can we pause, recognize we are activated, and become detectives, exploring what previous experiences may have led us to this reaction, then use our tools to modify and navigate through our habitual reactions?
    a. Calming activities, such as breathing techniques, journaling,

or other methods for self-soothing, can increase our awareness and bring us back to center.

    b.   Observations about our thoughts and feelings that emerge when we are in Trauma Land are useful to share with a therapist or trusted friend.

    c.   Changing our interpretations and reactions is hard work. Remember to give yourself patience and compassion.

4.   Visualizing a Safe Place or imagining a comforting hug from our Nurturer or a shielding gesture from our Protector can be helpful.

    a.   Imagine a place where you feel comfortable and safe. If that is hard to imagine, then have a place that is safe enough. It can be a place you know or a place you imagine. Make the image as vivid as possible using all five senses. What time of day is it? What season? What do you hear? See? Smell? Taste? Feel? Are there people around, or are you by yourself? What are you wearing? Are you sitting or standing?

    b.   Visualize your Nurturer. This is an entity who is there for you no matter what you are feeling or what you have done. They are the essence of compassion, understanding, and comfort. There is no judgment. If the image is someone you know, then make them an idealized image. This could be a Nurturing Parent that you are creating. Your Nurturer could also be an animal, a spiritual figure, or a tree. What works for you?

    c.   Visualize your Protector. This entity has your back and can keep you safe from any danger or foe. It could be a superhero image of yourself, someone you know, a warrior, or a protective animal. Imagine with as many details as possible. What are their powers?

    d.   Imagine yourself in your safe place, with your Nurturer and your Protector, all together or separately. You can do this at the end of a meditation. It is useful to take long deep breaths, and you can gently tap, right-left, right-left, to solidify the image.

    e.   Use these images as a way to counterbalance the forces pulling you into Trauma Land.

5.   Identify specific traumas in your life, either one-time events or chronic woundings.

    a.   What Sticky Beliefs about yourself, others, and life came from each trauma?

    b.   What Bodyguards were created to help you survive and feel safe?

    c.   Think of others you know and consider the traumas you suspect they have experienced.

    d.   How do you think those events impacted their Sticky Beliefs? Their Bodyguards?

....

CHAPTER 14

The Should-Be Self

When we become activated, we are definitely not in Should-Be Land, and there is a good chance that our identity feels threatened. When we ask ourselves, "What does the situation mean about me?" we may feel judged—by ourselves or others. If so, we are faced with a verdict issued by our inner judge: we are found guilty of not being our Should-Be Self.

1. How would you describe your Should-Be Self?
    a. What do they look like?
    b. How do they behave?
    c. What do they know?
    d. What are they able to do?

2. What and who influenced that image?
    a. How does your family impact your idea of who and how you should be?
    b. How are you impacted by your peers?
    c. What role does social media play?
    d. Which popular, powerful, political, or persuasive people impact your judgment?
    e. Which people do you admire?

3. How would you describe your As-Is Self?
    a. What do they look like?
    b. How do they behave?
    c. What are they able to do?

4. What would your current As-Is Self like to say to your current Should-Be Self?
    a. Imagine the conversation at different ages.
    b. Imagine a conversation between a past and current As-Is Self.

5. Practice compassion with your As-Is Self.
    a. Think of actions they took that led to disappointment, suffering, and pain.
    b. Tell your As-Is Self that you realize that they were doing the

best they could with who they were and the knowledge they had at the time.

    c.   Would your past As-Is Self be confused or disappointed by choices you are making now and how you are living your life?

    d.   Tell your past As-Is Self that life is different than you imagined then and you are doing the best you can.

6.   These can be useful tools, but my strongest suggestion and hope is that this book will encourage those who have experienced deep emotional wounding to seek out and work with a therapist who specializes in treating trauma.

....

CHAPTER 15

Circles of Compassion

The practice I call Circles of Compassion serves many purposes. It is a way to transform an experience of activation and antagonism into a vehicle for compassion and connection.

When we notice we are activated by the words, actions, and mere appearance of another person, we can choose to call for our Bodyguards or we can choose to practice Circles of Compassion.

It is useful to remember that *compassion* means to go toward and be with passion. Passion encompasses the energy of intense suffering and intense love. This requires courage.

1.   Find the common denominator between you and the other person. It may be that you are both angry, scared, disappointed, or confused. Perhaps there is reactivated suffering from old traumas. Probably they are annoyed that you are not being who they think you should be, and you are annoyed that they are not being who you think they should be.

    If nothing else, you are both humans, doing life the way you each know how to do life. The way you choose to be alive and the way they choose to be alive is different, and that may be upsetting—to both of you. Oh well. This means you have something in common.

2.   After you have established that you have something in common, give yourself a big dose of compassion because you are doing something hard. Or, maybe you find it easier to give compassion first to others rather than yourself. Fine. The practice works in both directions, simultaneously getting and giving compassion.

3.   Imagine the suffering you're each experiencing, then wish yourself and

them happiness and freedom from suffering. (To learn more about expanding this practice, research work by Pema Chodron or Sharon Salzberg and their metta and tonglen approaches.)

4. Imagine that compassion, light, or the energy of the Universe is shining on you or the other person.

5. Then, imagine that light traveling across the bridge built by the common denominator you have established between the two of you. Let that light shine on you, fill you, fill them, circling around you both. Feel the circular energy connection. Expand that circle of light-filled compassionate energy to include others you know who share the common denominator you have identified.

6. Then expand the circling energy to include all those anywhere in the world who right at the moment share that common denominator. Now expand it to include anyone who has ever lived and shares that human common denominator.

While you are doing this practice, it is useful to notice your breath. I use it after my morning meditation and when I have interacted with a troublesome person or anticipate such an interaction. It can also be used on the spot while you are actually interacting with that person. They don't have to know what you are doing. You can do it before, just after, or while you are in conversation. It will, I promise, change the energy and your experience of the interaction. They will feel it too, but not necessarily understand why the dynamic has changed. It is often difficult to give ourselves compassion. When we judge ourselves harshly, we perpetuate an attitude of rigidity and disdain toward others. Loving and accepting ourselves and others is crucial to our ability to be fully alive. Gossip and comparisons can create the illusion of connection but usually inhibit our sense of contentment and leave us with a toxic residue.

....

CHAPTER 16
The Courage to Lay Down Our Sword and Shield

We all get activated and respond with defenses that tend to fall under the heading of Fight, Flee, Freeze, or Fawn. When we know more about our style of activation, we have more control over our response. We can make behavioral choices that are more useful for us individually and more beneficial for our relationships.

1. What do you fear and react to the most—actions you interpret as aggression or actions you interpret as abandonment?

2. What actions leave you feeling like you are being abandoned?

3. What actions feel aggressive and attacking?
4. What actions feel like threats to your identity or sense of self?
5. When there has been an activation, what do you want and need? What helps bring your activation level down?
   a. Space and time to regain equilibrium before interacting?
   b. Physical contact such as a hug or sitting close or sexual intimacy as soon as possible?
   c. A verbal exchange such as Speaker-Listener, so you can better understand why the activation happened and what the other person thought and felt, and so that your position is understood and the Something Important is addressed?
6. Do you need time for your activation level to dial down before you attempt resolution, or do you feel that there must be a sense of resolution before your activation level can calm down?
7. Do you hold back anger and irritation and then explode?
8. Does it take a long time for you to deactivate once you have passed a certain level of activation?
9. Do you activate fast and hot, express your anger, and then deactivate just as quickly?
10. Are you hypervigilant, always at a low level of activation?
11. How do you react when you feel that others are activated?
12. Do you rely on other people, distractions, or substances to bring down your activation level? Do you have other possible responses?
13. Describe patterns you have with those who have activation styles similar to your activation style, and describe patterns of activation when you and the other person have different styles of activation.
14. What are your beliefs about apology, forgiveness, resentment, and punishment?

....

CHAPTER 17

Parent, Adult, or Child?

This concept posits that, at any age throughout life and even throughout each day, we find ourselves in roles identified as either Parent, Adult, or Child.

The Parent role can fall into the category of a Judgmental Parent or of a Nurturing Parent.

1. The Judgmental Parent doles out messages that result in pride or shame for the person in the role of Captive Child and others whom they view as needing their praise or guidance.
   a. We can be in the role of Judgmental Parent at any age.

b. We can interpret children as being in the role of Judgmental Parent when they tease, ridicule, and bully or use excessive praise as a way to ingratiate themselves to a peer.

c. A child in the role of Judgmental Parent can also be extremely focused on rules and adamant that others should do things the way they understand to be right, not wrong, and smart, not stupid.

d. We can be experienced by others as a Judgmental Parent when our intentions are to have an Adult-to-Adult conversation (just as we can experience others as Judgmental Parents when their intentions are to have an Adult-to-Adult interaction).

e. When we are overly focused on the opinions of others, there is a good chance that we were trained by a Judgmental Parent to be their Captive Child.

f. Can you identify times when you were in the role of Judgmental Parent?

g. Can you identify times you were in the role of Captive Child?

h. Whom do you experience as a Judgmental Parent or Captive Child?

2. The Nurturing Parent expresses care, concern, support, and interest in the experience of someone in the role of Free Child or another person in the position of Nurturing Parent.

   a. A Nurturing Parent can establish and enforce rules and boundaries and guide behavior, but with the recognition and validation of the other's experience: "I can understand why you want the third piece of cake and why you are upset that I won't let you have it."

   b. A Nurturing Parent aims to combine compassionate curiosity and respect with guidance and boundaries.

   c. Children can be in the role of Nurturing Parent when they care for a pet or peer.

   d. When children are regularly in the role of Nurturing Parent toward their own parents, they are identified as a "parentified child."

   e. A Free Child has a strong sense of agency and is comfortable with what they experience as the As-Is Self.

   f. Can you identify times when you were in the role of Nurturing Parent?

   g. Can you identify times when you were in the role of Free Child?

   h. Whom did you experience as a Nurturing Parent or Free Child?

3. The Adult role comprises activities such as taking care of business, solving problems, and working to act responsibly.

    a. When two people agree to a Pause or do Speaker-Listener, they are interacting as Adult to Adult. This is a way to shift out of a Parent-Child dynamic.

    b. What are times that you identify as "adulting?" How much of your life is spent in the category you would identify as Adult?

    c. Were there periods in your life when you spent fewer hours or more hours in the role of Adult?

    d. Is being in the Parent or Child role more comfortable than being in the Adult role?

    e. What is the hardest aspect for you of being in the Adult role?

4. The Child role is important to understand.

    a. In the Child role we access our playfulness, our creativity, our sexuality, and our ability to imagine and dream.

    b. Much of our aliveness is contained and expressed when we allow and encourage our Child Self to emerge and be expressed by our As-Is Self.

    c. There is much in society that shames, discourages, and dismisses expressions of the Free Child who is led by their Inner Camera more than their Outer Camera.

    d. Some cultures more than others reward with praise the directed performance of the obedient Captive Child when their accomplishments and behavior are perceived as successful by those in authority.

    e. Society can punish and/or reject the unruly Captive Child who fails to comply with the directives and norms established by those in authority (or reward them with notoriety for being daring rebels).

    f. Those in the Captive Child position are still dependent on and leashed by those experienced as in the role of Judgmental Parent, even though they may be oppositional, uncooperative, defiant, and even hostile toward those who hold the reins.

    g. When we are playful, having fun together, including being affectionate and sexual, then we are in what we consider to be Child to Child.

    h. What activities in your life would qualify as being in the role of Child?

    i. What memories do you have of Child activities when you actually were a child?

    j. Which activities from that time have carried over into adulthood?

k. Which have disappeared?

l. What new ones have emerged?

5. In relationships there are often repeated patterns of the roles we take on.

   a. Sometimes one person is usually in the role of Judgmental Parent and the other is in the role of Captive Child.

   b. In other relationships there can be a continual jockeying for the role of Judgmental Parent and an attempt to put the other in the role of Captive Child. The comment "Yeah, but you . . ." often indicates this dynamic is in play.

   c. Some relationships are great at Child-to-Child experiences but not so good for Adult-to-Adult or Parent-to-Parent activities.

   d. On the other hand, some usually find themselves in the roles of Adult to Adult or Parent to Parent, but have lost the vitality found in Child-to-Child interactions.

   e. Using the diagram to the right, map out three important relationships.

P   P

A   A

C   C

....

CHAPTER 18
Circularity and Vital Play

Bill and I call our projects, big and small, "mud pies." This emphasizes our Child-to-Child interaction. There may have been lots of planning and serious efforts that may feel more Adult to Adult, but our mud pies are a major source of Vital Play. Key elements are a sense of fun, joy, pleasure, connection, creation, collaboration, improvisation, and playfulness.

This book has been a *very* big mud pie!

1. Circularity is how we describe a felt sense of energetic connection.

   a. We say that, with certain people, places, objects, or actions, we feel a connection.

   b. There is a sense of energy flowing in a circular motion.

   c. We are simultaneously giving and getting.

   d. Breath in, breath out is the circularity of aliveness.

   e. When people, places, objects, or actions take on a heightened, ineffable meaning, we understand them to have a symbolic quality.

   f. Symbols can create a sense of wholeness; something lost has been brought back together.

2. What people, places, objects, or actions create that sense of special connection for you?

       a.   Write about one of those people.

       b.   Write about one of those objects.

       c.   Write about one of those places.

       d.   Write about one of those actions.

       e.   What ways can you bring more of those connections into your life?

       f.   What ways can you create more awareness of the connections already there?

3.   Vital Play is what we call actions that involve circular, energetic connection.

       a.   The word *vita* means "life."

       b.   Play involves actions that are self-directed, voluntary, fun, meaningful, spontaneous, flexible, and creative.

       c.   When play is relegated to the time of childhood, we adults lose an essential aspect of being alive.

       d.   The belief that play is only for children is one of the reasons why adult relationships can become dry and hollow.

       e.   Sexuality is under the category of Child-to-Child interactions in the Parent-Adult-Child model.

       f.   When we focus only on the product or goal to be gained through our actions, we lose the ability to take in the joy and satisfaction of the process.

       g.   Actions that exist for reasons beyond the need to survive are often our Vital Play.

       h.   Actions that are necessary for survival can also be experienced as Vital Play.

4.   Consider what you experience as Vital Play.

       a.   List activities you experience by yourself that you consider Vital Play.

       b.   What Vital Play experiences have you had in the past and would like to have again?

       c.   What experiences have you never had but think you might like to try?

       d.   List experiences you have with others that you consider Vital Play.

       e.   Do those Vital Play interactions with others feel like Child to Child? Why?

5.   An important Child-to-Child connection is our sexual aliveness.

    a. We may need to use our Adult-to-Adult skills to manifest some of those Child-to-Child interactions.

    b. Outer Cameras can shut down the experience and bring judgment into the room.

    c. Imagine you are connecting Inner Camera to Inner Camera, focusing on your present experience and attuned to the other person's experience.

6. One of the most devastating effects that trauma, stress, illness, or conflict can have on a relationship is the disruption of sexual intimacy.

    a. An unwanted and unexpected effect can be a decline in sexual desire.

    b. Even when partners want to resume sexual relations, a sense of self-consciousness can make it feel difficult. Instead of being spontaneous and playful, lovemaking can seem stilted and awkward.

    c. This can be disturbing, disappointing, and embarrassing to both partners.

    d. Sexual activity provides a physical connection that is vital to intimate relationships.

    e. Sometimes a person experiencing problems with sexual desire or performance will avoid physical affection due to fear of not being able to, or not having the desire to, have sex.

    f. Sometimes that person's partner will also avoid physical contact for fear of creating an awkward situation.

    g. This kind of hesitancy can add unnecessary tension and misunderstanding to an already stressful situation.

    h. What is needed is more comforting, connecting touch—not less.

    i. As a way to stay physically connected while removing fears and embarrassment, couples can use a nonsexual touching approach until spontaneous sexual desire and performance return.

GUIDELINES FOR NONSEXUAL TOUCHING:

1. Sexual stimulation is not the goal; in fact, it is not allowed.
2. Touching genitals is off limits.
3. Agreeing to temporarily suspend sexual touching allows you to explore other kinds of touching, like foot rubs, scalp massages, back rubs, and hand massages.
4. Take turns touching each other. Agree on a length of time—say between five and twenty minutes—and set a timer. When the timer goes

off, switch roles. The one who's been doing the touching becomes the one receiving the touching, and vice versa.

5. Plan your nonsexual touching sessions. Agree on a time and decide on a place where you won't be disturbed. Also agree on how long you will spend together and how many turns touching and being touched each person will get.

6. Create a sensual atmosphere for your nonsexual touching exercise with lighting, fragrance, music, fabric, etc.

7. When doing the touching, experiment with varying the kinds of strokes and the levels of pressure you use. Allow yourself to be creative, playful, and nurturing.

8. When receiving the touching, do not monitor your response. Instead, maintain a mindful focus on the physical sensation of being touched. If you find your mind wandering and thinking, gently bring it back to a focus on the physical sensation.

....

CHAPTER 19
Owning Our Choices

Choices that don't feel like choices can be a source of disappointment. Rather than lash myself with a torrent of stinging invectives for the left-on-the-counter shopping list, I choose to acknowledge my disappointment, decide how I can adapt to the current situation, and consider ways I may adjust my future behaviors. I also assure myself that I am still lovable and have value.

We also have a choice in how we respond to others who have made choices with unintended and inconvenient consequences. Bill and I choose to replace shaming and blaming with love and understanding. When a plane was missed on our way back from Europe, we were able to deal with the situation in the same way we deal with forgotten shopping lists. Yes, there was more activated energy in the initial moment of realization that the plane had left without us, but we were able to stay connected and make the best of the unfolding repercussions.

We owned our unconscious choices that led to the missed plane, and we owned our choices in how we reacted to the missed plane. None of us has the ability to look into the future and know exactly how our choices will unfold. We do the best we can with who we are and the data we have in that pivotal moment of choice. It is hard being human. We all need some compassion.

1. Repeated choices become our default choices.

a. What are some habitual choices you make, such as eating the whole bag of potato chips, scrolling on your phone, or thanking the person serving you coffee?

b. What proportion is conscious, and what proportion is unconscious or semiconscious?

c. Are there choices you'd like to change?

d. How can you make the unconscious choices more conscious?

e. Do you go to shame, judge yourself harshly, and attack your identity and worth when you realize you have made an unfortunate choice?

f. Do you bring in the Bodyguards? Blame others? Find excuses?

g. Or do you nurture change through gentle, increased awareness and responsibility?

h. How do you react to other people's seemingly unconscious choices that are disappointing or at odds with your choices?

2. What are some important choices you have made or are considering making that impact your life and possibly the lives of others? Examples could include getting married or divorced, having a child, leaving or starting a job or profession, choosing a school, moving, or staying.

a. What people influence your choices?

b. What beliefs influence your choices?

c. What fears influence your choices?

d. What hopes influence your choices?

e. What traumatic experiences from your past influence your choices?

3. How do you go about making choices?

a. Do you tend to be spontaneous and impulsive?

b. Do you tend to research and ponder?

c. Do you ask others' advice?

d. Do you go by intuition or more mystical tools?

e. Do you often have buyer's remorse and question your decisions?

f. Do you look for approval of your decisions or keep them secret?

g. What situations spring to mind with these questions?

4. With important choices, we often get stuck, wanting to know what is the "right" decision, as if we could somehow see into the future and know how all our choices will unfold.

a. What choices do you now regret?

b. What choices would confuse or disappoint your younger self?

      c.   Consider several important choices that impacted your life, and remember or research what else was happening in your life and in the world at that time.

      d.   What beliefs influenced your decisions?

      e.   Who and what was important in your life at that time? Why?

5.   What choices did you make in the past that you now appreciate?

      a.   Were they mostly conscious or unconscious?

      b.   Spontaneous or thought about and planned?

      c.   Influenced by others?

      d.   A product of the times?

      e.   A lucky chance?

6.   Draw up a contract with your future self.

      a.   The contract reads that your future self agrees to be understanding about choices you make now that will eventually become your past.

      b.   Remind your future self that the world keeps changing and what seems obvious in the present was often not even dreamed of in the past.

      c.   Suggest to your future self that they practice Circles of Compassion with your past self. Your future self may also need compassion to deal with repercussions that were set in motion by your past self.

      d.   Encourage your past self to also practice Circles of Compassion to extend empathy and compassion to your current self for choices that, to your past self, may feel disappointing, confusing, or even like an act of betrayal. There is likely to be a common denominator linking then and now.

We can also get caught trying to anticipate others' reactions, trapped by the belief that our choices need to meet everyone else's approval. We can choose to consider what the other person may feel in reaction to our choices, and that awareness may influence our decisions, but we are not responsible for the other person's interpretation or experience.

7.   When making choices, how aware are you of how your actions will impact others? Is there an image of your Should-Be Self that will never make a mistake and will meet with the approval of everyone?

      a.   Do you tend to feel responsible for other people's experience more than your own experience?

      b.   Do you consider your experience first and consider others only after you have made the choice that works best for you?

c.   Do you tend to seek a negotiation where all the needs of those involved are considered and some kind of compromise is reached?

d.   What comes up when you ask yourself these questions?

There are those in life who believe that whenever life is disappointing or uncomfortable, it is someone's fault. It is either your fault or my fault or the fault of someone outside of the tribe. Someone is guilty. Too often the fault-giver and fault-taker find each other, form a relationship, and reinforce the habitual, internalized patterns. The interaction feels normal, usually ingrained in early childhood, so the interpretations and reactions are difficult to identify and change.

8.   What are your beliefs about mistakes, fault, blame, and shame when making choices?

a.   Do you tend to take the blame and believe it is your fault?

b.   Do you tend to blame others?

c.   Do you tend to blame luck or circumstance?

d.   Do you tend to blame those whom you identify as outsiders or even enemies?

e.   Do you feel remorse when you are aware that your actions resulted in pain for others? Or do you feel defensive?

f.   Do you make amends, acknowledge the pain your actions may have caused others?

g.   Do you let others know that their actions resulted in pain or discomfort for you?

h.   Write about some specific situations.

9.   Identify interactions or relationships where you are impacted by each other's choices.

a.   Do you often feel responsible for another person's experience and guilty if they are unhappy or disappointed by your choices?

b.   Do you tend to blame others or circumstance for your unhappiness or disappointment?

c.   Do you often consider others' needs over your own needs when making decisions?

d.   Identify interactions and relationships where your experience and the other person's experience were or are both considered.

We are each responsible for our actions and our reactions. We are responsible for our choices and our reactions to those choices and our reactions to the choices of others. Our choices are what create our experience. We can't change the weather, but we can change our response.

....

CHAPTER 20

Your Way There

We are a Full Spectrum of different thoughts and feelings, and we are always going through Stages of Change. Different aspects of our life will be at different stages. We are never finished. There is always more to understand, more ways to adjust.

It is important to acknowledge and feel satisfaction when we realize that, in one area of our existence, we have moved to Stage Three or even Stage Four. Do not be discouraged when you realize that in certain areas of awareness you are in Stage One or that, yes, in those same old areas, you are still in Stage Two. The move from Stage Two to Stage Three is frustrating. Have patience. There is no skipping over the stages.

1. Change is difficult—and possible!
    a. Describe areas where you were in Stage One—Unconscious Incompetence.
    b. Describe areas where you often find yourself in Stage Two—Conscious Incompetence.
    c. Describe areas where you are often shifting from Stage Two to Stage Three—Conscious Competence.
    d. Describe areas where you realize you have moved into Stage Four—Unconscious Competence.

2. We can combine the Stages of Change with the idea that we move through life in different experience lanes.
    a. Different aspects of our personality can prefer different lanes.
    b. Relationships can impact what lane we are in.
    c. We are impacted by our environment and what we are doing.
    d. Compare the lanes you are in when you are doing different activities, in different environments, or in various relationships.
    e. We can revert to old habitual lanes when we find ourselves in familiar situations connected to our past, such as family of origin, high school buddies, or friends and acquaintances from a certain social tribe.

3. Examine the lane you identify as Stage One—Unconscious Incompetence.

a. What Bodyguards and Sticky Beliefs usually run the show?

b. Do you habitually react with anger and rage?

c. Do you Freeze and shut down, go numb, and possibly dissociate?

d. Do you Flee, run away, and avoid confrontation?

e. Do you focus on the needs of others, people please, and seek validation?

f. Does it feel like this is who you are and how you will always be?

g. Do you believe that other people and outside actions control your experience?

h. In what environments and in what relationships do you often find yourself traveling in this lane of Unconscious Incompetence?

i. Are there situations where you swerve back into this lane?

4. Explore the lane you identify as Stage Two—Conscious Incompetence.

a. What actions and reactions interpreted as Incompetent are you attempting to change but finding that old habits die hard?

b. Where and when do these actions and reactions usually occur?

c. Do others join and support those actions and reactions you consider Incompetent?

d. How do you react when you become aware of your Full Spectrum and realize you are, once again, in the lane of Incompetence?

e. Do you patiently, with compassion and curiosity, explore why you have found yourself in that lane and calmly move back into the Stage Three lane?

f. Do you berate and judge yourself harshly for not being who you should be and, with white knuckles, jerk the wheel back into the Stage Three lane?

g. What interpretations and Sticky Beliefs send you into the Stage Two lane?

h. Can you validate that moving from the Stage Two lane to the Stage Three lane is hard? Give yourself some encouragement!

5. Staying in the Stage Three lane—Conscious Competence—takes work and concentration. It's difficult staying mindful and conscious! There are so many forces ready to push us into another lane. Make sure you feel the satisfaction that comes with that lane!

a. In what areas of your life can you identify that you have made changes?

b. What and who were helpful in making those changes?

    c.   Are there changes that have happened over time that you now appreciate?

    d.   Can you identify others in your life who have moved through these stages?

    e.   Do others recognize the changes you have made and verbally validate those changes?

    f.   Do you validate the changes that others have made?

6.   The Stage Four Lane—Unconscious Competence—is a tricky one. We are often only aware that we have been smoothly sailing along in that lane when something moves us out of it! And when we get smug and self-righteous that we are doing it all right (as opposed to everyone else), we have shifted into an old lane of judgment and comparison.

    a.   In this lane you extend compassion to the other person or people because you realize they are all having their own reactions to deal with.

    b.   In this lane, we use our awareness of our Full Spectrum to give us more choice in how we respond to a situation, utilizing our tools and developing new skills.

    c.   In this lane, we travel through life aware of how opposites, birth and death, sorrow and joy, darkness and light, are inextricably entwined.

    d.   We develop practices such as meditation, journaling, psychotherapy, healing work with others, and additional mindful activities that increase our attunement with others, our world within, and the world without.

    e.   We read and listen to others who offer wisdom and useful maps that help us navigate life. We pass on that wisdom through our words and actions toward others.

We are all moving through our lives, from birth to death. The journey is our life. In which lanes do you want to travel? Life is full of joy and sorrow, satisfaction and disappointment. You are here, in As-Is Land. Oh well. Embrace it all—your Full Spectrum of thoughts and feelings. Be fully alive while you're alive. The choice is yours.

Fare Well

We are all in this life together, doing the best we can. May you have the strength, courage, and patience needed for your journey. We hope this book has served as support.

Thank you for joining us on your way there.

Gratitude

Especially during these recent trying times, when my life and the world have seemed to be spinning out of control, the practice of intentionally returning to a place of gratitude has been key to maintaining my equilibrium, finding my way back to the center of my Full Spectrum.

The following people have served as ballast, and my heart is filled with gratitude that I have such people in my life. They have inspired and supported me over the years and were especially essential during the long and arduous process of birthing this book, which has its roots in my mother's passion for reading and writing and my father's love of making things.

My New York City Writers' Group has been together since January 1997. They are: Anne Adams, JoAnne McFarland, Katherine Leiner, Lavinia Plonka, Bette Glenn, Marilyn Kaye, Michelle Willens, and the dear and departed Janie Furse. They all patiently read draft after draft and have been integral in the development of my life as a psychotherapist. I would not be who I am today without the relationships I have within this group.

The Saratoga Writers' Group has taken me into their fold, and I am so grateful to share in friendship, vitality, and exchange of ideas. Thank you, Eva Nagel, Courtney Reid, and Dianna Goodwin for your input on the book. I look forward to our continued work together.

Louise Penny gave me much needed encouragement. Bruce McCallister enthusiastically coached my return to writing, and Stuart Horwitz told me what to emphasize and what to cut. Both were instrumental in the formation of this book.

Julia Rothman shared her skills as an illustrator with Bill and inspired and encouraged us to make illustrations an essential aspect of the book. Elena Sabinson taught Bill some key technical lessons on the use of Photoshop. Francesca Richer and Hong Wu added their magic of book design.

Several friends have also been key supports and gave me important feedback on both content and style. Thank you, Martha Robins, Joan Sudmann, and Joan Hoeberichts!

Amy Quale, Hanna Kjeldbjerg, and Patrick Maloney at Wise Ink were gifted and enthusiastic navigators for our wild publishing adventure, and Sean Pratt, Ian Levitt, Anthony Roman, and Phil Palazzolo ably and enthusiastically guided us through the audiobook process.

Kayaking is a theme throughout the book, and Marshall and Dorothy

Changing Light

William Murray/Gretta Keene

William Murray

Slow and steady ♩ = 70

The sun is warm, I'm feel - ing glad. But I know that this will change.
The sky is grey, I'm feel - ing sad. But I know that this will change.
The night is dark, I feel a - fraid. But I know that this will change.
The morn - ing comes, I'm filled with hope. But I know that this will change.
I wel - come in what - ev - er comes For I know that all will change.

What - ev - er life may send me, how - ev - er life may bend me,
What - ev - er life may send me, how - ev - er life may bend me,
What - ev - er life may send me, how - ev - er life may bend me,
What - ev - er life may send me, how - ev - er life may bend me,
What - ev - er life may send me, how - ev - er life may bend me,

I trust the light I hold with - in to guide and to be - friend me.
I trust the light I hold with - in to guide and to be - friend me.
I trust the light I hold with - in to guide and to be - friend me.
I trust the light I hold with - in to guide and to be - friend me.
I trust the light I hold with - in to guide and to be - friend me.

Seddon at the River Connection taught us so much about kayaking and kayaks. Dr. Disha Mookherjee understands both the emotional and physical complexity of the heart, and Sara Cohen gave her heart as my brother Brad's social worker.

I have learned from my friends, therapists, and teachers along the way. I especially owe immense gratitude to Pema Chodron for her influence on my work and on my life. The resource page on our website, mindyourweather.com, has links to the many others who have influenced both my life and my work.

Two people who are invisibly woven throughout this book are my two daughters, Juliana and Elena. They made me a mom and continue to be important guides for how to be human. They expand my awareness, challenge old Sticky Beliefs, and fill my heart with their love and wisdom. And I so appreciate their partners, Matthew and Mike, and my brother, Jason, and sister-in-law, Gini, for being in my life.

Gratitude is a meager word and completely inadequate for describing how much I appreciate my Bill. In our personal and professional relationship, I am alive in ways I could barely imagine. Doing life, whether it be the mundane or the extraordinary, we have fun. I'm so glad we are together, finding our way.

Biographies

Gretta Keene is a licensed clinical social worker, psychoanalyst, and certified sandplay therapist, with further training in several modalities useful in the treatment of trauma. Her background as a writer, visual artist, and performer informs her work as a psychotherapist. Gretta was introduced to meditation many decades ago and utilizes a mindfulness approach to her life and therapy. Nature has always been a source of comfort and rejuvenation. You might find Gretta out drawing trees, kayaking, or working in the garden—some of her favorite ways to connect with the natural world.

William Murray is a clinical psychologist specializing in relationship counseling and the mindfulness-focused treatment of anxiety issues. He is a certified EMDR and sandplay practitioner. William is adept at holding a space of compassionate respect for those who embark on the journey of insight and transformation. He writes and plays music, draws and paints, and is out on the water kayaking with Gretta as often as possible.